Y0-DCD-340

WITHDRAWN
UTSA LIBRARIES

Tourist Activities in Multimodal Texts

Tourist Activities in Multimodal Texts

An Analysis of Croatian and Scottish Tourism Websites

Melani Nekić
Justus Liebig University, Giessen, Germany

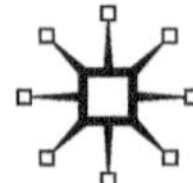

First published 2015 by
PALGRAVE MACMILLAN

Palgrave Macmillan in the UK is an imprint of Macmillan Publishers Limited, registered in England, company number 785998, of Houndmills, Basingstoke, Hampshire RG21 6XS.

Palgrave Macmillan in the US is a division of St Martin's Press LLC, 175 Fifth Avenue, New York, NY 10010.

Palgrave Macmillan is the global academic imprint of the above companies and has companies and representatives throughout the world.

Palgrave® and Macmillan® are registered trademarks in the United States, the United Kingdom, Europe and other countries.

ISBN 978–1–137–39790–4

This book is printed on paper suitable for recycling and made from fully managed and sustained forest sources. Logging, pulping and manufacturing processes are expected to conform to the environmental regulations of the country of origin.

A catalogue record for this book is available from the British Library.
Library of Congress Cataloging-in-Publication Data
Nekić, Melani, 1983–
Tourist activities in multimodal texts : an analysis of Croatian and Scottish tourism websites / Melani Nekić.
pages cm
Summary: "Tourist promotional material is a tool utilised by many people preparing to travel or planning an activity. How do we as readers make sense of the tourist promotional material that is available to us? How do we as users understand tourism websites? Awareness of how tourism websites function may enable business people to master the range of resources used as strategies to design websites in ways which more specifically target types of users. Tourist Activities in Multimodal Texts addresses these questions by analysing Croatian and Scottish tourism web pages to explore the ways in which tourist activities are represented in tourism websites and the ways in which tourism websites construct their recipients as media actors and cultural tourists"— Provided by publisher.
ISBN 978–1–137–39790–4 (hardback)
1. Tourism—Internet marketing—Case studies. 2. Tourism—Internet marketing—Croatia. 3. Tourism—Internet marketing—Scotland. 4. Web sites—Design. I. Title.
G156.5.I5N45 2014
381'.4591411—dc23 2014022929

Typeset by MPS Limited, Chennai, India.

Printed and bound in Great Britain by
CPI Antony Rowe, Chippenham and Eastbourne

My debt is to my loved ones whose endless love and understanding accompanied me through the gains and pains of this book.

Ova knjiga je posvećena Vama.

This book is dedicated to You.

Contents

List of Figures and Tables

Figures

Tables

Acknowledgements

This book has been informed by an interdisciplinary web of input. In particular, I am indebted to Wolfgang Hallet, Professor of Teaching English as a Foreign Language at the Justus Liebig University, Giessen, and John Bateman, Professor of Applied English Linguistics at the University of Bremen. They have offered sustained support and advice on methodological and theoretical issues throughout. To both, warm thanks. For intense conversations on the challenges of my book, I am also fortunate for having had the ear of Helmuth Feilke, Professor of German Linguistics and Language Teaching at the Justus Liebig University, Giessen.

Equally, I gratefully acknowledge being given the opportunity to become a member of the International Graduate Centre for the Study of Culture (GCSC), the Cusanuswerk, the DAAD, and the FAZIT foundations. They granted me funding, and enabled me to benefit from research on tourism studies at the Juraj Dobrila University in Pula, Croatia, and discuss work-in-progress with experts on the study of culture and functional linguistics at conferences and summer schools in Germany, Croatia, Slovenia, Great Britain, and Portugal.

Also I would like to acknowledge permission given for the use of figures in my book: by Dr Emilia Djonov, lecturer in Early Childhood Language and Literacy at Macquarie University, Sydney, Australia, to re-use a screenshot of a Figure Aon website structure as a hierarchy of Themes, permission given by John Bateman to include figures on differential use of leading, layout structure, and the correspondence between layout structure and area models, permission given by Scotland's National Tourism Organization, VisitScotland, to include screenshots of the Orkney and Perthshire region websites and a screenshot of an extract of the Orkney region website, permission given by the Istria Region Tourist Board, Turistička Zajednica Istarske Regije, to use screenshots of the Istria region and permission given by the Zadar County Tourist Board, Turistička Zajednica Zadarske Županije, to include screenshots of the Zadar county website and screenshots of extracts of the Zadar county website.

Last but not least, my thanks also needs to be recorded to Kate Oden for proofreading earlier versions of chapters and offering illuminating and constructive comments.

Acknowledgements

1
Introduction

1.1 Why tourism websites?

Culture has been identified as an academic buzzword (Schmidt, 2004, p. VII in Cha & Schmidt, 2004). Critical ink has been spilled over the question of whether tourism is a subject worthy of academic study (Page & Connell, 2006, p. 6; Sharpley, 2011, p. 6). The newness of the new media has been challenged (O'Neill, 2008, p. 16). Advertising has been categorised as an area where much debate has already taken place (Bendel & Held, 2008, p. 6 in Held & Bendel, 2008). In various research traditions, multiple meanings have been assigned to the concept of text (Adamzik, 2004, pp. 38 ff.).

In the face of these descriptions and evaluations, have the signifiers of culture, tourism, the new media, advertising, and text become short-lived, over-researched, and derogatory signs? In fact, as this book will demonstrate, there is space for a response in the negative. Contradictory though it may sound, it is precisely the popularity of culture in academic and popular discourses which points to the need for it to be systematically studied.

The study of tourism websites is important for several reasons. Firstly, it is highly socially relevant since research reveals that tourism is of huge economic importance. Thus, according to a report on EU tourism policy (Verheugen, 2005, p. 2), the tourist sector has been identified as a significant contributor to the EU economy (ibid.). The inclusion of Croatia within the European Union makes the country, referred to as one of the important tourist destinations in the Mediterranean (Ministry of Foreign Affairs and European Integration of the Republic of Croatia, 2006), a potentially significant contributor to the European tourist industry. Also, evidence that increasing financial means have been spent by the Croatian National Tourist Board (HTZ) on advertising Croatia as a tourist destination on global television networks such as CNN and Eurosport (Ministry of Tourism of the Republic of Croatia, 2010), suggests that the importance of Croatia as a tourist destination is also communicated through the global media. Similarly, tourism is one of Scotland's largest employment generating industries (The Scottish Government, 2011). The use of the Internet and television exposure also provides important avenues for attracting potential visitors to Scotland. The wealth of views registered for the homepage of the new UK and Ireland marketing campaign *Surprise Yourself* and the new television advert accompanying the *Surprise Yourself* campaign may serve as examples (Scotland's national tourism organization, 2011).

Secondly, the study of tourism is of huge importance for political reasons. More specifically, when it comes to intercultural communication and multilingualism, it has been seen as desirable to involve several languages and cultures in the idea of multilingualism and multiculturalism in Europe (Trim, 2002, pp. 12 f. in Tosi, 2002). Achieving this is attempted through the inclusion of cultures and languages, such as Croatian, which have only recently been represented in crucial political institutions, such as the European Union (European Parliament, 2014), and are under-represented in analyses of advertising on the Internet. The analysis of banner advertising on the Internet in German and Croatian may serve as an example (Filipan-Zignić, 2007).

Thirdly, while discussions of tourism among anthropologists reveal concerns related to the possible destruction of cultural diversity in local communities through tourism and travel (Salazar, 2012, p. 19), the study of tourism has been characterised as fundamental to grasping human interaction in multilingual and multicultural tourist language-learning settings (Phipps, 2007, pp. 19 ff.; Nekić 2009, review on Phipps, 2007). More specifically, as a site for issues of identity, it has the potential to encourage levels of self-reflexivity which enable the self to become aware of and question its established practices and routines in relation to the other in a dialogical way (Jack & Phipps, 2005, pp. 157, 161). In addition, there have been calls for the analysis of multimodal texts and meaning-making in teaching and learning contexts (Whittaker et al., 2007, pp. 2 ff. in McCabe et al., 2007; Jewitt, 2008, pp. 241–267); and their potential for the enhancement of students' writing and literacy achievement has been stressed (Hallet, 2008a, p. 8; Hallet, 2008b, pp. 167–183 in Müller-Hartmann & Schocker-von Ditfurth). For didactic purposes, tourism web pages may further be employed in the teaching and learning of foreign languages and cultures to promote reflection and critical thinking among students and raise their awareness of schematized representations of cultures.

In addition, while it is the case that, as part of multimedia convergence, knowledge has been assimilated from previous media forms, in that previous media forms have been integrated into newly convergent interactive media forms such as the layout from print material and the moving image from film (O'Neill, 2008, pp. 16, 20 f., 92 f.), it is equally the case that web pages as forms of new media cover obligatory and optional characteristics: the hypertextual organization in the World Wide Web platform accessible via the Internet, the multimodal coding, the dynamic nature, the interactivity potential and the support of computer-mediated communication (Storrer, 2008, pp. 211–227 in Janich, 2008). Besides, except for the study of identity construction on tourism websites, as conducted by Hallett & Kaplan-Weinger (2010), most studies on tourism and discourse, text, or language (Dann, 1996; Baider et al. 2004; Jaworski & Pritchard 2005; Antelmi et al. 2007; Held & Bendel 2008) have been concerned with an analysis of print material, rather than the new media. This lends merit to giving space to the analysis of the new media, in addition to print material. Also, research on destination marketing and communication reveals that, despite evidence that marketing budgets in many tourist destinations are spent on more conventional, print-based media, including brochures and leaflets (Dore & Crouch, 2003 in Fyall, 2010, p. 14; Foley & Fahy, 2004 in Fyall, 2010, p. 14), a new tendency towards using more electronic and web-based forms of communication has been identified (Fyall, 2010, p. 14 in Wang & Pizam, 2010).

Furthermore, although a wealth of research has been conducted in the area of advertising (Bendel & Held, 2008, p. 6 in Held & Bendel, 2008), a dearth of research has been noted when it comes to combining tourism studies with the study of language or discourse, in general (Pritchard & Jaworski, 2005, p. 1 in Jaworski & Pritchard, 2005), and systematic analyses of promotional tourist discourse, in particular (Held, 2008, p. 149 in Held & Bendel, 2008). Thus, the project is relevant to the areas of commerce and advertisements. In this context, a plea has been made for dealing with three subjects of investigation: first, the quality assessment of texts and suggestions for improvement, such as through website usability; second, the identification of latent textual meanings through use of psychological and sociological methods; third, the identification and critical assessment of social concepts and ideals constructed by promotional texts (Bendel, 2008, pp. 237 f. in Held & Bendel, 2008). When it comes to qualitative interpretation of latent meanings, a note of caution needs to be sounded. Textual analyses of promotional texts or discourse have been criticised for intuitive interpretations (Bendel, 2008, p. 234 in Held & Bendel, 2008). In application to this work, this is a methodological challenge which, rather than exclusively relating to websites, concerns empirical analyses of texts, in general. As it is known that qualitative interpretation of data is essential to hermeneutic activities (ibid.), this work seeks to offer plausible interpretations based on what has been defined as the strength of linguistic work, that is, the presence of a tool-kit suitable for in-depth analyses of meanings (Bendel & Held, 2008, p. 4 in Held & Bendel, 2008). This work is therefore intended to point to meaning potentials on the basis of an exemplary study of tourism websites, without making claims to cover all possible meanings and to be complete.

Moreover, the book is of potential practical application. When it comes to business studies, knowledge about what is represented on tourism websites, what is communicated to users as cultural tourists, and how users are involved in the creation of tourist meanings may allow business people to become more aware of the functioning of tourist promotional material. More precisely, it will enable them to master the range of resources used as strategies to design websites in ways which more specifically target types of users.

As a final point, the importance of the book to the progress of multimodal research needs to be pointed out. Within the area of multimodal research, the findings are expected to contribute to the understanding of the ways in which tourism websites function as examples of multimodal texts. In this context, despite the realization that language is merely one of several semiotic modes involved in the construction of meaning (Matthiessen, 2009, p. 14 in Halliday & Webster, 2009), it is only recently that studies have begun to apply multimodal text approaches to the empirical analysis of texts. This has included multimodal discourse analysis taken from a more systemic-functional perspective, the social semiotic theory of multimodality, the theory of multimodal actions (Bucher, 2010, pp. 46–64), and multimodal interaction analysis (Jewitt, 2009b, pp. 28–39 in Jewitt, 2009c).

Thus, following multimodal discourse analysis, meaning is construed through the interplay between semiotic resources themselves (Bucher, 2010, p. 52 in Bucher et al., 2010), with the interests of the sign-maker, as the person who makes meanings, being of less importance (Jewitt, 2009b, p. 36 in Jewitt, 2009c).

The social semiotic theory of multimodality views the construal of meaning as resulting from the ways in which sign-makers attribute meanings through use of semiotic resources for certain purposes. Multimodality is thus viewed as a dynamic and motivated social process which is closely tied to the socio-cultural context of use (Jewitt, 2009b, p. 30 in Jewitt, 2009c). The foundations of both multimodal discourse analysis and the social semiotic theory of multimodality were set by the theories of systemic functional linguistics and social semiotics, as advanced by Halliday (1978, 1985). Historically, social semiotics has been influenced by researchers in the area of interactional sociology. For instance, Foucault's (1980, p. 119) notion of 'power' which creates knowledge and discourse has been used as a means for elaborating explorations of the interdependence of language and social and political issues through an exemplary analysis of the function of language in a state of war (Hodge & Kress, 1993, pp. 153 f.). Bernstein's (1972, 1975) investigations of language and power relations across social classes have been used to explore the link between utterances, classifications or 'judgments about qualities of intelligence, character, etc.' (Hodge & Kress, 1993, p. 66) and class expectations (ibid.).

In multimodal interaction analysis, meanings of identity are created through the interaction between social actors through the use of semiotic resources. There is a focus on the situated nature of interaction in the socio-cultural context; that is, social interaction is bound to a given point in time with certain social actors (Jewitt, 2009b, p. 33 in Jewitt, 2009c). Multimodal interaction analysis has been influenced by interactional sociolinguistics, mediated discourse, and multimodality. For example, approaches to the function of communication in the construction of power and social identity (Gumperz & Cook-Gumperz, 1982, p. 1 in Gumperz, 1982) and the sociological notion of (inter) action as performance (Goffman, 1959, p. 17), rather than signs which 'constantly change as they circulate in different contexts for different groups with different histories' (Hodge & Kress, 1993, p. xii), were crucial to the development of multimodal interactional analysis. In particular, the works of Norris (2004, 2009, 2011) and Norris & Jones (2005) have been devoted to the analysis of the ways in which meaning is made through the interaction of modes, such as gaze and body movement, in people's everyday interactions and contemporary communication technologies such as the Internet, software, CD-ROM, and video from a discourse analytical perspective.

According to the theory of multimodal action, meaning is construed through the communicative context of use of semiotic resources and the state of knowledge of the communication partners, rather than the semiotic resources themselves (Bucher, 2010, pp. 52, 54 in Bucher et al., 2010). Thus, the communicative use of language by Searle (1969), Heringer (1974), Fritz (1982), and Gloning (1996) and of images by Muckenhaupt (1986), Scholz (2004), and Stöckl (2004) can be related to Austin (1962), who set the foundations for a theory of multimodal action (Bucher, 2010, p. 59 in Bucher et al., 2010). In particular, the theory is informed by Austin's (1962, pp. 6 f.) notion of speech acts, that is, the fact that speakers perform actions with utterances. Adopting a social semiotic perspective on tourism websites, this book is also expected to offer newly developed concepts, tools, and methodological approaches to the empirical analysis of data, which may be applicable to the analysis of websites with other social contexts of use than tourism.

The importance of the above-mentioned signifiers of culture, tourism, the new media, advertising, and text calls for their investigation. This will be realized through an analysis of tourist activities – such as visiting natural heritage sites, doing sports activities, experiencing history and heritage, and benefiting from gastronomy – in multimodal texts. It is intended to understand the ways in which contemporary multimodal texts such as complex cultural communicative acts may function in a specific communicative situation – that is, tourism communication online – through an in-depth, exemplary analysis of regional Croatian and Scottish tourism web pages. In order to give an impression of the kind of websites which will be explored, screenshots of the homepages of the Zadar, Orkney, Istria and Perthshire region websites are shown in Figures 1.1–1.4.

A first glance at the homepages of the four regional websites reveals that they differ in terms of layout. When it comes to layout elements, many more elements can be noted on the Zadar region homepage (covering a wealth of text fragments, text passages, menu items, boxes, separators, icons, and photographs) and the Istria region homepage (involving a wealth of text fragments, menu items, drawings, maps, icons, menu areas, and boxes) than on the Orkney region homepage (including text fragments, photographs, icons, boxes, and menu areas) and the Perthshire region homepage (predominantly embracing text fragments, text passages, menu areas, and icons). Also, some elements are made more prominent than others, as indicated by textual cues related to salience and framing. Examples on the Zadar region website include a visually and spatially prominent landscape photograph, repetitive representation of landscape environments in smaller static photographs, lexical references to seascapes and landscapes in groups and clauses, the large size and prominent placement in the upper part of the page of a wealth of sports activities photographs, and the repetitive

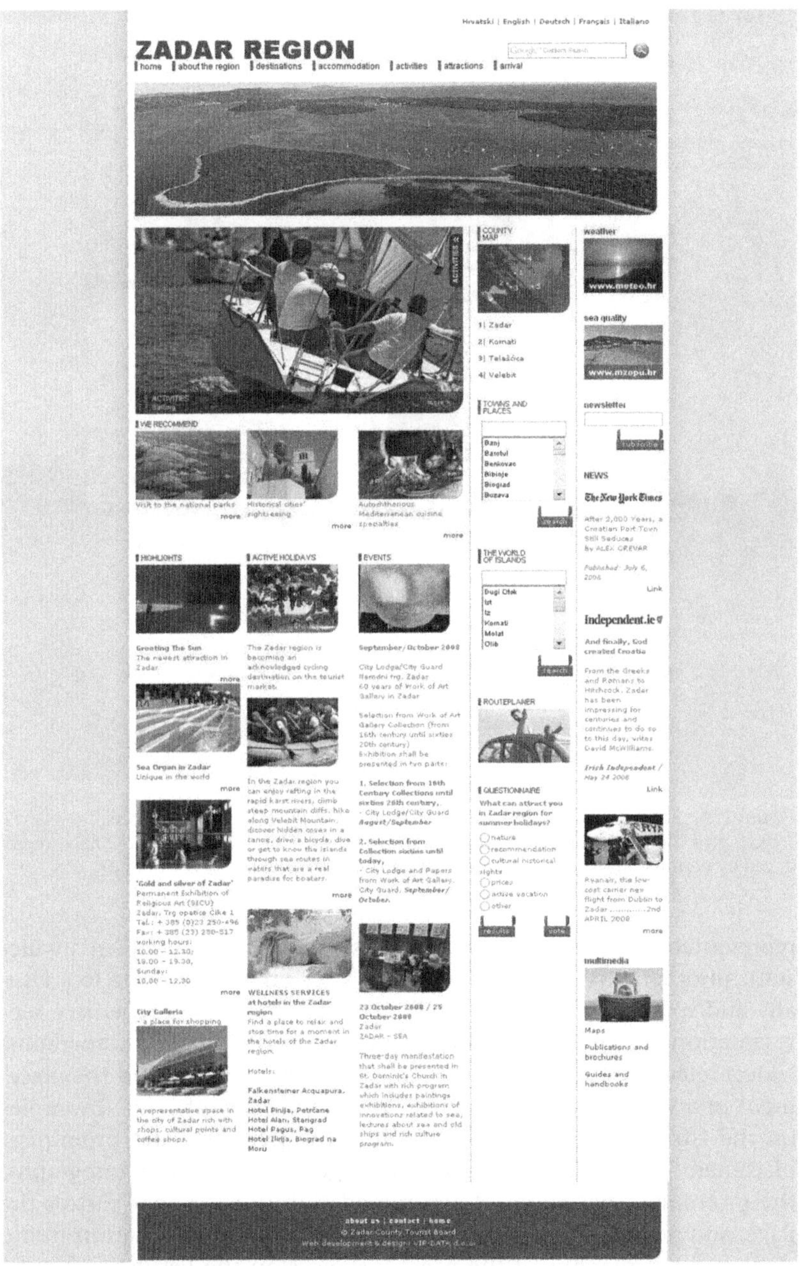

Figure 1.1 Screenshot of the homepage of the Zadar county website

Source: http://www.zadar.hr/English/Default.aspx (accessed on 10 September 2009); reproduced by permission of the Zadar County Tourist Board.

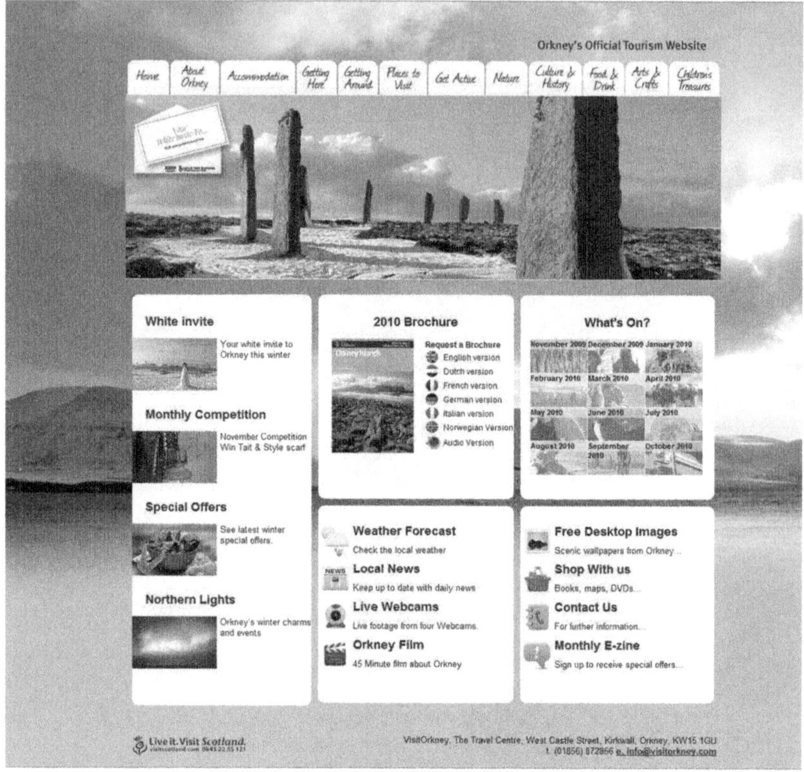

Figure 1.2 Screenshot of the homepage of the Orkney region website
Source: http://www.visitorkney.com/index.html (accessed on 10 December 2009); reproduced by permission of Scotland's national tourism organization, VisitScotland.

representation of activities and wellness in interplays between smaller static photographs. Instances on the Orkney homepage relate to a visually and spatially prominent landscape photograph, the repetitive representation of landscape environments in smaller static photographs, lexical references to white winter in groups and phrases, and the placement of a wealth of types of media in separate layout units. Examples on the Istria homepage revolve around the large size and prominent placement in the upper part of the page of landscape photographs, the prominent placement of accommodation in the upper part of the page, and repetitive references to accommodation in layout units in the right and left margins of the page. Instances on the Perthshire homepage involve the large size and prominent positioning of a landscape

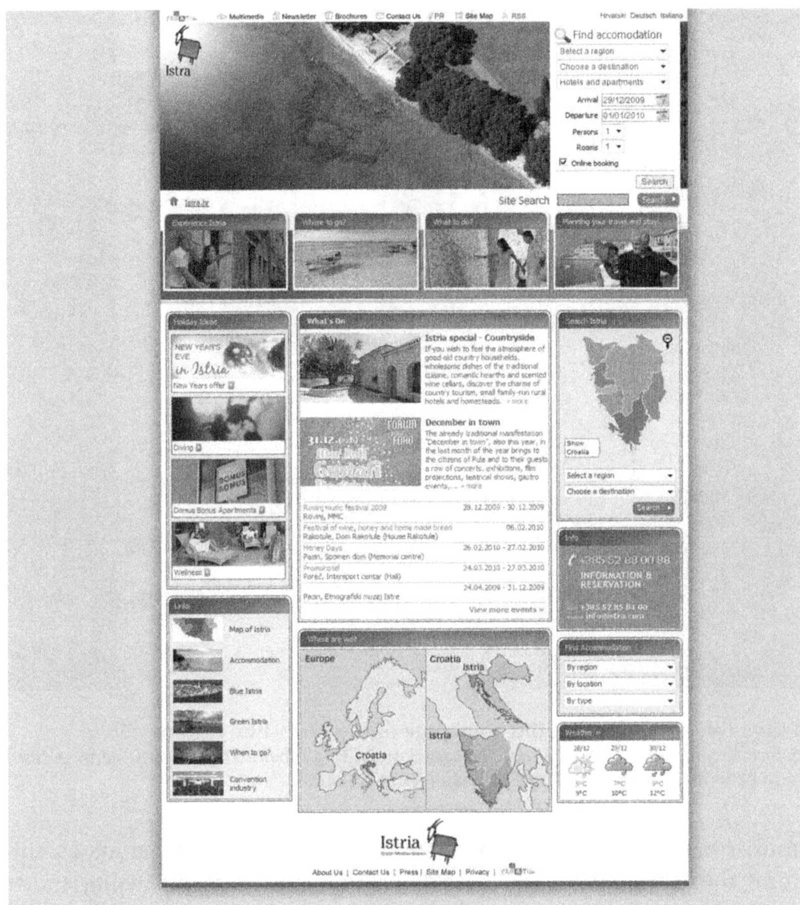

Figure 1.3 Screenshot of the homepage of the Istria region website
Source: http://www.istra.hr/en (accessed on 26 December 2009); reproduced by permission of the Istria Region Tourist Board.

photograph in the upper part of the main viewing area of the page, repetitive references to activities, events, natural heritage and conference tourism in the form of interplays between photographs, groups and/or groups and clauses in the main viewing area of the page or as menu items in the menu bar, and reference to events in a unit in the upper part of the left margin of the page.

Furthermore, the homepages differ in their representation of thematic meanings in the virtual world which can be conceived of as

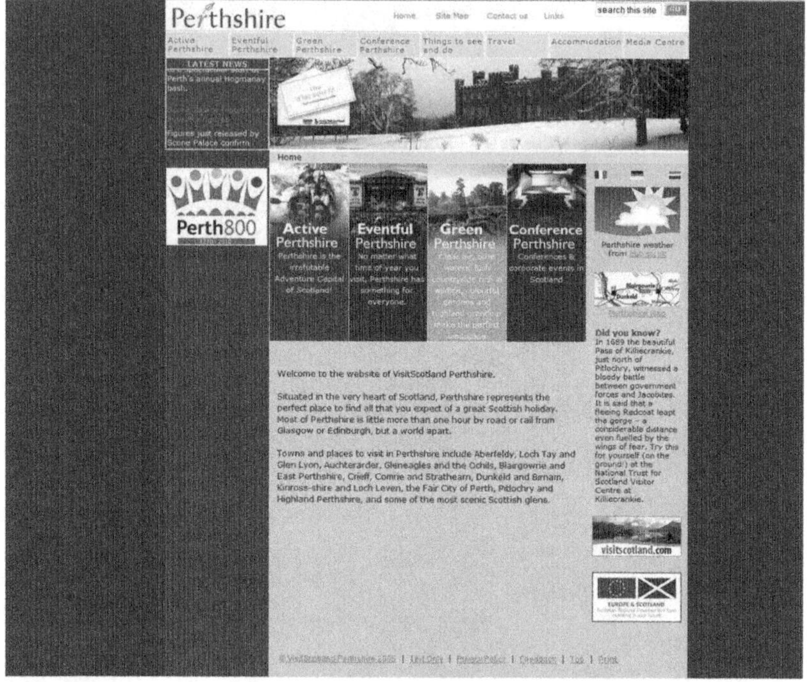

Figure 1.4 Screenshot of the homepage of the Perthshire region website
Source: http://www.perthshire.co.uk (accessed on 26 December 2009); reproduced by permission of Scotland's National Tourism Board, VisitScotland.

tourist activities, since tourist activities are practiced by users as cultural tourists in the social world. Examples include practising sports activities, visiting natural and cultural heritage sights, and benefiting from gastronomy. The above-listed textual cues indicate that certain thematic meanings are privileged over others. Thus, the Zadar region website places emphasis on more recreational tourist themes, such as Central Mediterranean landscape imagery in spring or summer and outdoor and water sports activities; the Orkney region website gives more space to different types of media and North Atlantic landscape imagery; the Istria region homepage focuses more on inland Mediterranean landscape imagery, the social experience of the region, and holiday planning through searching for accommodation; and the Perthshire region website concentrates on recreational tourist activities, such as sports activities, music events, and green natural heritage, and conference tourism.

This initial description and characterization of the homepages gives us our first insights into meaning-making in tourism texts. First, diverse elements and resources, such as text fragments and photographs, work together to represent and construct thematic meanings. Second, meaning is made by users as both media actors and cultural tourists who attribute meanings to multiple elements on the web pages due to their intertextual and cultural knowledge and the relative prominence of elements on the homepages. It follows from this that tourism can be studied by analysing multimodal tourist texts from a social semiotic perspective. In sum, a first glance at the homepages has given us our first insights into meaning-making and the final goal of the empirical analysis of Croatian and Scottish tourism web pages. Thematic meanings *represented* for users as *media actors* in the virtual world can be conceived of as tourist activities, since tourist activities are practiced by users as *cultural tourists* in the social world. Meaning is thus made by users as both media actors and cultural tourists. More precisely, they activate multiple elements on the web pages through types of user actions and attribute meanings to them due to their intertextual and cultural knowledge and the relative prominence of elements. The research goal is to understand the ways in which contemporary multimodal texts such as complex cultural communicative acts may function in a specific communicative situation, that is, tourist communication online, through an in-depth, exemplary analysis of tourism web pages. The term 'modes' will be used to denote communicational modes and semiotic resources for making meaning, shaped by society and culturally given (Jewitt, 2009a, p. 1 f. in Jewitt, 2009c; Kress, 2009a, p. 54 in Jewitt, 2009c).

Chapter 2 will further deal with the methodological approach applied to the empirical website analysis. This will be followed in Chapter 3 by an empirical website analysis of website layout. Moving from layout to meaning-making, an overview will be given of diverse tourist activities, with a focus on walking activities, natural heritage, history and heritage, and gastronomy in Chapter 4. These thematic meanings will be explored in terms of representation, and cultural tourist and user communication. Each subsection of Chapter 4 will conclude with a sub-subsection summarizing the main findings in response to the initial research questions and hypotheses. The conclusion in Chapter 5 will summarize the main findings and implications, and make suggestions for future work.

In sum, the study of the signifiers of culture, tourism, the new media, advertising, and text is of huge significance for scientific, business, and didactic reasons. Culture has been identified as crucial to both academic and popular discourses. A dearth of research has been noted when it comes to combining tourism studies with the study of language or discourse and systematic analyses of promotional tourist discourse. Web pages as forms of new media are of particular research interest due to their hypertextual organization in the World Wide Web platform accessible via the Internet, their multimodal coding, their dynamic nature, their interactivity potential, and the support of computer-mediated communication. This calls for the systematic analysis of culture through the investigation of tourist activities in multimodal tourist texts. The analysis is intended to reveal the ways in which tourism websites function as instances of multimodal texts.

1.2 Research questions and hypotheses

Against the background of the above-delineated research goal, the primary question is: In what ways do websites socio-semiotically, that is, through use of diverse resources such as language or types of visuals, realize the communicative purposes of representation, tourist communication and user communication? More specifically, in what ways do websites represent themes, such as tourist attractions, events, or information on user orientation, to users? How do websites construct users as cultural tourists who participate in diverse tourist activities, such as visiting natural and cultural heritage sights, doing sports activities, and benefiting from gastronomy? In what ways are users as media actors invited to interact with tourism web pages through diverse types of user actions, such as rollover, mouse-click, or type-in? This triggers four core research questions:

The first core research question is: To what extent are tourist activities important as tourist themes for the images constructed for the regions, users as cultural tourists, and media actors? Are there themes which are of more, less, or equal importance for the image constructed for the regions and, if so, how is this socio-semiotically realized?

The second core research question is: Which image is represented of the Zadar, Orkney, Istria, and Perthshire regions? This can further be divided into the related subquestions: Which aspects of these regions are shown as tourist activities practised by tourists in the tourist regions and in the form of themes on the tourism web pages? How is each theme represented? For example, is history materialized through cultural heritage sights and artefacts or represented as a set of historical events? Are statements about themes represented as indisputable facts or is the force of statements tempered? Which semiotic tools, such as clause types, are used to realize these representations?

The third core research question is: Which meaning potentials are communicated to tourists as cultural actors who participate in tourist activities? This can further be divided into the subquestions: In what ways do types of visuals, such as photographs, position users? For example, when it comes to the theme of history, are they constructed as observers or explorers of cultural heritage sights and public institutions? Which types of users as cultural tourists are addressed? How is this realized socio-semiotically?

When it comes to web user interaction potential, the fourth core research question is: Which type of user profile is constructed? For example, are users constructed as observers of tourist promotional material or social actors in social media such as Facebook or Twitter? More precisely, do the websites make use of more units with accessible or with inaccessible elements? Is media interaction made more or less salient? In what ways can users interact with elements on the web pages?

Finally, the question arises as to whether (and if so, in what ways) representation, tourist communication, and user communication interact to construe certain tourist profiles. The core research questions, in turn, allow for the formulation of initial hypotheses through reference to previous research and evaluations.

With regard to the first research question, research reveals that meaning-making on websites depends on the interplay between the categories of navigation, design, and function (Djonov, 2005, p. 131). Thus, it can be expected that the degree of importance of tourist activities to the ways in which regions are represented, and the way in which users are addressed as cultural tourists and engaged as media actors, is influenced by the compositional principles of the layout.

In addition, when it comes to the first and second research questions, rather than being restricted to travel texts themselves, features of tourism offers, such as nautical and trekking tourism, are embedded in a wider social context of use: tourism communication, as part of which destinations are advertised to prospective customers on the part of website producers and tourism authorities such as the Ministry of the Sea, Transport and Infrastructure, Ministry of Tourism" (2008, p. 8) and the National Development Agency and Managing Authority for International Cooperation (2011, p. 76). Socio-linguistic research further suggests that the language of tourism combines several registers of language, the most frequent ones being 'ol' talk', the language of nostalgia tourism, 'spa', the register of health tourism, 'gastrolingo', the language of food and drink, and 'greenspeak', the register of eco-tourism (Dann, 1996, pp. 211–218). Dann (1996, pp. 241–249) also identifies characteristic lexical items, principles and themes which interact to construe the register of ecotourism. Lexical items capture notions of simple, expert knowledge and an escape of the individual to unspoilt places. Principles include ideas of the sustainable, sections of landscape which are set apart and preserved for future generations, patriotic feelings towards landscape protection, biodiversity through diversification, and limits to tourism growth. Themes cover nature, with reference to notions of the natural, authentic, pure, and unaffected; nostalgia, in the sense of a longing for the supposed warmth and safety of the past, and people who are closely related to nature; and nirvana, as the state of happiness of the individual who is conceived of as being at one with nature.

Similarly, it is productive to identify other aspects of the manner in which each region is represented. Croatia, in general, and the Adriatic sea coast, in particular, are commonly represented as traditional Mediterranean tourist destinations by authorities such as the Ministry of Foreign Affairs and European Integration of the Republic of Croatia (2006). It can therefore be assumed that Mediterranean landscapes, sunny weather conditions, outdoor and water sports activities in Mediterranean landscapes, various artistic and religious, as well as modern and contemporary tourist attractions and events, indigenous seafood and crafts offers, and ancient history and monuments are of central importance for the image constructed for the Zadar region. Similarly, as Istria is commonly described as a popular wine and olive oil region by travel companies (Istraturist, 2013), it can be expected that, on the Istria region website, landscapes which present the Istria region as a blue-green peninsula, and depict Mediterranean gourmet food and wine for *bon-vivants*, gastronomic and music events, sports activities and ancient monuments in Mediterranean landscapes, and the location of Istrian tourist destinations are of particular relevance. As Orkney and Perthshire are Scottish regions, a geographic closeness can be expected to the Atlantic Ocean and the North Sea (Scotland map, 2014). In addition, Scotland's national tourism organization (2011) has launched new marketing campaigns to promote Scottish destinations in online and other electronic media. This may indicate that North Atlantic landscapes, activities and prehistoric remains in these landscapes, stark weather conditions, food and drink from local sources, and types of print and online media are crucial to image construction on the Orkney region websites. Equally, as Perthshire is referred to as 'a popular destination for business, leisure, and tourism' (Hazeldene Guest House, 2013) by accommodation companies, it may be the case that tourist themes, such as green landscapes, adventure sports, music events, benefiting from gastronomy, sightseeing, and activities for commercial and professional purposes, such as shopping and conference tourism, are crucial to the image constructed for the Perthshire region.

Moreover, research reveals that there is a relationship between realistic expectations about tourist destinations on the part of tourists as customers, on the one hand, and customer satisfaction, on the other hand (O'Neill et al., 2004, p. 32). Thus, in the context of tourist-wildlife encounters, O'Neill et al. (2004) note that '[...] unrealistic expectations about wild dolphins may lead to dissatisfaction. [...] It is assumed that the education offered by operators during the brief helped to create realistic expectations, and hence enabled tourists to be more satisfied with their experiences.' It is thus expected that all four regional websites predominantly represent statements about thematic meanings as facts, rather than creating space for their questioning and challenging. This may have to do with the social context of use in which websites are embedded, that is, tourism communication, as part of which destinations are advertised to prospective customers by the website producers. The websites are therefore expected to create realistic tourist experiences for users as media actors in the virtual world, thus suggesting that users can expect what is promised on the websites as cultural tourists in the social world.

In terms of the third research question, functional-linguistic studies into English and German travel texts have identified the following experiential and interpersonal features of English travel texts: fact-orientedness, as suggested by the predominance of relational over other process types; the lack of instructions, as suggested by the dearth of clauses in imperative mood; an impersonal mode of expression, as indicated by the frequent use of passive constructions (Neumann, 2003, p. 88 f. in Abeillé et al., 2003); and a more descriptive character, as suggested by the frequent use of complex noun phrases (Nilsson, 2000, pp. 267, 272 in Mair & Hundt, 2000). Thus, it can be expected that all four websites will give less space to addressing the user or to clauses, phrases, groups or photographs. They may show photographs which present information about diverse tourist themes as objects of observation, rather than inviting users to establish an imaginary relation with the represented information. Equally, however, there may be differences in the degree to which users are addressed as cultural tourists in clauses, phrases or groups between the websites of the Zadar and Istria region and the websites of the Orkney and Perthshire regions. The latter may create more space for directly addressing users as lovers of sports and landscape, animal observers or visitors of sights and events. Also, as a by-product, an analysis of the representation of thematic meanings can reveal which process types and modality features are more prominent, thus giving more insight into possible features of travel texts.

Finally, when it comes to the fourth research question, research into the use of the web by tourism organizations distinguishes between different levels of functionality and interactivity of websites in three main stages (Burgess et al., 2009, p. 523). Higher levels of functionality imply more sophisticated use of technologies (ibid., p. 525). In order to identify the degree of adoption of web technologies for destination marketing, a corresponding model has been developed. For ease of reference, this is shown in Table 1.1.

The model shown in Table 1.1 will be used as a reference point for identifying the types of user profiles constructed on the four regional websites. Stages 1 and 3 of the model have been omitted since only Stage 2 will be relevant here. Lower levels of interactivity, as exemplified by the provision of more basic information on thematic meanings, hyperlinks to further information and contact forms, will be related to the construction of more individual users as traditionally print-literate tourists. By contrast, higher levels of interactivity, as illustrated by social media, such as chat rooms and discussion forums, will be linked to the creation of more contemporary, technologically advanced, media-interactive social actors. Against the background of research into the functionality and interactivity of websites, and since it is generally questionable whether websites fully reach their interactivity potential, it can be assumed that, on all four websites, users are constructed more

Table 1.1 Stage 2 of the extended Model of Internet Commerce Adoption (eMICA)

eMICA	Examples of functionality
Stage 2 – Provision	
Layer 1 – low level interactivity	basic product catalogue, hyperlinks to further information, online enquiry form
Layer 2 – medium interactivity	higher-level product catalogues, customer support (e.g. FAQs, sitemaps), industry-specific value-added features
Layer 3 – high interactivity	chat room, discussion forum, multimedia, traveller reviews newsletters or updates by email

Source: Adapted from Doolin et al. (2002) and from Burgess and Cooper (2000) in Burgess et al. (2009, p. 523).

as traditional and individual readers of websites than contemporary and technologically advanced social actors who visit social network sites.

1.3 Conclusion

In sum, the study of the signifiers of culture, tourism, the new media, advertising, and text is of huge significance for scientific, business, and didactic reasons. Culture has been identified as crucial to both academic and popular discourses. A dearth of research has been noted when it comes to combining tourism studies with the study of language or discourse and systematic analyses of promotional tourist discourse. Web pages as forms of new media are of particular research interest due to their hypertextual organization in the World Wide Web platform accessible via the Internet, their multimodal coding, their dynamic nature, their interactivity potential and the support of computer-mediated communication. This calls for the systematic analysis of culture through the investigation of tourist activities in multimodal tourist texts. The analysis is intended to reveal the ways in which tourism websites function as instances of multimodal texts. Against the background of this research goal, the primary question is: In what ways do websites socio-semiotically realize the communicative purposes of representation, tourist communication, and user communication? More specifically, in what ways are themes represented and types of users constructed as cultural tourists and media actors?

Any empirical analysis of texts would be insufficient without an explanation of the methodological basis. Also, the wealth of modes and layers that can be identified for tourism websites requires a complex analytical framework which will model the types of multiple modes, criteria according to which they can be grouped into larger units, ways in which the modes relate to one another, and dimensions of meanings which can be identified for each mode. Thus, the following chapter, on methodology, will deal with the selection and characterization of tourism websites, the development of an analytical framework, and the steps taken to reveal how to proceed in the empirical analysis of the tourism websites on the basis of the relevant concepts and theoretical principles.

2
A Multi-Layer Approach to the Website Analysis

2.1 Selection and characterization of tourism websites

The investigation involves an in-depth study of 48 Croatian and Scottish tourism web pages, covering the Scottish regions of Orkney and Perthshire and the Croatian regions of Zadar and Istria. These are extracted from the homepages of the Croatian National Tourist Board, 'Hrvatska Turistička Zajednica', and the Scottish National Tourist Board, as part of 'Visit Britain', which are in charge of the national promotion of Croatia and Scotland, respectively, as tourist destinations. The four regional websites are compared with one another. They have been selected as they coincide in bases of comparison as part of parallel textual analyses which have been agreed upon by researchers in the area of contrastive media studies suitable for comparing texts (Lüger & Lenk, 2008, p. 19 f. in Lüger & Lenk, 2008). Thus, all four websites are embedded in tourist communication in which the same text types (regional tourist texts), in the same media realization (websites), dealing with the same tourist activities in the form of thematic meanings (doing activities, visiting natural and cultural heritage, and benefiting from gastronomy), fulfil the same communicative function; that is, they are designed to inform and appeal to users who opt for visiting the regions advertised on the websites as holiday destinations. Although websites in other languages and of other tourist organizations may equally display common bases of comparison, the choice of Croatian and Scottish websites is motivated by their general underrepresentedness in multimodal analyses of texts. The homepages will serve as a starting point for the analysis for two reasons. Firstly, they serve as 'the user's point of entry, to a website and its meanings' (Baldry & Thibault, 2006, p. 118). Secondly, they display the highest representativeness with regard to the overall message of the websites; that is, depending on whether they appeal to them, users can be assumed to either navigate or not to further web pages of the overall websites.

Moreover, when it comes to the analysis of types of processes, clauses, and modality features in clauses, such as modal adjuncts and finites (cf. definitions in subsection 2.2, Chapter 2), the clause will serve as the unit of analysis. This type of analysis will give insight into the ways in which tourist activities are represented. The texts can be divided into 1,470 clauses. With regard to the analysis of representational structures, value, and realizations of the systems of contact, attitude, and social distance in types of visuals, the type of visual will serve as the unit of analysis. The analysis of representational structures and value in types of visuals will tell us more about the nature of representation of tourist activities. By contrast, the analysis of realizations of the systems of contact, attitude, and social distance in types of visuals will be relevant to the following question: How are users addressed and positioned as cultural tourists? For the four regional websites, 253 visuals can be identified. The analysis of clauses and visuals will be done manually. In addition, for the analysis of units of user address as cultural tourists, groups, phrases, and clauses will be analysed. More specifically, the analysis of clause types and personal pronouns will point to the ways in which users are addressed as cultural tourists. The analysis of units with accessible and inaccessible elements will cover both clauses and types of visuals. Accessible elements can be activated by users through types of user actions, such as mouse click, rollover and mouse click, type in and click, and up, down, left and/or right movement. Inaccessible elements cannot be activated by users through these types of activity potential (cf. subsection 3.1, Chapter 3). In order to give insight into the variety of ways in which users are addressed as cultural tourists in terms of activities, such as viewers of landscape and activities or lovers of dynamic sports (cf. sub-subsection 4.2.2, Chapter 4), and verbal indications of media interaction, the corresponding instances will be identified. If the possibility of users becoming engaged as media actors is equally suggested verbally through processes in imperative mood, such as *search*, this will be referred to as *verbal indication of media interaction*. The analysis of accessible and inaccessible elements, types of user actions and verbal indication of media interaction will give insight into the types of user profiles which are constructed. Overviews of statistics of clauses and types of visuals on diverse tourist activities, sports activities, natural heritage, history and heritage, and gastronomy for the four regional websites are given in Tables 2.1–2.2.

Table 2.1 Overview of statistics of clauses for the four regional websites

Region websites / Clauses	Zadar	Orkney	Istria	Perthshire
Total	320	311	490	349
Tourist activities	31	9	15	21
Sport activities	35	43	51	70
Natural heritage	19	124	85	74
History and heritage	90	76	205	79
Gastronomy	145	59	134	105

Table 2.2 Overview of statistics of types of visuals for the four regional websites

Region websites / Types of visuals	Zadar	Orkney	Istria	Perthshire
Total	106	56	60	31
Tourist activities	40	33	29	14
Sport activities	13	5	4	6
Natural heritage	17	7	7	3
History and heritage	26	5	5	4
Gastronomy	10	6	15	4

Also, in order to compare the values, some standardizing of frequency is necessary. Thus, depending on the type of analysis, relative (%) or absolute figures (instances) will be given. Graphs and tables will be given to allow the reader to compare the values directly. For ease of reference, an overview of types of figures, analyses, graphs (subsections 4.1–4.5, Chapter 4) and tables (subsection 3.2, Chapter 3) is given in Table 2.3.

Investigations at this scale and level of detail raise the following question: How can the organization of information offerings on tourism web pages be adequately addressed? In response, the analysis does not aim to include all aspects present in the 48 web pages. As hypertext media are characterized by indefiniteness in terms of textual boundaries (Djonov, 2005, pp. 4, 116), they allow for the unlimited accumulation of meanings. This calls for boundaries to be made: The analysis will include the layout subunits on the four homepages and the visually and spatially more prominent base units positioned in the main viewing areas of the opening pages at the first, second, and third hierarchical levels of the website structures which more directly deal with walking,

Table 2.3 Overview of types of figures, analyses, graphs, and tables for the four regional websites

Types of figures / Types of analyses	Relative (%)	Absolute (instances)
Types of representational structures	–	–
Types of processes	cf. Figures 4.5 (subsubsection 4.1.2, Chapter 4), 4.9 (subsubsection 4.2.1, Chapter 4), 4.13 (subsubsection 4.3.1, Chapter 4), 4.17 (subsubsection 4.4.1, Chapter 4) and 4.21 (subsubsection 4.5.1, Chapter 4)	–
Types of clauses	–	–
The type, value and orientation and manifestation of modality features in clauses	cf. Figures 4.6–4.7 (subsubsection 4.1.2, Chapter 4), 4.10–4.11 (subsubsection 4.2.1, Chapter 4), 4.14–4.15 (subsubsection4. 3.1, Chapter 4), 4.18–4.19 (subsubsection 4.4.1, Chapter 4) and 4.22–4.23 (subsubsection 4.5.1, Chapter 4)	–
The value in visuals	–	–
Realizations of the systems of contact, subjective and objective attitude and social distance in visuals	cf. Figures 4.8 (subsubsection 4.1.3, Chapter 4), 4.12 (subsubsection 4.2.2, Chapter 4), 4.16 (subsubsection 4.3.2, Chapter 4), 4.20 (subsubsection 4.4.2, Chapter 4) and 4.24 (subsubsection 4.5.2, Chapter 4)	–
Units of user address as cultural tourists	–	–
Units with accessible and inaccessible elements	cf. Table 3.1 (subsection 3.2, Chapter 3)	–
Types of user actions	cf. Table 3.2 (subsection 3.2, Chapter 3)	–
Experiential meanings in groups and phrases	–	–
Instances of user address as cultural tourists	–	–
Instances of verbal indication of media interaction	–	cf. Table 3.4 (subsection 3.2, Chapter 3)

natural heritage, history and heritage, and gastronomy. The analysis will exclude units which give less direct insight into representation and cultural tourist and user communication, as placed in the marginal areas of the opening web pages.

Furthermore, criteria need to be identified to define which elements capture thematic meanings on walking activities, natural heritage and history and heritage, and gastronomy in the relevant layout units on the four homepages. In response, the following criteria will be considered: salient lexical references to the relevant thematic meanings in captions or experiential meanings on the themes in photographs and elements as part of content-oriented layout units or menu items of menu bars as functional layout units. Also, they will include hidden lexical references in the captions and experiential meanings in photographs which can be uncovered on the web pages which open at subsequent levels of the website structure through activation of anchors on the homepages.

Thus, on the homepage of the Zadar region website, as presented in Figure 1.1, elements cover the embedded text fragments or captions of the corresponding content-oriented layout units or the menu items of the menu bar as a functional layout unit. The text fragments or captions of the content-oriented layout units explicitly refer to thematic meanings, such as *Activities, Historical cities' sightseeing* and *Autochthonous Mediterranean cuisine specialties*, together with smaller static photographs which experientially relate to the thematic meanings on sports activities, cultural heritage, and gastronomy. The menu items explicitly indicate that they deal with the respective thematic meanings, such as *Activities*. If activated by clicking, users are directed to a page portraying types of activities, such as walking or birdwatching. If the thematic meanings are less salient, users have to navigate the website to find out in which ways they can be accessed. Examples include the *About the region* menu item which, if activated by clicking, leads to the opening of a page enumerating natural heritage, history, cultural heritage, gastronomy, and indigenous products, and other subthemes as further thematic meanings.

On the homepage of the Orkney region website, content-oriented layout units are predominantly not devoted to the portrayal of activities, natural heritage, history and heritage, and gastronomy. Rather, these thematic meanings can be accessed by activating them in the menu bar as a functional layout unit through menu items explicitly denoting the thematic meanings captured by menu items such as *Get Active, Nature, Culture & History*, and *Food & Drink*.

On the homepage of the Istria region website, elements include the menu items *Blue Istria* and *Green Istria* which, in concert with smaller static photographs, experientially denote seaside Istrian and Central Istrian regions as instances of natural heritage as part of content-oriented layout units. Also, they relate to menu items explicitly denoting the respective thematic meanings, such as *History, Food & wine, Natural attractions* and *Sport*; or users have to navigate to the website to find out that *Blue Istria, Green Istria* and *Arts and culture* deal with natural heritage and cultural heritage sights. This is indicated in the menu bar as a functional layout unit. If activated through rollover, the menu bar suggests that these menu items serve as subheaders of the headers *Experience Istria* and *What to do?*.

On the homepage of the Perthshire region website, elements denoting the respective thematic meanings include titles which denote activities and natural heritage, such as *Active Perthshire* and *Green Perthshire*, together with photographs on activities and natural heritage as part of content-related layout units. Also, they cover menu items as part of the menu bar as a functional unit, such as *Active Perthshire* and *Green Perthshire*. These are embedded in photographs with clauses, such as *Perthshire is the irrefutable Adventure Capital of Scotland* and *Clear air, pure waters, lush countryside rich in wildlife, colourful gardens and Highland grandeur make the perfect landscape*, or have to be identified by users as dealing with activities and gastronomy by navigating the website. For instance, if activated by clicking, the *Things to see and do* menu item leads to the opening of a corresponding page listing *WalkingWild* and *Shopping, eating and nightlife* as menu items.

Following these criteria, an overview of elements on activities, natural heritage, history and heritage, and gastronomy on the four homepages is presented in Table 2.4.

Finally, for readers to get an idea of where all of the tourism web pages fit, which will be analyzed in the empirical parts of Chapter 4, an overview is presented in Table 2.5. The horizontally-running rows represent the names of the web pages which deal with tourist activities, that is, sports activities, natural heritage, history and heritage, and gastronomy. The vertically-running columns exhibit the names of the web pages which belong to the four regional websites, that is, the Zadar region website, the Orkney region website, the Istria region website, and the Perthshire region website.

To analyse multimodal texts, it will be assumed that the regional Croatian and Scottish websites constitute *multimodal and multilayered tourist texts*. This raises several questions: How far can tourism websites serve as instances of multimodality? How far can the attribute 'multilayered' be ascribed to them? And how far does it make sense to

Table 2.4 Overview of elements on walking activities, natural heritage, history and heritage, and gastronomy on the four homepages

Thematic meanings / Homepages	Zadar region	Orkney region	Istria region	Perthshire region
Sports activities	- *Activities* menu item - *Activities* unit - Unit on rafting	- *Get Active* menu item	- *What to do?* menu item	- *Active Perthshire* menu item - *Active Perthshire* unit
Natural heritage	- *About the region* menu item - *Visit to the national parks* unit	- *Nature* menu item	- *Experience Istria* menu item - *Blue Istria* unit - *Green Istria* unit	- *Green Perthshire* menu item - *Green Perthshire* unit
History and heritage	- *About the region* menu item - *Historical cities' sightseeing* unit	- *Culture & History* menu item	- *Experience Istria* menu item	- *Things to see and do* menu item
Gastronomy	- *About the region* menu item - *Autochthonous Mediterranean cuisine specialties* unit	- *Food & Drink* menu item - *Special offers* unit	- *What to do?* menu item	- *Things to see and do* menu item

Table 2.5 Overview of tourism web pages

Regional websites / Tourist activities	Zadar region	Orkney region	Istria region	Perthshire region	Total regional web pages with tourist activities
Overview	Homepage	Homepage	Homepage*	Homepage**	**4**
Sports activities	*Activities* page *Trekking and mountain-bike trail maps* page	*Get Active* page *Walking* page	*What to do?* page *Sport* page *Trekking* page	*Active Perthshire* page *Walkingwild* page	**9**
Natural Heritage	*About the region* page *Birdwatching* page	*Nature* page	*What to do?* page *Natural attractions* page *Unique Play of Nature* page *Experience Istria* page *Green Istria* page *Blue Istria* page	*Green Perthshire* page *Wildlife and nature* page	**11**
History and Heritage	*About the region* page *History* page *Cultural heritage* page	*Culture and history* page	*Experience Istria* page *Prehistoric people in Istria* page *Prehistoric settlements* page *Romans in Istria* page *Byzantine period* page *Medieval towns* page *What to do?* page *Arts and Culture* page *Cultural sights* page *Archaeological sites* page *Museums and collections* page	*Things to see and do* page*** *History and heritage* page	**17**

(*continued*)

Table 2.5 Continued

Regional websites / Tourist activities	Zadar region	Orkney region	Istria region	Perthshire region	Total regional web pages with tourist activities
Gastronomy	*About the region* page *Gastronomy* page *Indigenous products* page	*Food and drink* page	*What to do?* page *Food and wine* page *Istrian cuisine* page *His majesty the truffle of Istria* page *Restaurants* page *Agritourisms and Taverns* page *Wine routes* page *Olive-oil trails* page	*Things to see and do* page *Shopping, eating and nightlife* page	**14**
Total Regional Web Pages	9	6	25	8	**55** / **48**

Note: *: The homepage saved on 26 December 2009 has been analysed, not the updated version of the web page.
**: Just as for the Istria region website, for the Perthshire region website, the older version of the homepage has been analysed.
***: The clauses and types of visuals identified for the *Things to see and do* page have been analysed as part of section 4.4 on history and heritage in Chapter 4. In order to avoid repetition, they will not be analysed as part of section 5 on gastronomy.

read them as texts? The reply to the first question is more straightforward. Thus, previous research reveals that documents can be viewed as multimodal in that they combine multiple modes, including verbal aspects, visual elements, and layout (Bateman, 2008, pp. 1–19). More specifically, in her recent introduction to multimodality, Jewitt (2009a, p. 1 f. in Jewitt, 2009c) conceptualizes multimodality as:

> the whole range of representational and communicational modes or semiotic resources for making meaning that are employed in a culture – such as image, writing, gesture, gaze, speech, posture. Multimodality starts from the position that all modes, like speech and writing, consist of sets of semiotic resources (semiotic resource refers to resources that people draw on and configure in specific moments and places to represent events and relation).

In application to the Croatian and Scottish tourism websites, representational and communicational modes or semiotic resources for making meaning can be divided into two interrelated types of meaning potential: first, various visual resources of meaning potential, such as static and moving photographs, advertising banners, drawings, maps and icons as graphical symbols in a graphical user interface, language in the form of text fragments and coherent text passages, and typography; second, haptic and aural resources of meaning potential, that is, some of the above-mentioned visual resources responding to rollover, type in, and/or mouse click.

At this point, a brief digression into the notion of visual, haptic, and aural resources of meaning potential is necessary. Baldry and Thibault (2006, p. 104) describe web pages as visual-spatial units which are displayed on the screen, and as activity potentials of mouse click, rollover, type-in, and other forms of user actions. These descriptions are important for capturing the particularities of websites and highlighting the fact that meaning-making is an active process which involves various sense systems. It is the user's hands, which are active in the process of making sense of websites by *touching, moving, and clicking* on the mouse. If users are not deaf-mute or blind, their ears are *listening to* mouse clicks. Their eyes are *watching* the screen. Various possible constellations of inter*action* between these senses result in brain *activity*. The active nature of these human senses may become most obvious when considering more or less extreme bodily symptoms of a pathological type, such as eyestrain, headache, earache, and backache experienced when spending a huge amount of time in front of the computer. Also, the saying 'to have a trained eye for' something may precisely illustrate the active nature of meaning-making. For further investigations of the user's bodily interactions with the screen, more profound digressions into psychology and cognitive linguistics may be useful. In fact, although a relationship between the reader's looking at multimodal texts and their cognitive processing of multimodal texts has been identified through use of the methodology of eye tracking (Just & Carpenter, 1980, pp. 329–354), a dearth of research has been noted when it comes to the nature of actual interaction between users and multimodal texts (Holsanova & Nord, 2010, p. 93 in Bucher et al., 2010). However, this line of thought will not be taken further in this work, as it would exceed its scope, but may be of interest for future investigations. Nevertheless, a conclusion can be drawn in terms of website characterization. It is in favour of a characterization of web pages as visual, haptic, and aural activity potentials resulting from interplays of diverse human senses in meaning-making.

The second response is more challenging. Thus, a framework with multiple layers of description, involving basic elements on a page, the layout structure, a rhetorical base, and elements relating to navigation in the page, has been suggested to empirically explore multimodal documents (Bateman, 2008, p. 108). The establishment of an analytical framework which separates, rather than connects, various layers of analyses, is motivated by criticism of previous analyses of multimodal texts. Following Bateman (2008, pp. 22, 45, 50), these have been informed by pretheoretical ideas of, rather than the actual functioning of, multimodal texts. To exemplify this view, Bateman (2008, p. 47) refers to analyses of information value as an area of meaning potential in which one-to-one correspondences have been drawn between layout compositions and ideological meanings, such as those conducted by Kress & van Leeuwen (2007, p. 47) and Baldry & Thibault (2006, p. 82). As this is elaborated on in a detailed way in Bateman (2008, p. 47), a brief example will suffice to follow his line of argument.

For instance, in an analysis of printed biology textbook pages, Baldry & Thibault (2006, pp. 71–90) read the drawing of frog blood cells as ideal/given, and of medium salience and high importance on the basis of their positioning in the upper left of the page, while the image of human blood cells is interpreted as ideal/new, and of high salience and importance due to its positioning upper right on the page. However, rather than reliably accounting for layout compositions, the ascription of notions of the ideal and real appear as 'stories to be told about the functioning of the elements on the page' (Bateman, 2008, p. 49) which may appear plausible in some instances, but may lack plausibility in others. Following this line of argument, in application to the analysis of tourism websites, greater caution will be used in drawing direct correlations between layout compositions and ideological implications. Rather, as will be exemplified in the discussion of the analytical framework and steps in subsection 2.2 of Chapter 2, the importance of the positioning of elements on a page in certain rather than other ways for meaning-making activities will be captured through perceptual Gestalt psychology.

Also, the websites will be analyzed following multiple layers, rather than the clusters used by Baldry & Thibault (2006, p. 31). A cluster as 'a local grouping of items' (ibid.) is inappropriate as a unit of analysis, since Baldry & Thibault offer no comment on the ways in which a cluster can be determined. By contrast, the analysis of multiple layers allows for the explicit identification of the types of elements and criteria according to which they have been grouped together to form larger units. Thus, it is expected to enhance the degree of reproducibility and reliability of multimodal text analysis, in general.

The final challenge of characterizing websites consists in reading them as texts. This is due to the wealth of suggestions for the definition of 'text' which are observable in various research traditions dealing with texts in the humanities. The German-speaking research tradition, a discipline whose name may suggest that it demonstrably looks into the features and meanings of texts – text linguistics – and the discipline which has recently been suggested for approaching discourse through a multilayered analysis of texts, knowledge, and actors – discourse linguistics – may serve as examples. In these disciplines, the predominant view of text has emerged as a more narrow, communicative-functional one in which texts are conceptualized as 'more or less self-contained, coherent communicates' (Spitzmüller & Warnke, 2011, p. 82) or, more precisely, '*eine begrenzte Folge von sprachlichen Zeichen, die in sich kohärent ist und die als Ganzes eine erkennbare kommunikative Funktion signalisiert*' (Brinker, 2001, p. 17), that is, 'a limited sequence of linguistic signs which is coherent and which, as a whole, signals a visible communicative function' (own translation). Rather than commencing with the impossible attempt of providing an exhaustive definition of text which is generally acceptable for all text types and research traditions, as was the case in earlier text linguistic research in the 1980s, a tendency towards summarizing aspects of texts which may be of interest with regard to the subject of investigation has developed (Adamzik, 2004, pp. 38 ff.). It follows from this that with regard to the above-identified purpose of this analysis, a view of text will be selected which does justice to the dynamic and procedural nature of meaning-making within and across websites and the context of use in which they are embedded.

In sum, texts will be characterized as 'meaning-making events whose functions are defined by their use in particular social contexts', as was done by Baldry & Thibault (2006, p. 4) in reference to Halliday (1989, p. 10 in Halliday & Hasan, 1989). Following the Classifier as any feature which may classify the Thing in terms of material, scale, purpose, function, status, rank, origin, and other features (Halliday & Matthiessen 2004, p. 320), that is, *meaning-making* in this characterization, texts will thus be viewed as dynamically developing in the process of website traversal. The Thing as the element denoting a class of things (ibid., p. 312), that is, *events*, will be used to express the idea that the meaning potential of texts allows for different readings which may be similar, but may also vary among users. Following the notion of social contexts, as introduced above, and part of the notion of multimodality as a social practice which covers multiple layers, such as the planning, production, design, and distribution of texts (Kress & van Leeuwen, 2001 in Leander & Vasudevan, 2009, p. 129), the *social context of use* will be one of tourism communication. More specifically, users as prospective tourists to the respective destinations advertised on the part of website marketers, agencies, and tourist boards will be thought of as attributing meanings to the multiple modes accessible on tourism websites.

2.2 Analytical toolkit and empirical procedure

Concepts which have been developed in the field of hypermedia design and the research tradition of systemic functional linguistics and social semiotics will serve as starting points for studying meaning-making in tourism websites. These include website structure, base layer, layout structure, and metafunctions. Thus, more structurally-oriented areas of analysis will be combined with more meaning- and activity-related areas of analysis. They will describe tourist activities in terms of representation and cultural tourist and user communication. More specifically, more structurally-oriented areas of analysis will include accounts of global website structure and micro-analyses of base elements and layout. The accounts of global website structure will give insight into the following question: Where are themes positioned within the overall structure of a website? Micro-analyses of base elements and layout will respond to the following question: To what extent are tourist themes important for the images constructed for the regions, and users as cultural tourists and media actors? More meaning- and activity-related areas of analysis will involve different modes of meaning characterized by 'metafunctions'. This will tell us more about the following questions: How are themes represented? How are users positioned and addressed as cultural tourists? How are users involved as media actors?

In brief, the notion of website hierarchy, as advanced by Djonov (2005, pp. 137 ff.), will be used in order to identify the positioning of themes within the overall structure of a website. It is based on the idea that information organized in a website is predominantly hierarchical, with web pages and navigation options in a website being unequal in terms of status (ibid., p. 136). Djonov (2005, p. 137) proposes to combine insights from two perspectives on website hierarchy, which she sums up as the holistic perspective and the segmental perspective, to conceptualize website hierarchy as a hierarchy of themes from the perspective of periodicity.

Thus, the holistic perspective is drawn upon to stress the type and structure of information within the website as a whole (ibid., pp. 134, 138), the concomitant potential of semiotic resources in web page design to structure information and web pages into meaningful semantic units (ibid., pp. 135, 155), and the idea that website hierarchy is based on a scale of containment. This allows levels of the hierarchy to be optional in the sense that 'a website *may* consist of sections, which *may* consist of subsections, which *may* consist of sub-subsections and so on' (ibid., p. 134). While this subordination of levels below the homepage in a website's hierarchy represents its vertical dimension, the horizontal dimension is specified by sections in a website or subsections in a section, and so on (ibid., pp. 149, 155).

Insights from the segmental perspective are used to emphasize the function of hyperlinks in showing this structure of information by connecting individual web pages as 'building blocks' (ibid., pp. 133, 155) of a website. Both perspectives are called upon to highlight the function of the homepage as the topmost level in a website's hierarchy. Following the notion of 'hierarchy of periodicity' (Thibault, 1987, p. 612, cited in Djonov, 2005, p. 85) in the sense of 'a hierarchy of waves built by resources for realising textual meaning' (Djonov, 2005, p. 85) and as a tool for explaining information flow in verbal texts (ibid., p. 85), a website's hierarchy is specified as a hierarchy of themes. The notion of theme in verbal texts is identified as 'the point of departure for the message. It is the element the speaker selects for "grounding" what he is going on to say' (Halliday & Matthiessen, 2004, p. 58) and a resource for accounting for information packaging (cf. Martin, 1992 in Djonov,

2005, p. 86). The notion of macro-Theme is referred to as 'an element or group of elements predicting the thematic development of the page' (cf. Thibault, 2001, p. 296, cited in Djonov, 2005, p. 89). Applied to the analysis of the structuring of information on web pages into meaningful units, this conceptualization of theme allows for the following conceptualization of website structure:

> What that means for websites is that a main page below the level of the homepage can function as a higher-level Theme only to webpages belonging to the same section, subsection, subsubsection, and so on. In other words, the subdivision of a website section into subsections can be seen as giving rise to a separate hierarchy of Themes. Each subdivision thus creates a new sequence of webpages available for users to explore or branch away from to visit webpages in other such sequences. All such hierarchies of Themes, however, are united by the homepage as the website's highest level macro-Theme. (Ibid., p. 148)

This conceptualization of website structure as a hierarchy of Themes is schematized in Figure 2.1 as follows:

In order to deal with the complexity of multimodal texts, a multilayer approach will be applied to the empirical analysis of tourism websites. This will decompose web pages according to several distinct,

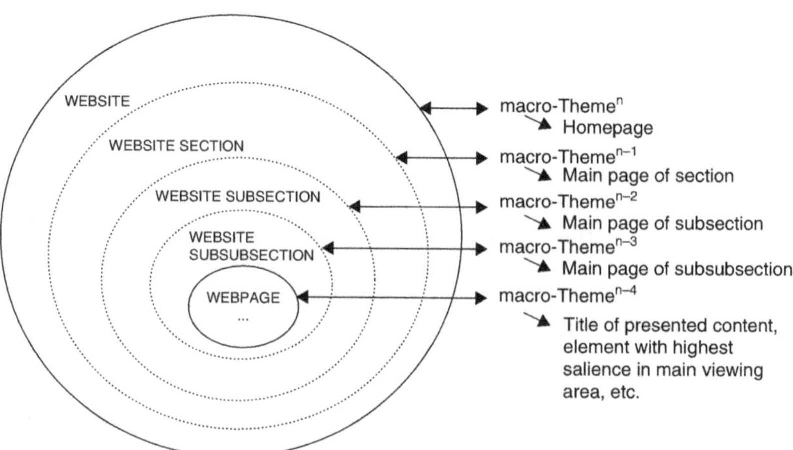

Figure 2.1 Website structure as a hierarchy of themes
Source: Following Djonov, 2005, p. 147; reproduced with permission of the author.

but related levels of analytical abstraction. The concept of base layer will serve the function of a common ground which provides the smallest verbal and graphical elements visually perceptible on a multimodal text for the analysis of elements in the layers to follow (Bateman, 2008, p. 110). More specifically, the identification of base elements will include graphical elements, such as photographs, advertising banners, drawings, maps, icons as graphical symbols in a graphical user interface, and verbal elements, such as text fragments and text passages. Together, they will present the smallest elements on the page which are visually, haptically, and aurally accessible. Verbal elements will be analyzed in terms of experiential meanings. When it comes to graphical elements, a distinction will be made between those with predominant presence and those with limited presence or absence of salient linguistic elements. Those with predominant presence of salient linguistic elements, such as *search* buttons and menus on towns and places, will be analyzed as groups, phrases, and clauses in terms of experiential meanings. By contrast, those with limited presence or absence of linguistic elements, such as maps, icons, or photographs, will be explored in terms of types of representational structures.

Significantly, as there may be a relationship between the choice of modes of communication and the kinds of meanings expressed, it may be useful to point to some differences between verbal and graphical elements. Thus, it has been suggested that language and image differ in their cognitive and communicative potential:

> *'Sprache zeichnet sich in erster Linie durch eine überlegene semantische Flexibilität aus-über alles und jedes kann vermittels Sprache kommuniziert werden. [...] Bilder hingegen zeigen vorwiegend im Bereich der Wahrnehmung Vorteile. [...] Aufgrund ihrer Zeichendichte „bewegen" sie in kleinen Wahrnehmungszeiten und –räumen relativ große Informations- und Assoziationsmengen.'* (Stöckl, 2004, p. 248)
>
> 'Language stands out due to a superior semantic flexibility-everything and anything can be communicated about through language. [...] By contrast, images predominantly show advantages in the area of perception. [...] Due to their packing density, they "move" relatively huge quantities of information and association in small times and spaces of perception.' (Own translation)

Having established the basis for the analysis of subsequent layers, the next layer of analysis is concerned with grouping the above-identified base units into larger layout units and elements to provide a layout structure. The relation between base elements is conceived of as one of correspondence, rather than a part-whole relation (Bateman, 2008, p. 109). As the second layer in Bateman's (2008) GeM model, this stage of analysis can be regarded as a first step towards accounting for the reasons *why* certain base units are grouped into larger layout units and elements which are directly visually perceptible following genre knowledge and layout properties or features. In response, two main schools of thought will be useful for the analysis of the homepages of the four regional websites.

The first relates to the perceptual Gestalt psychology which has been advanced (Koffka, 1935 and Köhler, 1947 in Bateman, 2008, pp. 59 ff.) to account for the functioning of the visual perception of readers and its relation to design. In this context, seven key criteria for organizing pages into layout units have been suggested. These refer to proximity, similarity, continuity, symmetry, closure, relative size, and figure-ground. The second is multimodal linguistics, as presented by Kress & van Leeuwen (1996) following Halliday & Matthiessen (2004), according to which three main areas of the textual metafunction have been developed to identify the layout composition of pages. These include salience, framing, and information value.

Salience, whereby an element draws attention to itself, will be analyzed according to perceptual features, such as spatial proximity, similarity due to the form of visual realization, types of visuals, commonality of typographical features and colour of letters, continuity assumed by entities in a visual field, symmetry of shapes, closure (whereby a recognizable contour in the visual field forms itself into a continuous loop), relative size (whereby elements share a common area of the visual field), and figure-ground, that is, elements as figures which are picked out from some background as ground. By contrast, in terms of framing as a form of disconnection, separating regions on a page, empty space, discontinuous areas of colour, and particularly recognizable shapes that create boundaries will be identified (Koffka, 1935 and Köhler, 1947 in Bateman, 2008, pp. 59 ff.)

The criterion of information value will not be considered in analysing the layout structure of the homepages. It has been excluded as it has been criticized for providing readers with unreliable layout interpretations, based on assumptions of one-to-one correspondences between layout groups and ideological import (Bateman, 2008, p. 45). Rather, the organization of resources on the page within the main viewing area and marginal areas will be considered. This will be crucial to the investigation of the relation between the degree of importance ascribed to certain (sub)themes on the tourism websites for the images constructed for the regions, and users as cultural tourists and media actors. More specifically, in her discussion of web page design as a crucial area in the field of hypermedia design (Djonov, 2005, pp. 10, 37), Djonov suggests that web pages use diverse resources for informational and compositional purposes:

> Webpage design makes use of verbal, visual, audio and kinetic resources (i) to present information and (ii) to present its organization within the website. Every webpage usually has a main viewing area, which excludes the anchor to the homepage, the navigation bars which occur on most webpages within a website, website section or subsection, and any advertising banners. These elements typically frame the main viewing area as they occupy the marginal areas of webpages. The dominant function of the main viewing area is to present information. (Ibid., p. 114)

Thus, web pages will be distinguished in terms of verbal, visual, audio, and kinetic resources used and the ways in which they are arranged on the page, that is, within the main-viewing area and marginal areas. In the terminology adopted in this work, instead of web page design, the term 'layout' will be used. In addition to the category of main viewing area and marginal areas, the category 'throughout the page' will be used to refer to elements which are spread throughout the web page in a more flexible way. When it comes to verbal, visual, audio, and kinetic resources, a distinction will be made between several types of elements or resources. 'Verbal elements with(out) colour and with(out) haptic and aural activity potential' will cover brief elements, such as groups and phrases, and long elements, such as text passages. 'Verbal and graphical elements with(out) colour and with(out) haptic and aural activity potential' will include contact forms. 'Less varied elements' will encompass text passages and photographs or text passages and scroll bars. 'More varied elements' will relate to logos, photographs, text passages, scroll bars, links, search boxes, charts, and maps. 'Graphical elements with(out) colour and with(out) haptic and aural activities potential' will involve photographs or maps. 'Audio resources' will include audio brochures and live webcams. The resulting system network for the organization of layout resources within web pages is presented in Figure 2.2. Double arrows (↕) will be introduced. These signal that combinations of types of resources are possible in the analysis of the tourism web pages.

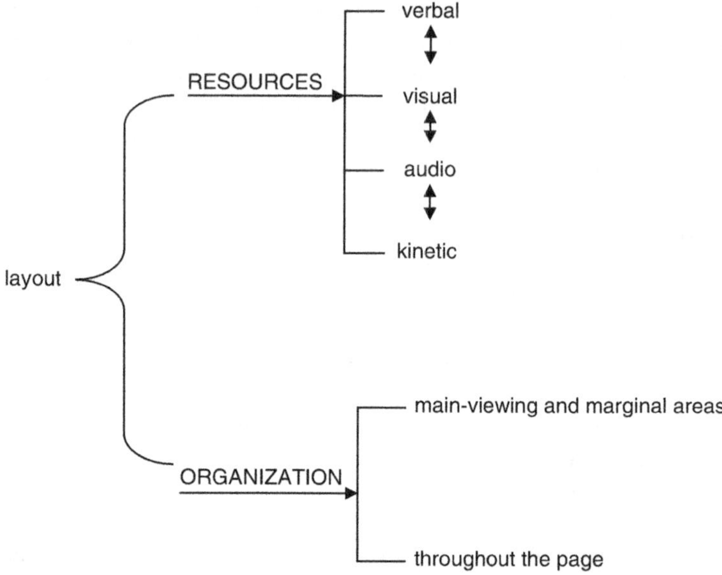

Figure 2.2 System network for the organization of layout resources within web pages

In order to facilitate the understanding of the layout analysis of the Perthshire homepage in subsection 3.2, Chapter 3, in the following, an example analysis of the layout structure of a Gannet page, as conducted by Bateman (2008, p. 123), will be referred to. This allows for inferring useful instructions for procedure and criteria for the identification of the layout structure. Four main steps can be observed. First, as exemplified in Figure 2.3, for ease of reference (ibid., p. 119), *spatial proximity* through leading, that is, the vertical line spacing between verbal text parts (ibid., p. 118), has been identified. This has led to the classification of the page into three main textual regions.

Second, the *forms of visual realization*, that is, textual and graphical elements (ibid., p. 117), have been determined and differences in the forms of visual realization have resulted in their placement in separate layout units. The forms of visual realization have covered three verbal, textual elements and one graphical element. The first verbal element includes the base units Gannet, Sula Basana, Family Sulidae, Gannets, No. 27. The second involves the paragraph starting with 'This great bird' and ending in 'with dark spots'. The third refers to the paragraph starting with the bold text fragment 'Haunt' and ending in 'Residents'. The

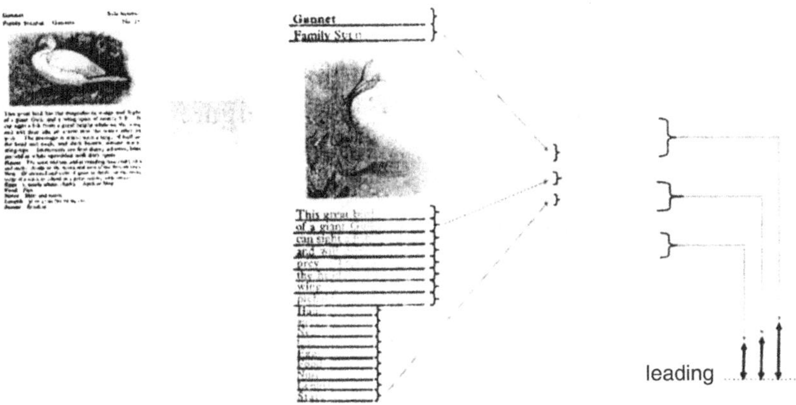

Figure 2.3 Example of differential use of leading in the example Gannet page
Source: Following Bateman, 2008, p. 119; reproduced with permission of the author.

graphical element encompasses a visual of the Gannet. These two steps have resulted in the identification of four horizontally running bands: the first layer of the hierarchical structure of the segmentation procedure 'XY-tree', with the page itself as the root of the tree. For reference purposes, the layout structure for the 1972 Gannet example page (ibid., p. 123) is illustrated in Figure 2.4. The root of the tree has been captured in L1, with L standing for layout unit. The four bands in the first layer of the tree have been labelled L1.1, L1.2, L1.3, and L1.4.

In a third step, the textual bands have been divided into further subunits on the basis of *commonality of typographical features* – such as type face, style of type, and type size – and the *colour of letters and graphical effects*, such as shadows, glows, and 3D textures (ibid., p. 117 f.). Thus, the base units of the first textual band, L1.1, have been grouped together into three layout units, L1.1.1–L1.1.3, at the second layer of the tree, as they display the same type face, size, and leading. Equally, the base units of the fourth textual band have been grouped into seven layout units, L1.4.1–L1.4.7, at the second layer of the tree, due to commonality of the style of type, that is, list headers in bold. In contrast to the fourth textual band, the third textual band, L1.3, has not been subdivided into further layout or base units, as it exhibits the same leading and typographical features within a paragraph.

Analogous to the identification of commonality of typographical features in textual elements, in a final step, the visual has been classified according to *types of visuals* (ibid., pp. 121, 124), including photographs,

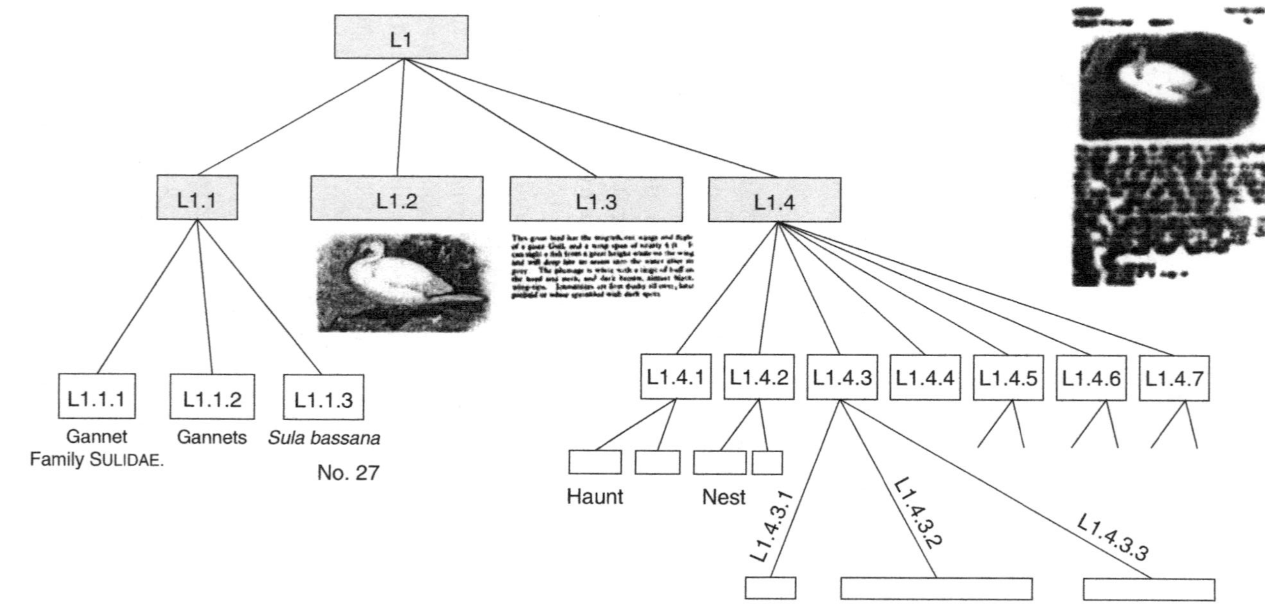

Figure 2.4 Layout structure for the 1972 Gannet example page according to the GeM model
Source: Following Bateman, 2008, p. 123; reproduced with permission of the author.

drawings, or diagrams. Accordingly, the image of the Gannet in L1.2 has been classified as a drawing.

Furthermore, in order for sub-areas of a page to identify the position of each unit that will be identified at the layers of the layout structure as abstract locations, a graphical overview in the form of an 'area model', as developed by Bateman (2008, p. 124 f.), will be used. The simplest version of it divides page space into rectangular sub-areas in a table-like fashion. Thus, in application to the layout structure of the Gannet page, as presented above, the three layout units L1.1.1, L1.1.2 and L1.1.3 can be identified as occupying the top of the page, while L1.2–L1.4 are positioned in the three horizontally running sub-areas below it. Figure 2.5 illustrates the correspondence between units located at the first and second layer of analysis of the layout structure and their positioning in the area model.

Significantly, rather than layout properties themselves, it is genre considerations which frame users' interpretations of documents. Using the element 'section heading' as an instance, Bateman exemplifies this view, as follows:

> In short, when we see a text fragment shown slightly spatially offset in the text-flow, slightly larger and bolder than the text surrounding it, perhaps with a number before the text, this is *not* a section heading because of these features – it is (possibly) a section heading because there is an established body of documents in which this particular collection of typographical, visual and spatial properties is regularly deployed with the intention of signalling a textual division and a point of access into the navigation structure. Only then can we label this functionally as a 'section heading'. (2008, p. 177)

Thus, the grouping of elements into larger layout units and the identification of their functions is informed by users' genre knowledge.

Moving from structurally-oriented to more meaning- and activity-related areas of analysis, the concept of metafunction, as developed in the field of systemic functional linguistics, will be used to analyse experiential and interpersonal dimensions of meaning of layout units. In general, the analysis of websites from a social semiotic perspective will show two aspects. First, diverse modes and constellations of modes are involved in the construction of meanings. Second, the construction of meanings is a complex and dynamic activity as part of which users interact with elements on web pages. In particular, the analysis of experiential and interpersonal dimensions of meaning of layout units will

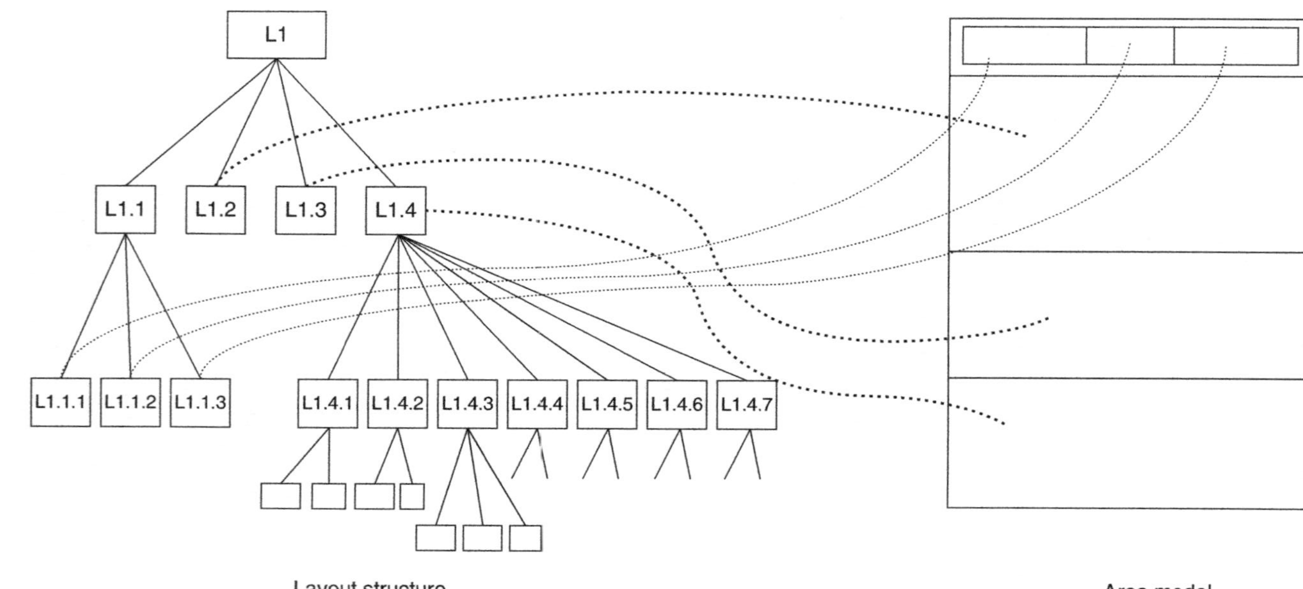

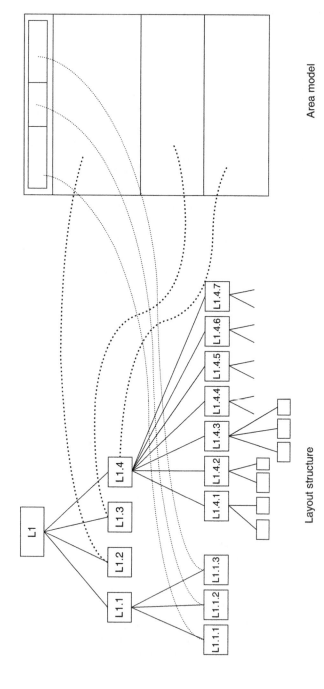

Figure 2.5 Correspondence between the layout structure and the area model of the 1972 Gannet page
Source: Ibid., p. 128; reproduced with permission of the author.

give insight into the ways in which tourist activities are represented, and users are addressed as cultural tourists and involved as media actors.

Systemic functional linguistics rests on the assumption that language is a system of meaning potentials (Halliday & Matthiessen, 2004, p. 26 f.) that has evolved to fulfil two main functions in human life: the ideational metafunction which, covering experiential and logical components, serves to construe human experience; and the interpersonal metafunction with the purpose of enacting interpersonal relationships among people (ibid., pp. 24 f., p. 29 f.). These two functions, in turn, are said to depend on a third function of language: the textual metafunction to arrange information as text (ibid., p. 30). These metafunctions are correlated with dimensions of structure which, in turn, correspond to different meanings, as realized in clause structure. Thus, in its meaning as representation, the clause is predicated on a segmental type of structure with clearly defined constituent parts. As exchange, the clause depends on prosodic features. As message, the clause builds upon culminative patterns. Logical components will not be considered, since they are not relevant for the purpose of exploring representation and cultural tourist and user communication. For ease of reference, the correspondences between the metafunctions, their kind of meanings and statuses in clauses, and the favoured type of structure are illustrated in Table 2.6 (ibid., p. 60 f.).

The metafunctions are viewed as working together simultaneously within the clause. The clause *The Istrian Peninsula has managed to preserve true and original natural values,* as taken from the layout unit entitled *Eco Oasis in the Heart of Europe* on the *What to do?* page of the Istria region website, will serve as an example. It is illustrated in Table 2.7.

The experiential metafunction is realized in the grammar by the transitivity system. This construes human experience as a set of process

Table 2.6 Metafunctions and their reflexes in grammar

Metafunction (technical term)	Definition (kind of meaning)	Corresponding status in clause	Favoured type of structure
Experiential	construing a model of experience	clause as representation	segmental (based on constituency)
Interpersonal	enacting social relationships	clause as exchange	Prosodic
Textual	creating relevance to context	clause as message	Culminative

Source: Adapted from Halliday & Matthiessen, 2004, p. 61.

Table 2.7 Metafunctional dimensions of meaning in an English clause

	The Istrian Peninsula	**has managed to**	**preserve**	**true and original natural values**
Experiential	Actor	Process: material		Goal
Interpersonal	Subject	Finite	Predicator	Complement
	Mood		Residue	
Textual	Theme	Rheme		

types. More specifically, experiential meanings are construed as three functional constituents: Processes, Participants and Circumstances, which denote *events* or *goings-on*. The major process types cover material, behavioural, mental, verbal, relational-attributive, relational-identifying, and existential processes (Halliday & Matthiessen, 2004, pp. 170 ff.).

Thus, material processes are referred to as clauses which denote doing or happening and relate to prototypical action events. The Participants covers an Actor as the performer of the action, and a Goal as that which is affected by the action; in addition, it may involve other Participants, such as Scope, Recipient, Client, and Attribute (ibid., pp. 179–196).

Behavioural processes refer to the outer expressions of the inner world of consciousness and physiological states; that is, they express physiological and psychological behaviour. The Behaver as the typically conscious being that is behaving serves as the first Participant, and the Behaviour is similar to the Scope of a material process and functions as a second Participant (ibid., pp. 248–251).

Mental processes express experiences in the inner world of consciousness. The Participants involve a human-like Senser 'endowed with consciousness' and the Phenomenon as the thing, act, or fact experienced (ibid., pp. 201–203).

Verbal processes refer to clauses of saying and the relationships between human consciousness and its manifestations in the form of language. Participant functions involve the Sayer as the Participant who is speaking and, in addition, the Receiver as the person to whom the saying is directed, the Verbiage as the message that is said and the Target as the entity that is the object of the saying (ibid., pp. 252–256).

Relational processes express a relation of characterization and identification between two concepts or entities. Further distinctions can be made between relational-attributive processes, which construe relationships of class-membership and relational-identifying processes, which create relationships of identity. The Participants in relational-attributive processes are: Carrier, as the class assigned to an entity, and Attribute, as the entity to which it is assigned. The Participants in relational-identifying processes are the Identified, as the entity which is to be identified, and the Identifier, as the entity which functions as the identity. Every identifying clause consists either of the structure Identified/Token and Identifier/Value or Identified/Value and Identifier/Token, with Token and Value representing a stratal difference in terms of expression and content. Both relational-attributive and relational-identifying clauses can further be categorized into intensive, possessive, and circumstantial processes. In intensive processes, classes are identified by naming an entity or a quality; the processes unfolding through time remain unspecified – that is, neutral, or phased – that is, specified with regard to time, appearance, or sense-perception – or there is a difference in domains of attribution relating to material versus semiotic. In possessive processes, the relationship between two entities is one of ownership. In circumstantial processes, the two entities relate to one another in terms of time, place, manner, cause, accompaniment, role, matter, or angle (ibid., pp. 210–248). Minor clauses fulfil speech functions, such as exclamations, calls, and greetings, and lack subject finite configuration that marks mood, therefore remaining unanalyzed for transitivity (Matthiessen et al., 2010, pp. 134, 140). An example of a minor clause may be *Welcome to the website of VisitScotland Perthshire*, as identified on the homepage of the Perthshire region website.

To experiential processes, states of existing and happening can be assigned, with the entity referred to as existing being called the Existent (Halliday & Matthiessen, 2004, pp. 256–259).

The interpersonal metafunction is realized by the relation between the Subject and the Finite of the clause, that is, the constituent entitled 'Mood' (ibid., p. 113 ff.). The remainder of the clause is referred to as 'Residue' (ibid., p. 114). The textual metafunction is realized by the positioning of elements in a clause; that is, the Theme as 'the point of departure of the message' (ibid., p. 64) occupies clause-initial position, while the Rheme covers the rest of the clause (ibid.).

The above-delineated grammar can be applied to the clause on metafunctional dimensions of meaning, as delineated in Table 2.7. The choices of website marketeers and the Croatian National Tourist Board to express the clause as they did exemplifies the conceptualization of language as a system of meaning potentials, as noted above. Thus, *the Istrian Peninsula* and *true and original natural values* are Participants. More specifically, while the former functions as the Actor, the latter serves as the Goal, both of which are embedded in a material process type. From the potential of meanings that they could have chosen, the website marketeers and Croatian National Tourist Board have selected this particular way of expressing the proposition that the Istrian Peninsula has succeeded in keeping a pristine and natural-looking environment. Furthermore, as the Subject precedes the Finite in the Mood block, interpersonally, the clause structure is therefore in declarative mood. If the position between Subject and Finite was reversed in the clause, this could have resulted in another configuration of mood, that is, interrogative mood, such as in *Has the Istrian Peninsula managed to preserve true and original natural values?*, or imperative mood, such as in a context in which tourists could have been asked to keep true and original natural values with a clause of the type *Manage to preserve true and original natural values in the Istrian Peninsula*. In addition to mood, the interpersonal metafunction is realized through modality, that is, the resources which attitudinally position readers due to the possibility, probability, and certainty expressed by modal adjuncts, modal finites, comment adjuncts, and attitudinal Epithets (Halliday & Matthiessen, 2004, pp. 146 ff.; Royce, 2007, p. 69 in Royce & Bowcher, 2007). More specifically, polarity and modality are conceptualized as follows:

> Polarity is [...] a choice between yes and no. But these are not the only possibilities; there are intermediate degrees, various kinds of indeterminacy that fall in between, such as 'sometimes' or 'maybe'. These intermediate degrees, between the positive and negative poles, are known collectively as MODALITY. What the modality system does is to construe the region of uncertainty that lies between 'yes' and 'no'. (Halliday & Matthiessen, 2004, pp. 146 f.)

The element which is responsible for the arguability of the clause is the Finite since '[i]t relates the proposition to its context in the speech event' (ibid., p. 115) by locating the statement of a clause in time, as in tensed, finite clauses, or by referring to the speaker's judgement of the proposition, as in finite clauses with modality features (ibid., p. 116). By contrast, non-finite clauses such as 'to' clauses, '-ing' clauses (Martin et al., 1997, pp. 70 ff.), and imperatives lack a finite element, thus not being arguable. Modal adjuncts and finites as modality features in finite clauses can further by distinguished according to the systems of type, value, orientation, and manifestation. Types of modality cover modalization as the scales of probability and usuality, and modulation as the scales of obligation and inclination (Halliday & Matthiessen, 2004, p. 147) or, more specifically, readiness; inclination and readiness;

ability (Martin et al., 1997, p. 70). Values of modality can be high, low, or median (Halliday & Matthiessen, 2004, p. 149). For instance, on the gastronomy web pages of the Zadar region website, the clause *The cheese must be dipped in oil* realizes a high obligation, while, on the natural heritage pages of the Perthshire region website, the clause *what you might see or hear* realizes a low probability. Orientation and manifestation refer to subjective or objective realizations of modality, with speakers explicitly or implicitly expressing the source of the conviction (Halliday & Matthiessen, 2004, pp. 149 ff.). For instance, when it comes to probability, congruent realizations of modality such as *must* and *certainly* are implicitly subjective (Impl sub), as realized by finites, and implicitly objective (Impl obj A/Impl obj P) forms of realization, as realized by adjuncts (A) or Predicators (P) (Martin et al., 1997, pp. 68 ff.). By contrast, metaphorical realizations which cover mental processes of cognition such as *I know* and attributive processes such as *it is certain* are explicitly subjective (Expl subj) and explicitly objective (Expl obj) forms of realization (ibid.).

Significantly, the interactivity potential of the websites, as indicated by types of user actions such as rollover or mouse click, will be expressed by the modal finite *can* in the analysis of modality features. Thus, the clause *User can* (Finite: readiness: ability: median: implicitly subjective) *click By region scroll box in menu* on the homepage of the Istria region website may serve as an example. Also, instances such as *Not rarely* in *Not rarely do visitors decide to take the trail from Velika Paklenica Canyon, across Jurlina and Njiva to Mala Paklenica* will be counted once and classified as high value modality, since they equate with modal adjuncts such as *often*. For ease of reference, Table 2.8 gives an overview of congruent and metaphorical realizations of modality.

As mentioned above, the types of modality listed in Table 2.8 can further be analyzed for low, high, and median value. For illustrative purposes, values of implicitly subjective realizations of modality can be seen in Table 2.9.

Apart from modal adjuncts and finites, diverse types of comment adjuncts express attitude, as shown in Table 2.10. Their difference from modal adjuncts is described as follows:

> [C]omment Adjuncts are less closely tied to the grammar of mood; they are restricted to 'indicative' clauses (those functioning as propositions), and express the speaker's attitude either to the proposition as a whole or to the particular speech function. (Halliday & Matthiessen, 2004, p. 129)

Table 2.8 Congruent and metaphorical realizations of modality

Kind of MODALITY	Congruent realizations			Metaphorical realizations	
	Finite implicitly objective	**Adjunct (mood) implicitly objective**	**Predicator Implicitly Subjective**	**mental clause explicitly objective**	**attributive clause explicitly subjective**
Probability	can/could, may/might, will/would, should, ought to must	possibly probably certainly		I guess, I think, I know	it is probable... it is possible it is certain...
usuality		sometimes usually, always,			
obligation		necessarily	be allowed to, be supposed to, be obliged to	I´m willing for... I expect... I want... (him to leave)	it is permitted it is expected it is necessary (...for him to leave
readiness: inclination		willingly, eagerly	be willing to, be keen to, be deter-mined to	I´d like to leave I want to leave	it´d be lovely to leave
readiness: ability	can/could		be able to	–	it is possible for him to leave

Source: Adapted from Martin et al., 1997, p. 70.

Table 2.9 Values of modality

Values	Implicitly subjective realizations of modality
High	Must, ought to, need, has to, is to
Median	Will, would, shall, should
Low	May, might, can, could

Source: Adapted from Halliday & Matthiessen, 2004, p. 624.

In addition to comment adjuncts, at the clause level, attitude can also by expressed by diverse types of comments, as shown in Table 2.11.

Equally, nominal groups can express attitude (ibid.). In fact, Halliday & Matthiessen (2004, p. 607) indicate that 'categories of modal assessment correspond to categories of appraisal'. Yet, as the analysis of

Table 2.10 Examples of adverbs serving as comment Adjuncts

Type					Examples of adverbs
propositional	**on whole**	**asseverative**	**natural**		**naturally, inevitably, of course**
			Obvious		**obviously, clearly, plainly, of course**
			Sure		**doubtless, indubitably, no doubt**
		qualificative	prediction	Predictable	unsurprisingly, predictably, to no one´s surprise
				Surprising	surprisingly, unexpectedly
			presumption	hearsay	evidently, allegedly, supposedly
				Argument	Arguably
				Guess	Presumably
			Desirability	desirable: luck	luckily, fortunately
				desirable: hope	Hopefully
				Undesirable	sadly, unfortunately
	on Subject	wisdom	Positive		wisely, cleverly
			Negative		foolishly, stupidly
		morality	Positive		rightly, correctly, justifiably
			Negative		wrongly, unjustifiably

(*continued*)

Table 2.10 Continued

Type				Examples of adverbs
speech-functional	unqualified	Persuasive	Assurance	truly, honestly, seriously
			Concession	admittedly, certainly, to be sure
		Factual		actually, really, in fact, as a matter of fact
	qualified	Validity		generally, broadly, roughly, ordinarily, by and large, on the whole
		personal engagement	Honesty	frankly, candidly, honestly, to be honest
			Secrecy	confidentially, between you and me
			Individuality	personally, for my part
			Accuracy	truly, strictly
			Hesitancy	Tentatively

Source: Adapted from Halliday & Matthiessen, 2004, p. 130.

Table 2.11 Examples of clauses serving as comments

Type					**Examples of clauses**
Comment: propositional	on Subject	wisdom	Wise		x is wise to…; it is wise of x [[to…]]
			unwise		x is foolish to…; it is foolish of x [[to …]]
		morality	moral		x is right to…; it is right of x [[to…]]
			immoral		x is wrong to… it is wrong of x [[to…]
	on whole	asseverative	natural obvious		it is natural [[that…]] it is obvious [[that…]]
			sure		I + not+ doubt
		qualificative	prediction	predictable	I + expect
				unpredictable	I + not + expect
			presumption	hearsay	they + say; I hear
				argument	I + argue
				guess	I + presume
			desirability	desirable: luck	I + rejoice
				[desirable: reaction]	it is wonderful/it fascinates + me [[that …]]
				[desirable: composition]	–
				[desirable: valuation]	–
				[undesirable: security]	I + am confident [[that …]]
				[desirability: dissatisfaction]	It is interesting/
				desirable: hope	It interests me [[that…]]

(*continued*)

Table 2.11 Continued

Type					Examples of clauses
				undesirable	I + hope
				[undesirable: reaction]	I + regret
				[undesirable: composition]	it is horrible/it disgusts + me [[that…]]
				[undesirable: valuation	–
				[undesirable: insecurity]	–
				[undesirability: dissatisfaction]	I + am anxious [[that…]] it is tiring/it displeases + me [[that…]]
comment: speech-functional	unqualified	persuasive	´I grant you´		I + admit
			I assure you´		I + assure
		factual			I + tell + you
	qualified	validity (degree of)			I + tell + you + in general terms
		personal engagement (claim for)	honesty		I + tell + you + honesty
			secrecy		I + tell + you + in confidence
			individuality		
			accuracy		I + tell + you + strictly
			hesitancy		I + suggest + to you

Source: Adapted from Halliday & Matthiessen, 2004, pp. 608 ff.

attitudinal lexis through application of appraisal theory, as advanced by Martin & Rose (2003), would exceed the scope of this work, it will not be considered here.

In addition to tempering the force of verbal statements, the force of visual statements can be moderated. Thus, photographs as visuals of higher modality represent objects in a more realistic way, while stylized representations of objects, as in sketch caricatures 'in which the main features of the represented participants have been emphasized to present them from particular attitudinal viewpoints' (Royce, 2007, p. 90 in Royce & Bowcher, 2007), are visuals of lower modality than photographs or realistic sketch drawings (ibid., p. 91). Thus, the visuals on the region websites will be distinguished according to photographs as visuals of higher modality, and stylized representations of objects, as in icons and maps, as visuals of lower modality. Yet, it seems important to note at this point that, if users are repeatedly exposed to the icons, they 'begin to look at things through the glasses of iconic convention' (Eco, 1976, p. 205); the icons may be perceived as more realistic than photographs due to their 'stereotypical simplicity' (Chandler, 2007, p. 66).

To recap, in subsection 1.2, Chapter 1, it was hypothesized that the websites construct more realistic tourist experiences for users as media actors, thus suggesting that users can expect what is promised on the websites as cultural tourists in the social world. To test whether this is the case or whether the websites leave limited space for questioning or challenging verbal and visual propositions, a quantitative analysis of the frequency of clause types, that is, non-finite, tensed finite, and finite clauses with modality features, will be conducted. A clause which makes use of one or more instances of modality features will be referred to as a clause with modality features. Within clauses with modality features, modality features, such as modal finites and mood adjuncts, will further be analyzed for value, type, orientation, and manifestation. Modality features, such as comment adjuncts and comments, will be analyzed for type, orientation, and manifestation. Types of visuals, such as photographs, icons, and maps, will be investigated for value.

Furthermore, while systemic functional linguistics has explored various 'modes of metaphorical expressions' (Halliday & Matthiessen, 2004, pp. vii, 586–658), such as the metaphorical realizations of modality introduced above, limited attention has been devoted to the integration of metaphors in the traditional sense, that is, lexical metaphors, and their analysis within the systemic functional linguistic framework (Goatly, 1997, p. 4; Simon-Vandenbergen, 2003, p. 223 in Simon-Vandenbergen et al., 2003). As will be demonstrated in some examples in this work, such as in sub-subsection 4.3.1, Chapter 4, lexical metaphors and figurative language can equally give insight into experiential and interpersonal meanings related to the representation of natural heritage.

Finally, in terms of the textual metafunction, the Theme of the clause is *The Istrian Peninsula* as occupying the beginning of the clause. The clause is presented in active voice, but could equally have been presented by the choice of passive voice, such as in *True and natural original values have managed to be preserved (by the Istrian peninsula).* All these metafunctions have been illustrated using the grammatical unit of a clause as an example, since this constitutes 'the primary channel of grammatical energy' (Halliday & Matthiessen, 2004, p. 31). More specifically, 'it is in the clause that meanings of different kinds are mapped into an integrated grammatical structure' (ibid., p. 10). Thus, the focus of the analysis of metafunctions will predominantly be at clause rank. Throughout, however, other systems of rank, including phrase, group, and their associated complexes, will be considered (ibid.). For instance, in the above clause, *The Istrian Peninsula* and *its true and original natural values* are nominal groups, while *has managed to preserve* is a verbal group. Further categories of membership within the nominal group may cover the Thing as the element denoting a class of things, a Deictic as some specific or non-specific subset of the Thing, the Numerative as a numerical feature in terms of quantity or order in an exact or inexact manner, the Epithet as an objective property or the speaker's subjective attitude towards a Thing, and the Classifier as any feature which may classify the Thing in terms of material, scale, purpose, function, status, rank, origin, and other features (ibid., pp. 309–320). Thus, the above-mentioned nominal groups can further be divided into the Deictic *The*, the Classifier *Istrian*, the Thing *Peninsula* and the Deictic *its*, the Epithets *true* and *original*, the Classifier *natural*, and the Thing *values*. Furthermore, examples such as *Things to see and do*, as can be observed on the Perthshire region website, will be classified as macro-Things – as 'acts' bigger than Things (Matthiessen et al., 2010, p. 60) – with *to see and do* qualifying the Thing *Things* as a constituent of the overall macro-Thing. Also, other elements, such as the website URL (Uniform Resource Locator) *www.outdooraccess-scotland.com* on the *Walking* page of the Orkney region website, will be added to groups and phrases. The exploration of metafunctions will give insight into the types of tourist themes which are represented, the ways in which these are represented, and the ways in which users are addressed as cultural tourists and involved as media actors.

Kress & van Leeuwen (2007, p. 44) suggest that, similarly to language, images can be analyzed ideationally, interpersonally, and textually. With regard to the ideational metafunction, two types of representational structures have been distinguished: a narrative one and a conceptual one. When it comes to narrative representational structures, in their summarizing comparison between narrative processes in language and images, they further identify processes in images – including non-transactional action processes, unidirectional action processes, events, non-transactional reaction processes, transactional reaction processes, mental processes, and verbal processes – for which correspondences can be found in language. These include material processes with one Actor as a Participant, material processes with two participants, passive transactional clauses with agent deletion, behavioural processes, mental processes related to perception, mental processes related to cognition and affection, and verbal processes related to quotation (ibid., p. 78). Similarly, in terms of conceptual processes, they further identify conceptual structures in images, such as classificational, analytical, and symbolic processes as comparable equivalents to relational and existential process types (ibid., p. 109). As considering these subcategories would go beyond the scope of this work, the relevant images on the tourism web pages will be characterized ideationally as conceptual or narrative in representational structure. As conventionally used in systemic functional linguistics, the paradigmatic order of a set of options – *a system* – will be represented in the form of abstract models of these options – *system networks* (Halliday & Matthiessen, 2004, pp. 22 ff.). Curly braces will be used to express simultaneous choice, square brackets to denote alternatives, and capital letters to express the names of the systems. Shown from left to right in system networks, the relationship between systems is one which increases in *delicacy*, that is, which becomes more specific in the sense of expressing a kind-of relationship (ibid., p. 22). The types of representational structures are shown in the form of a system network in Figure 2.6.

When it comes to the interpersonal metafunction, Kress & van Leeuwen (2007, p. 149) have developed a system network for interactive meanings in images, as shown in Figure 2.7.

Figure 2.6 Main types of representational structures in images
Source: Adapted from Kress & van Leeuwen, 2007, p. 59.

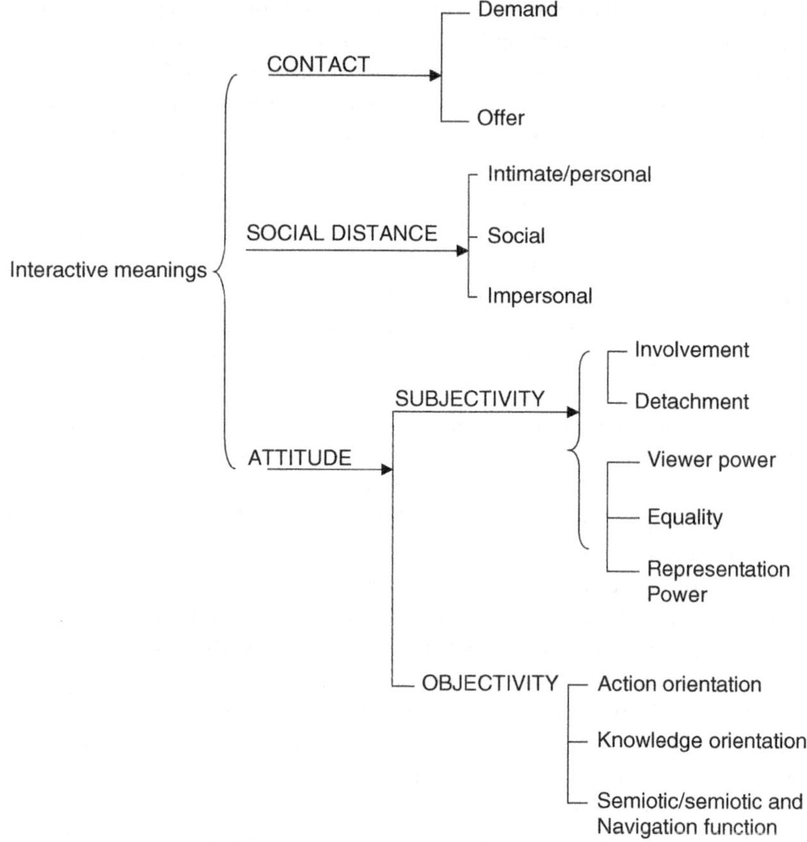

Figure 2.7 Interactive meanings in images
Source: Adapted from Kress & van Leeuwen, 2007, p. 149.

In terms of contact, images either demand something from viewers if human or quasi-human participants are represented as gazing at the viewer, or they offer something to viewers if there is an absence of gaze at the viewer. Several types of shots have been tested as creating diverse types of meanings in terms of social distance: intimate/personal meanings are expressed by close shot; social meanings are realized by medium shot; impersonal meanings are accomplished by long shot. In terms of realizations of the systems of contact and social distance in visuals, if types of visuals are split into further units, the embedded units will serve as units of analysis. The embedded geographical units of the *Where are we?* layout unit on the homepage of the Istria region website entitled *Europe* and *Istria* (cf. Figure 1.3, subsection 1.1) may serve as an example.

A distinction is further made between subjective images where the design of the image positions viewers in certain ways and objective images where the design of the image expresses an objective attitude and neutralizes perspective (ibid., pp. 143–147). The presentation of a *shopping basket* icon as part of the *Shop with us* unit on the homepage of the Orkney region website (cf. Figure 1.2, subsection 1.1) may exemplify this distinction. As users are not subjected by the website producers and marketeers to a particular position in relation to the icon – as the icon can be viewed from the front and from a vertical angle, the icon is portrayed as something that simply exists, uninfluenced by perspective. Thus, the icons encode an objective attitude on online shopping. If the icon had encoded a subjective attitude, this would have been indicated by manipulating these angles so that users view the icons from the side and from above or from below. Several sizes of frame indicate subjectivity in terms of attitude: involvement is indicated by a frontal angle; detachment is realized by an oblique angle; viewer power is accomplished by a high angle; equality is achieved by an eye-level angle; represented participant power is suggested by a low angle. With regard to objectivity in terms of attitude, a distinction is made between action orientation, as realized by a frontal angle, and knowledge orientation, as indicated by a top-down angle (ibid., p. 145). In addition to action orientation and knowledge orientation, the category of *semiotic/ semiotic and navigation function* of types of visuals will be introduced. This will capture representational meanings and navigational meanings related to the indication of rapid transference to other web pages. For instance, a *shopping basket* icon is neither action-oriented in the sense of communicating to users '"this is how it works", "this is how you use it", "this is how you do it"' (Kress & van Leeuwen, 2007, p. 145), nor knowledge-orientated in the sense that is 'contemplates the world from a god-like point of view, puts it at your feet' (ibid.), but a simplified representation of an object. If accessible through types of user actions, it enables users to navigate quickly to the corresponding internal or external web pages. Thus, it will be classified as encoding a semiotic/ semiotic and navigation function.

In addition, cultural and intertexual knowledge will be considered in the analysis of the meaning potential of graphical elements, such as photographs. This is due to the fact that it has been acknowledged that, rather than ascribing firm meanings to layout elements, layout elements derive their meaning potential from other factors, including the context and shared knowledge between the producers and receivers (Bucher, 2010, p. 57 f. in Bucher et al., 2010). In particular, when it comes to intertextual knowledge, the study of the ways in which thematic meanings on activities, history and heritage, natural heritage, and gastronomy are represented may usefully benefit from knowledge of specialized field language in future research. Thus, as explored in sub-subsection 4.5.1, subsection 4.5 (Chapter 4), due to intertextual knowledge, representational structures in visuals on Istrian gastronomy are coded with certain, rather than other, meanings in other texts. For instance, the following signifiers are commonly coded with notions of more formal social gatherings in other texts: drinking vessels with more delicate, as more easily breakable, glass material and a more refined shape of glass for enjoyment; an uplifted posture of a hand holding a truffle; the dropping of a small quantity of liquid out of the neck of a bottle; and an eating establishment with a sit-down option and careful table setting with napkins and precise arrangement of cutlery and glasses on the table. In fact, research into wine-speak, for instance, reveals that the accessibility or reliability of readings of the language of wine appreciation depends on knowledge of specialized field language (Hommerberg, 2011, p. 250). Thus, knowledge of 'gastro-lingo', the register of food and drink (Dann, 1996, pp. 212, 235–238), may give more detailed insight into the nature of representation of gastronomy in tourist promotional material.

Finally, in terms of the textual metafunction, Kress & van Leeuwen (2007, p. 210) propose a system of composition which relates the hitherto presented representational structures and interactive meanings to one another. It consists of the three parameters of information value, salience, and framing, each of which is further divided up into subcategories. Just as for the layout composition of pages, as mentioned in this subsection, for the organization of elements in images, the category relating to information value will be omitted to avoid drawing a direct relation between layout compositions and ideological meanings (Bateman, 2008, p. 45). Thus, the system network, as suggested by Kress & van Leeuwen (2007, p. 210), as shown in Figure 2.8, will be partially adopted. Maximum or minimum salience of objects in an image is shown by textual cues, such as prominent positioning, visual prominence, colour, contrast, differences in sharpness, and other features. Maximum disconnection and maximum connection is indicated by framing devices, including dividing lines and frame lines (ibid., p. 176 ff.). In application to this work, the observation of salient objects in types of visuals will be crucial to the identification of functional

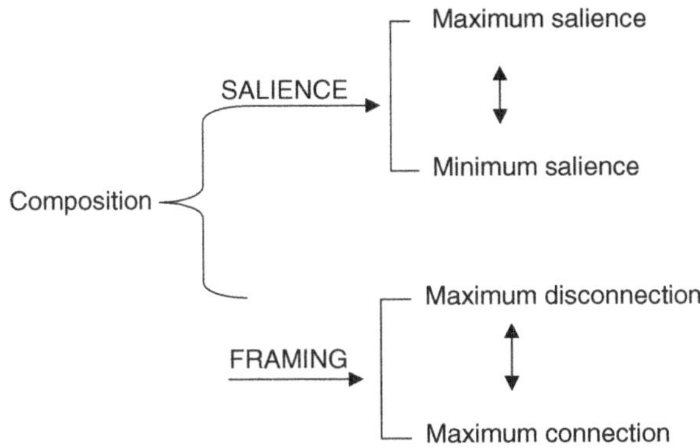

Figure 2.8 The meaning of composition
Source: Adapted from Kress & van Leeuwen, 2007, p. 210.

constituents as part of the conceptual and narrative representational structures which can by assigned to the types of visuals.

When it comes to the general question of the reliability of empirical analysis to ensure consistency of results and accuracy of the codings across coders, the requirements and recommendations of corpus-based work, in general, including issues of inter- and intra-coder reliability (Leetaru, 2012, p. 2), will not be considered more explicitly. This would have increased the amount of work substantially. Rather, from a qualitative, interpretative view, the classification of visuals will be based on what is most plausible and supported by textual evidence. Equally, in terms of the validity of the result, it needs to be said that the graphs which will be used in the empirical website analysis will not be subjected to standard significance tests which function to measure validity and reliability (Deacon et al., 2007, pp. 102–133). This would have gone beyond the scope of this book.

For analytical purposes, the empirical analysis will proceed in several steps. The first two steps relate to the analysis of the layout of web pages, as shown in Table 2.12. First, the base elements will be identified. Second, the base elements will be grouped into larger layout units following genre knowledge and layout properties. As mentioned at the beginning of this subsection, for pragmatic reasons, the identification of lists of base elements will be limited to the four homepages of the region websites. This will be followed by an analysis of meaning-making within and across pages. As modelled by Table 2.12, meaning-making requires reference to the base elements and layout structures which

Table 2.12 Steps in the empirical analysis of base elements, layout structure, and meaning-making

Base elements:
- Identify the smallest elements on a page which are visually, haptically and aurally perceptible.
Layout structure:
- Group the base elements into larger layout units following genre knowledge and layout properties, that is, framing and salience.
Meaning-making:
- Analyse layout units in terms of salience, framing and positioning.
- Identify meaning dimensions of verbal and graphical elements for all web pages.

have been identified. Thus, in a third step, layout units will be analyzed in terms of salience, framing, positioning, and organization. In a further step, meaning dimensions of verbal and graphical elements will be identified for all web pages. Table 2.13 further shows the relations between the core research questions, socio-semiotic tools to respond to them and the more specific socio-semiotic realizations of these tools. In addition, the table concerned with meaning-making also covers the categories of genre, intertextual knowledge, and cultural knowledge. It follows from Tables 2.12–2.13 that meaning-making depends on the interaction between several parameters: layout, meaning dimensions of elements and genre, and intertextual and cultural knowledge of the functions which elements commonly fulfil in other texts.

In terms of the specific means of analysis and integration of analyses, a toolkit for the analysis of representation and cultural tourist and user communication has been developed to capture the interaction between several parameters. As mentioned above, the parameters include layout, meaning dimensions of elements and genre, and intertextual and cultural knowledge of the functions which elements commonly fulfil in other texts. As shown in Table 2.12, the empirical analysis of base elements, layout structure, and meaning-making has proceeded in several steps.

Table 2.13 gives more detailed insight into meaning-making. It shows the relation between the core research questions, the types of tools to respond to them, and the more specific realizations of these tools.

2.3 Conclusion

The hitherto delineated relevance and scientific importance of the study of tourism websites, hypotheses and research questions, and analytical

Table 2.13 Analysis of meaning-making within and across pages

Meaning-making		
Research questions	**Tools**	**Realizations**
To what extent are tourist themes important for the images constructed for the regions, users as cultural tourists and media actors?	- Salience, framing and organization of layout units.	- Disconnection (through separating regions on a page, empty space, discontinuous areas of colour, particular recognizable shapes that create boundaries). - Perceptual features (spatial proximity, similarity due to the form of visual realization, types of visuals, commonality of typographical features and colour of letters, continuity assumed by entities in a visual field, symmetry of shapes, closure whereby a recognizable contour in the visual field forms itself into a continuous loop, relative size whereby elements share a common area of the visual field and figure-ground, that is, elements as figures which are picked out from some background as ground).
Which tourist themes are put into the layout units and subunits which have been identified in the analysis of the layout structure?	- Relation between experiential and textual dimensions of layout units.	- Positioning and organization of layout units within the main-viewing and marginal areas as well as throughout the page. - Relation between thematic meanings and the layout structure of the layout units.

(*continued*)

Table 2.13 Continued

Meaning-making		
Research questions	**Tools**	**Realizations**
Which tourist themes are represented and in what ways are they *represented*?	- Experiential meaning dimensions of layout units. - Interpersonal meaning dimensions of layout units.	- Intertextual and cultural knowledge. - Conceptual and narrative representational structures and process types. - Modality in clauses, as realized through modal adjuncts, finites, comment adjuncts and comments in clause types, and visuals, as realized through the type of visual in question.
In what ways are users addressed as *cultural tourists*?	- Interpersonal meaning dimensions of graphical elements. - Interpersonal meaning dimensions of verbal elements.	- Intertextual and cultural knowledge. - Social contact, as realized through gaze, social distance, as realized through size of frame, and attitude, as realized through camera angle. - Mood, as realized through clause types.
How are users involved as *media actors*?	- Interpersonal meaning dimensions of verbal and graphical elements.	- Accessibility of elements. - Salience of media interaction. - Types of user actions. - Levels of functionality. - Types of thematic meanings.

framework call for a social semiotic theoretical perspective on tourism web pages. At the heart of this perspective are two ideas. First, diverse elements and resources, such as text fragments and photographs, interact to represent and construct meanings. Second, meaning-making is not a static and purely grammatical phenomenon, but the active ascription of meanings to elements on web pages by users as cultural tourists and media actors due to their intertextual and cultural knowledge and the prominence of elements on web pages. More specifically, cultural meanings are construed in the act of media use. Web pages can thus be conceived of as visual, haptic, and aural activity potentials which are realized in the act of media use and embedded in tourism communication as their socio-cultural context of use.

In the following chapters, the tables giving insight into the analytical framework and the empirical procedures which have been developed hitherto will be applied to the empirical analysis of the regional Croatian and Scottish tourism websites. Thus, after analysing the homepages in terms of layout in Chapter 3 and the ways in which the layout development within and across pages gives insight into image construction in sub-subsection 4.1.1, Chapter 4, each subsection dealing with tourist activities in the form of thematic meanings, that is, subsections 4.2–4.5, will further be investigated in terms of the following three main areas: an analysis of the ways in which thematic meanings are represented on the web pages; an analysis of the ways in which users are addressed as cultural tourists on the web pages; and an analysis of the ways in which users are actively engaged in the creation of tourist meanings as media actors on the web pages.

3
Analysis of Website Layout

3.1 Base elements

The four homepages of the region websites have been decomposed into base units. The mode of base unit representation will adhere to the conventions introduced by Bateman (2008, pp. 133 ff.). For subsequent reference, the units are numbered and abbreviated with the prefix 'U' in order to distinguish them from units which will be introduced in the analysis of subsequent layers. Before listing the base elements which have been identified for the homepages of the four regional websites in tables, all the variables used in the tables need to be introduced and exemplified. Although this sort of genre-specific labelling belongs to the layout layer which will be dealt with in subsection 3.2, for ease of identification of the respective units, the following abbreviations will be used in the tables to correspond to the following variables which have been identified during analysis of the homepages and the web pages on walking, natural heritage, history and heritage, and gastronomy: *AB* for advertising banners, *B* for *box*, *Bl* for *block*, *D* for *drawing*, *G* for *grid*, *I* for *icon*, *M* for *map*, *P* for *photograph*, *S* for *separator*, *T* for *text* in the sense of all linguistic units, that is, *single words*, *phrases*, *sentences* and *paragraphs*, and *Tab* for *table*. This more broad understanding of texts as encompassing various linguistic units will suffice as detailed linguistic analyses will be restricted to the (sub)themes of walking activities, natural heritage, history and heritage, and gastronomy in the analysis of meaning-making in subsections 4.1–4.5, Chapter 4, rather than all (sub)themes introduced on the homepages. For ease of reference and reasons of readability, the homepages of the four regions' websites are magnified, and portrayed in the form of screenshots in Figures 1.1–1.4 in subsection 1.1, Chapter 1.

In addition, for some of the text fragments, arrows as icons, and boxes, terminology related to computer and Internet technology (Webopedia, 2012) will be used. Thus, text fragments will be referred to as *menu item* if they are part of a type of menu, such as a menu bar, a radio button menu or a pull down menu, and abbreviated as *MEI*. Arrows as icons to be scrolled will be denoted as *scroll arrows* and abbreviated as *SCAR*. Arrows as icons which cannot be scrolled and other types of icons will be referred to as icons and abbreviated as *I*, as mentioned above. Boxes will be referred to as scroll area and abbreviated as *SCA* if they are part of a scroll bar. If boxes or tables are part of a menu bar, they will be referred to as *menu areas* and abbreviated as *MA*. Smaller boxes in the scroll bar will be referred to as *scroll box* and abbreviated as *SCB*. Also, those types of visuals which neither represent photographs nor icons will more generally be referred to as *types of visuals* and abbreviated as *V*. Examples of these variables as types of base elements are extracted from the homepages of the Zadar and Orkney region websites (see Figures 3.1–3.4).

An example of a photograph is given in Figure 3.5. An example of a separator can be seen in Figure 3.6. Figure 3.7 shows an example of a text fragment. An example of a table is given in Figure 3.8.

Except for identifying types of base elements, for each base element, the nature of activity potential will be determined. In this context, a

Figure 3.1 Screenshot of an example of a block (Bl) on the Zadar county website
Source: http://www.zadar.hr/English/Default.aspx (accessed on 10 September 2009); reproduced with permission by the Zadar County Tourist Board.

Figure 3.2 Screenshot of an example of a grid (G) on the Zadar county website
Source: http://www.zadar.hr/English/Default.aspx (accessed on 10 September 2009); reproduced with permission of the Zadar County Tourist Board.

Figure 3.3 Screenshot of an example of an icon (I) on the Zadar county website
Source: http://www.zadar.hr/English/Default.aspx (accessed on 10 September 2009); reproduced with permission of the Zadar County Tourist Board.

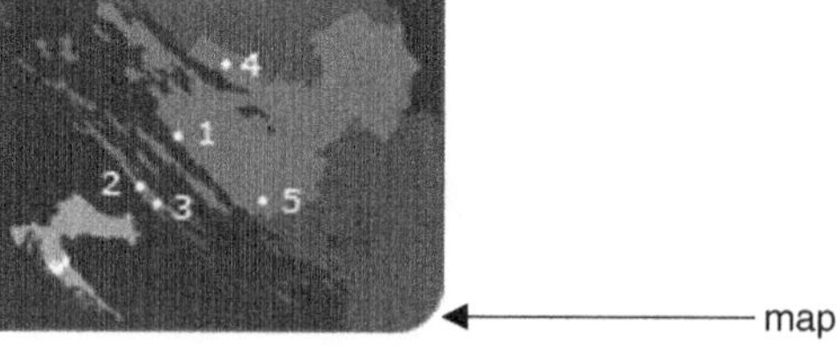

Figure 3.4 Screenshot of an example of a map (M) on the Zadar county website
Source: http://www.zadar.hr/English/Default.aspx (accessed on 10 September 2009); reproduced with permission of the Zadar County Tourist Board.

higher degree of interactivity potential can be identified for websites as digital multimodal texts than for print material, such as the page from a Darling Kindersley guide to Paris, as analyzed by Bateman (2008, pp. 130–135). Thus, those elements which are exclusively visually accessible by users, but not haptically and aurally, will be referred to as

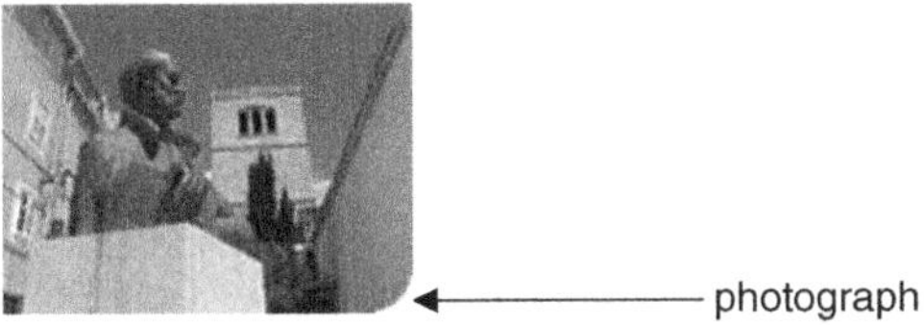

Figure 3.5 Screenshot of an example of a photograph (P) on the Zadar county website
Source: http://www.zadar.hr/English/Default.aspx (accessed on 10 September 2009); reproduced with permission of the Zadar County Tourist Board.

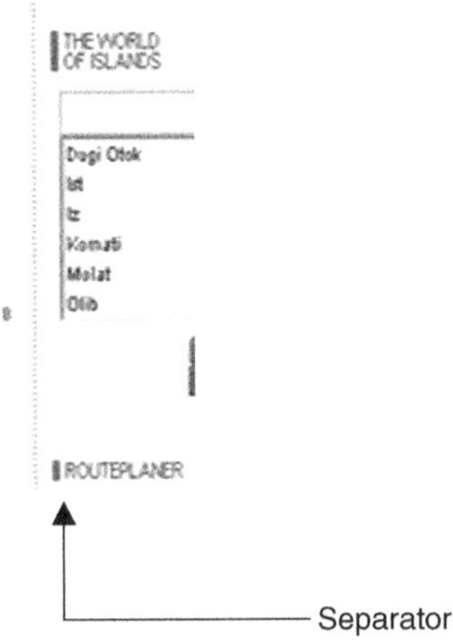

Figure 3.6 Screenshot of an example of a separator (S) on the Zadar county website
Source: http://www.zadar.hr/English/Default.aspx (accessed on 10 September 2009); reproduced with permission of the Zadar County Tourist Board.

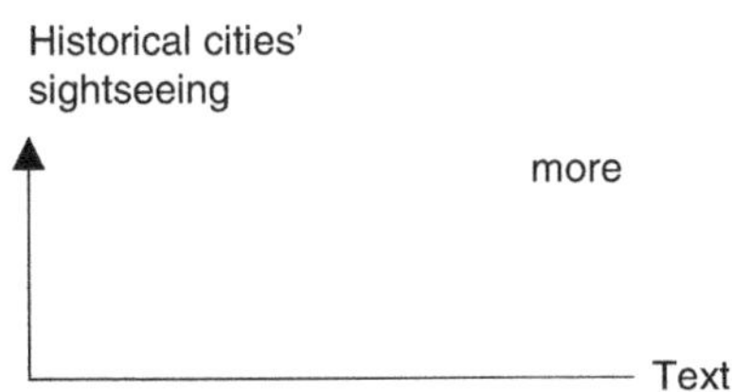

Figure 3.7 Screenshot of an example of a text in the form of text fragments (T) on the Zadar county website
Source: http://www.zadar.hr/English/Default.aspx (accessed on 10 September 2009); reproduced with permission of the Zadar County Tourist Board.

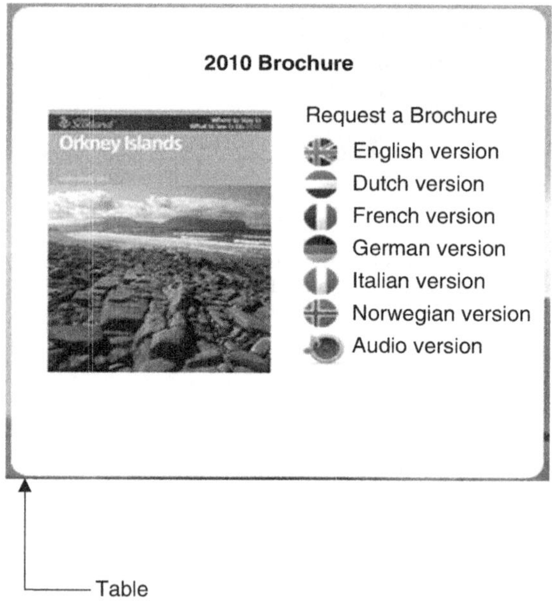

Figure 3.8 Screenshot of an example of a table (Tab) on the Orkney region website

Source: http://www.visitorkney.com/index.html (accessed on 10 December 2009); reproduced with permission of Scotland's National Tourism Organization, VisitScotland.

haptically and aurally inaccessible. By contrast, for those elements which, in addition to being visually accessible are also haptically and aurally accessible, a distinction will be made between the following types of visual, haptic, and aural activity potential: responding to mouse click, responding to rollover and mouse click, responding to type in and responding to click and up, down, left and/or right movement. These have been found to be main types of activity potential for the web pages that have been analysed. The analysis of a larger and different collection of websites may require the addition of further types of user action. The numbering of base units, as displayed on the four homepages, runs from top-to-bottom and left-to-right. Yet, this is arbitrary as the web page can be accessed non-sequentially. Following the rules introduced in subsection 2.2 of Chapter 2, the base units of the homepages of the four region's websites are listed as in Tables A1.1–A1.4 in Appendix B. For ease of reference, for one of the four homepages, the Zadar region homepage, the upper part has been extracted and the base units

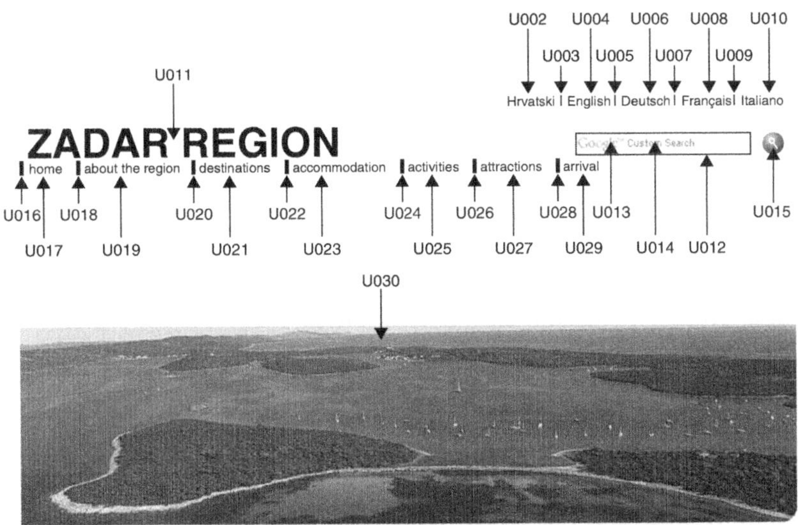

Figure 3.9 Screenshot of an extract from the homepage of the Zadar county website with marked units
Source: http://www.zadar.hr/English/Default.aspx (accessed on 10 September 2009); reproduced with permission of the Zadar County Tourist Board.

identified in the table have been marked. The extract with marked units relating to the upper part of the homepage can be seen in Figure 3.9.

3.2 Layout units

The layout analysis will work through hierarchically in isolating layout units, that is, from the root to the first, second, third, and fourth layers of the layout structure. For users to get an idea of the positioning of layout units, correspondences between the layout units of each layer in the layout structure and their positioning and organization within the main viewing area and marginal areas in the area model will be shown. The analysis will result in a layout structure for the homepage. For illustrative purposes, the homepage of the Perthshire region website will be explored. For the homepages of the Zadar, Orkney, and Istria region websites, presentation of the layout analysis will be omitted. The resulting layout structures will be presented on their own. This is due to the fact that the layout units shown in the layout structures will give insight into the positioning of elements which will serve as textual cues for the identification of types of thematic meanings in

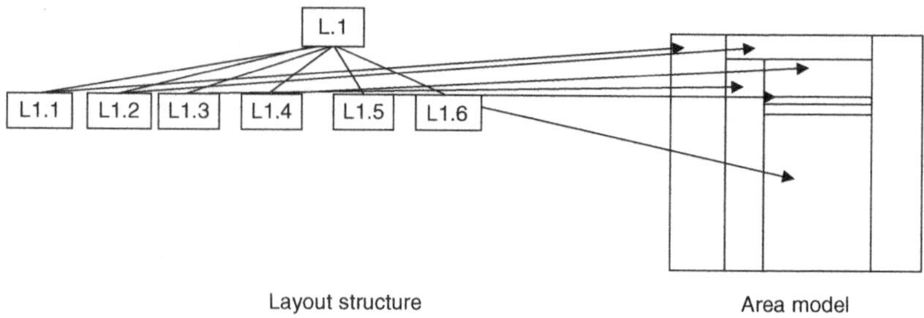

Figure 3.10 Correspondence between the first layer of the layout structure and its positioning in the area model for the homepage of the Perthshire region website

Figures 4.1–4.4 (cf. sub-subsection 4.1.1, Chapter 4). To recall, screenshots of the four homepages are shown in Figures 1.1–1.4 in subsection 1.1, Chapter 1. They enable readers to see to what the layout units which will be identified in the area models, such as L1.1–L1.6 in Figure 3.10 refer to. For ease of reference, the base units (U) which will be considered in the continuous text below are listed in Tables A1.1–A1.4 in Appendix B. To recap, the tables show what each unit is. For example, base unit U001 on the homepage of the Perthshire region website is a coloured block.

On the basis of separating lines, for the layout of the homepage of the Perthshire region website, six main layout bands at the first layer of the layout structure can be identified: as constituting background blocks which are separated from the remaining bands, the base units U001 and U392 form L1.1; the base units U002–U315 can be grouped into L1.2 as they are held together by a separating line which is running horizontally over the entire front page of the overall page; L1.3 consists of the base units U316–U328 due to a separating line running vertically to L1.4 and L1.5; L1.4 is made up of the base units U329–U337 as being separated from L1.5 by virtue of a white, horizontally-running line; L1.5, covering U338–U339, constitutes a separate layout band due to its continuous spread of grey; L1.6 involves the base units U340–U392. L1.1–L1.6 represent the first layer in the layout tree as direct descendants of L1. The correspondence between the first layer of the layout structure and its positioning in the area model can be seen in Figure 3.10.

L1.2 can further be divided into the base units U002–U005, U006, U007–U010, and U011–U315 in L1.2.1–L1.2.4 as they are spatially

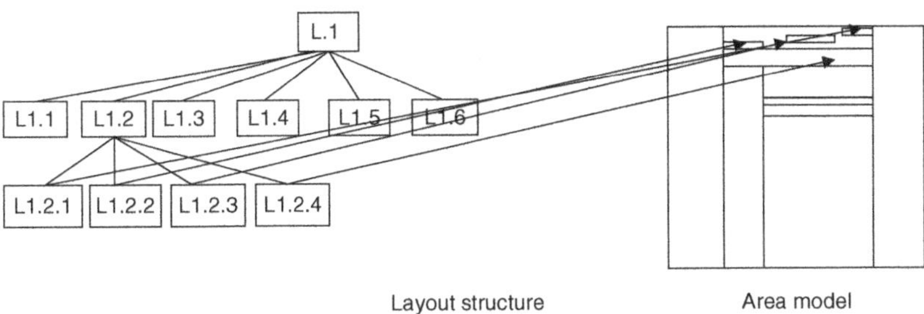

Figure 3.11 Correspondence between the descendants of L1.2 of the layout structure and their positioning in the area model for the homepage of the Perthshire region website

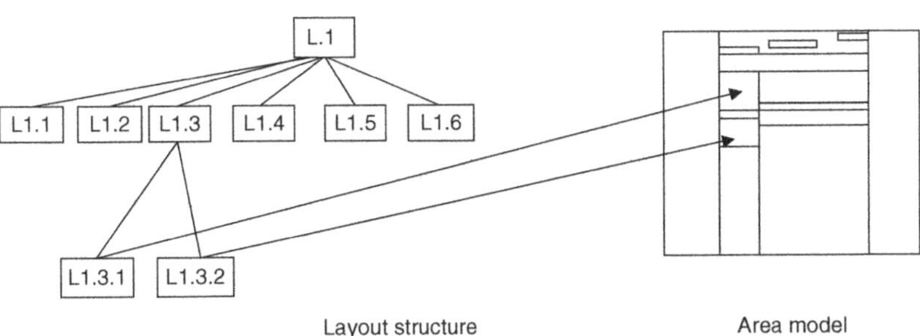

Figure 3.12 Correspondence between the descendants of L1.3 of the layout structure and their positioning in the area model for the homepage of the Perthshire region website

distant from one another. The correspondence between the descendants of L1.2 and their positioning in the area model is shown in Figure 3.11.

L1.3 is divisible into the base units U317–U322 and U323–328 in L1.3.1–L1.3.2 since they are framed by different boxes. The correspondence between the descendants of L1.3 and their positioning in the area model is shown in Figure 3.12.

L1.4 can further be divided into L1.4.1–L1.4.2. The base units U329 and U330–U337 in L1.4.1–L1.4.2 can be separated from one another as representing different types of visuals, that is, a landscape photograph and a drawing. The correspondence between L1.4.1–L1.4.2 and their positioning in the area model can be seen in Figure 3.13.

L1.5 cannot be further divided as this would directly lead to its base elements. The layout units L1.6.1–L1.6.7, as listed in the base units U340–U351, U352–U353, U354–U356, U357–U365, U366–U367,

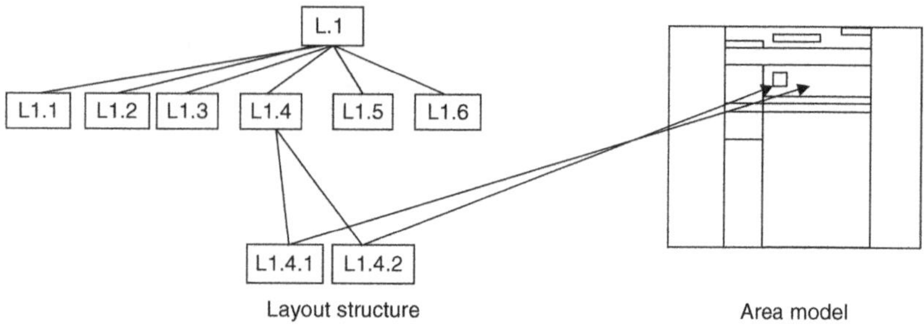

Figure 3.13 Correspondence between the descendants of L1.4 of the layout structure and their positioning in the area model for the homepage of the Perthshire region website

U368–U375 and U376–U392 constitute L1.6. They derive their separate status from the ways they are spread over the front page, as constituting different types and constellations of visuals. Thus L1.6.1 is a separate layout unit representing four types of visuals of the same size, shape, and proximity to one another, at the same height, with headers and brief clauses or captions of the same typography, in white. It is spatially separated from L1.6.2, a long coherent text passage in black which occupies the space below it. Moving to the right margin of the page, L1.6.3 is a separate unit consisting of a motif of icons of the same size and shape. Equally, L1.6.4 is a separate unit consisting of a motif of types of visuals, both of which contain embedded text fragments in an orange box. L1.6.5 is a separate layout unit as it contains another type of visual, that is, a text passage. L1.6.6 is, similar to L1.6.4, a separate layout unit presenting a motif of similar types of visuals, that is, logos. L1.6.3–L1.6.6 are arranged as if representing a horizontally-running column, despite the lack of a separating line which typically marks a column. Finally, L1.6.7 is spatially separated from the other layout units and encloses an interplay of verbal and graphical elements. L1.6.1–L1.6.7 are to be positioned in the second layer of the layout tree as direct descendants of L1.6. Their positioning in the layout tree and area model is shown in Figure 3.14.

At the third layer of the layout tree, the base units U317–U318 in L1.3.1.1 and U320–U323 in L1.3.1.2 as direct descendants of L1.3.1, the base units U340–U342, U343–U345, U346–U348 and U349–U351 in L1.6.1.1–L1.6.1.4 as direct descendants of L1.6.1, the base units U357–U361 and U362–U364 in L1.6.4.1–L1.6.4.2 as direct descendants of L1.6.4 and the base units U367–U370 and U371–U375 in L1.6.6.1–L1.6.6.2 as

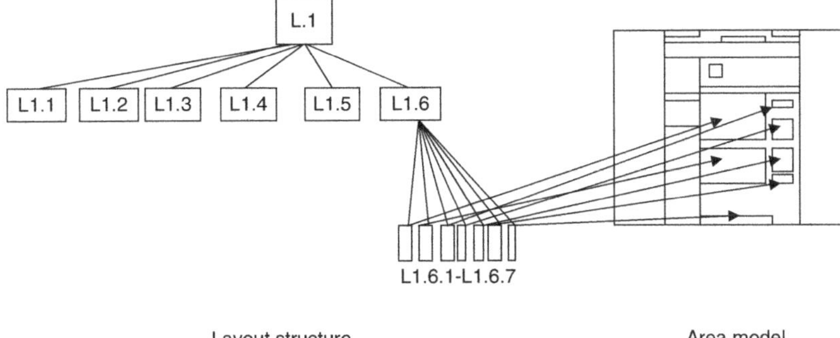

Figure 3.14 Correspondence between the descendants of L1.6 of the layout structure and their positioning in the area model for the homepage of the Perthshire region website

direct descendants of L1.6.6 are to be placed in relation to each other. L1.3.1 can be divided into L1.3.1.1 and L1.3.1.2 as they occupy different boxes and contain text fragments of different typography. While the subdivision of L1.6.1 is characterised by the above-mentioned repeated motif of four interplays between types of visuals and headers and brief sentences or captions of the same size and typography, L1.6.4 and L1.6.6 can further be subdivided due to a repeated motif of two photographs with boxes and underlined verbal elements, as in L1.6.4.1–L1.6.4.2, or of two logos, as in L1.6.6.1–L1.6.6.2. The correspondences between the descendants of L1.3.1, L1.6.1, L1.6.4 and L1.6.6 of the layout structure and their positioning in the area models can be seen in Figures 3.15–3.18.

L1.3.1.1 can further be divided into U317 in L1.3.1.1.1 and U318 in L1.3.1.1.2 since the former represents a dark green box as a possible access point to the overall layout box in terms of navigation, while the latter relates to the verbal text fragments as header of the overall layout box, as shown in Figure 3.19.

The resulting layout structure for the homepage of the Perthshire region website is schematized in Figure 3.20.

As mentioned above, the layout analysis of the homepage of the Perthshire region website serves as an example. The layout analysis of the homepages of the Zadar, Orkney and Istria region websites will be omitted here. The resulting layout structure of the homepage of the Zadar region website is illustrated in Figure 3.21.

The resulting layout structure of the homepage of the Orkney region website is illustrated in Figure 3.22.

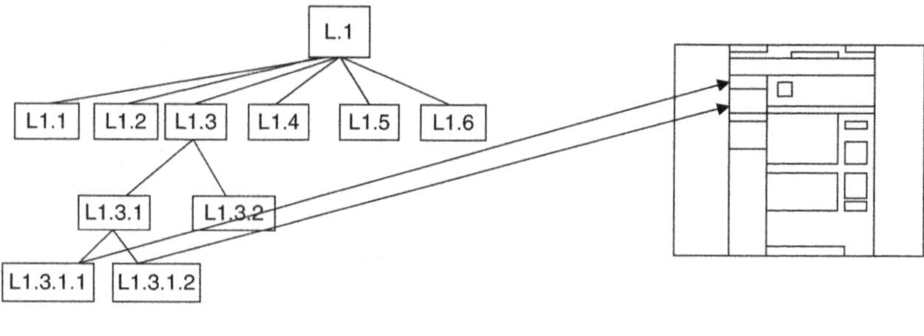

Figure 3.15 Correspondence between the descendants of L1.3.1 of the layout structure and their positioning in the area model for the homepage of the Perthshire region website

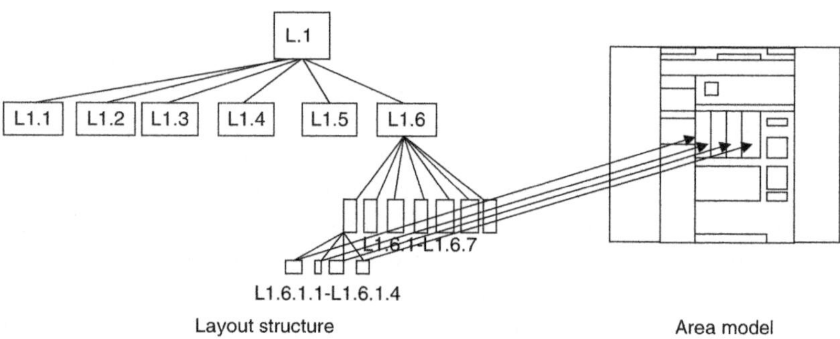

Figure 3.16 Correspondence between the descendants of L1.6.1 of the layout structure and their positioning in the area model for the homepage of the Perthshire region website

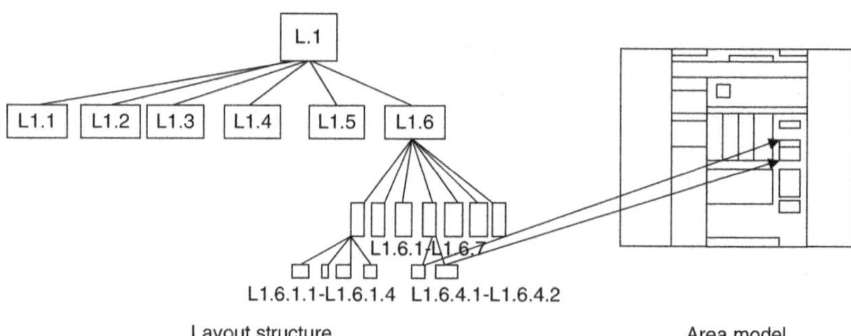

Figure 3.17 Correspondence between the descendants of L1.6.4 of the layout structure and their positioning in the area model for the homepage of the Perthshire region website

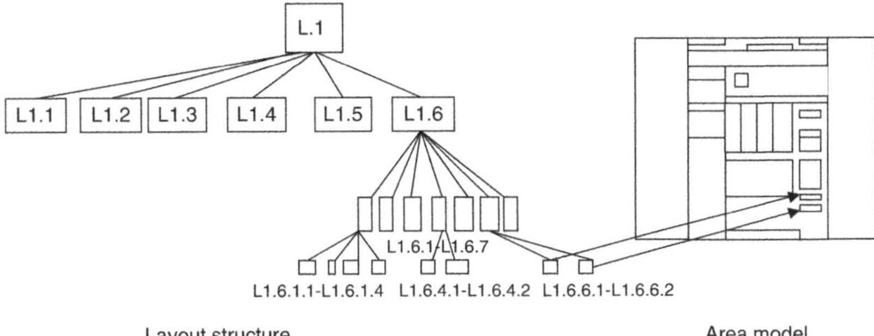

Figure 3.18 Correspondence between the descendants of L1.6.6 of the layout structure and their positioning in the area model for the homepage of the Perthshire region website

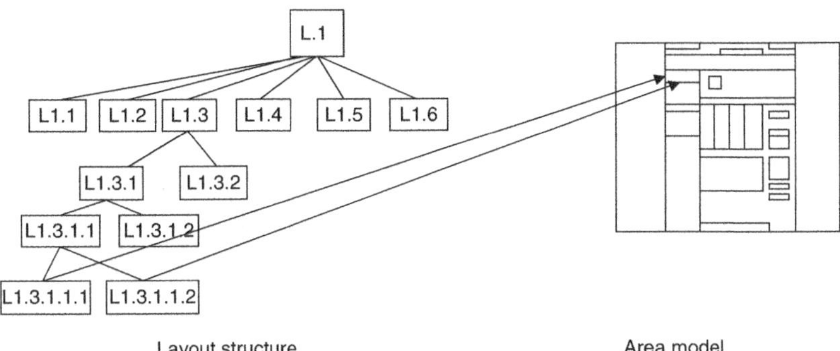

Figure 3.19 Correspondence between the descendants of L1.3.1.1 of the layout structure and their positioning in the area model for the homepage of the Perthshire region website

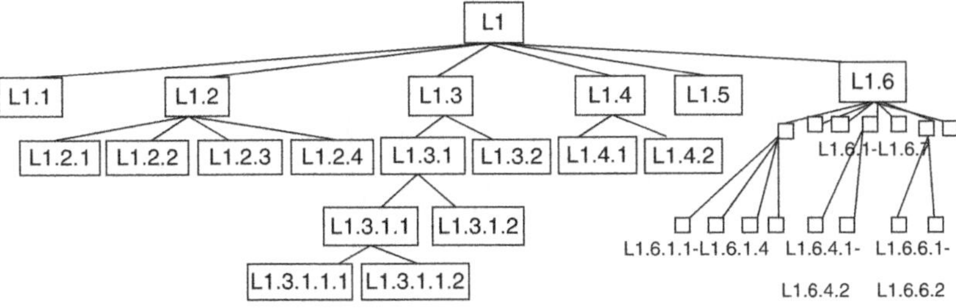

Figure 3.20 Layout structure for the homepage of the Perthshire region website according to the GeM model

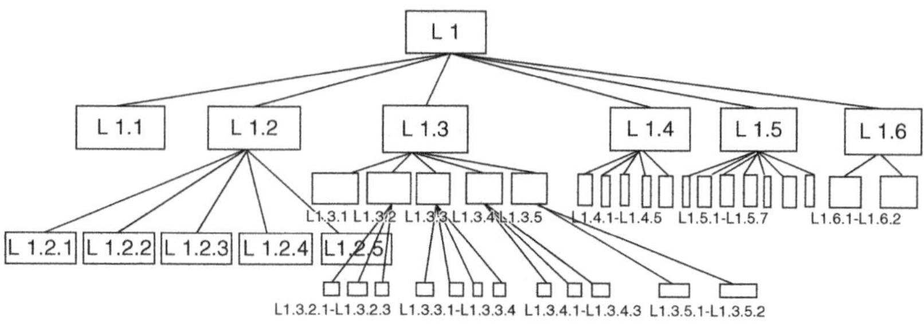

Figure 3.21 Layout structure for the homepage of the Zadar county website according to the GeM model

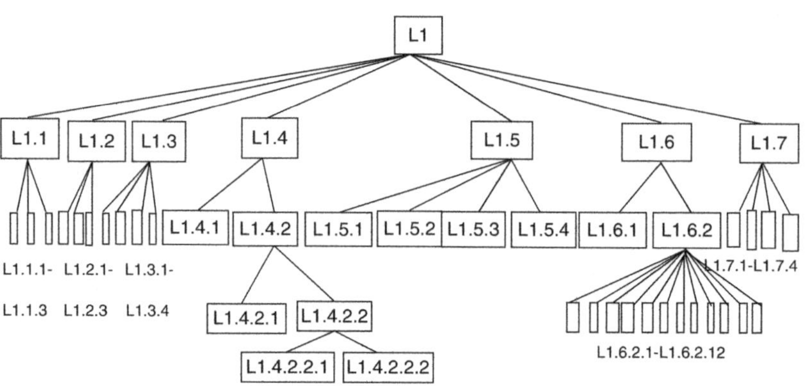

Figure 3.22 Layout structure for the homepage of the Orkney region website according to the GeM model

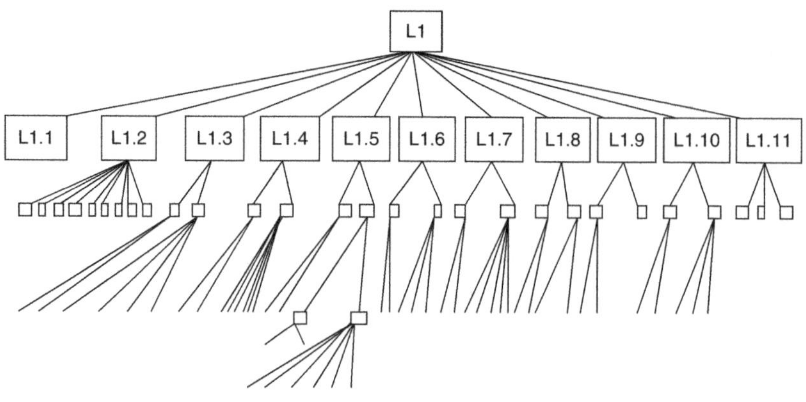

Figure 3.23 Layout structure for the homepage of the Istria region website according to the GeM model

All layout bands, elements, and subunits as components of the homepage of the Istria region website can be discerned in the layout structure in Figure 3.23.

For readers to get a sense of the statistics of base units (cf. definition in subsection 2.2, Chapter 2), accessible and inaccessible elements (cf. definition in subsection 2.1, Chapter 2), types of user actions (cf. definition in subsection 2.1, Chapter 2), types of elements (cf. definition in subsection 2.2, Chapter 2), and instances of verbal indication of media interaction (cf. definition in subsection 2.1, Chapter 2), overviews will be given in breakdowns for each of the four homepages in Tables 3.1–3.4 below.

In the process of decomposing pages into base units and subsequently grouping them into layout units, it has become clear that the homepage of the Zadar region website makes use of the highest number of base units, that is, 502 base units. For the other three homepages, a decrease in base units, starting with the homepage of the Istria region website with 458 base units, to the homepage of the Perthshire region website

Table 3.1 Overview of statistics of accessible and inaccessible elements on diverse tourist themes for the four regional websites

Homepages	**Zadar region**	**Orkney region**	**Istria region**	**Perthshire region**
Total base units	(502) 100%	(142) 100%	(459) 100%	(393) 100%
Inaccessibility	(192) 38.25%	(36) 25.35%	(103) 22.44%	(37) 9.41%
Accessibility	(310) 61.75%	(106) 74.65%	(356) 77.56%	(356) 90.59%

Table 3.2 Overview of statistics of user actions on diverse tourist themes for the four regional websites

Homepages	**Zadar region**	**Orkney region**	**Istria region**	**Perthshire region**
Total accessible units	(310) 100%	(106) 100%	(356) 100%	(356) 100%
Mouse click	(276) 89.03%	(12) 11.32%	(165) 46.35%	(60) 16.85%
Rollover and mouse click	(28) 9.03%	(94) 88.68%	(190) 53.37%	(296) 83.15%
Type in	(4) 1.29%	(0) 0%	(1) 0.28%	(0) 0%
Click and movement	(2) 0.65%	(0) 0%	(0) 0%	(0) 0%

Table 3.3 Overview of statistics of elements on diverse tourist themes for the four regional websites

Homepages	Zadar region	Orkney region	Istria region	Perthshire region
Total base units	(502) 100%	(142) 100%	(459) 100%	(393) 100%
Boxes	(54) 10.76%	(12) 8.45%	(23) 5.01%	(12) 3.05%
Blocks	(2) 0.4%	(0) 0%	(2) 0.44%	(2) 0.51%
Drawings	(5) 1%	(2) 1.41%	(42) 9.15%	(2) 0.51%
Grids	(2) 0.4%	(0) 0%	(0) 0%	(0) 0%
Icons	(44) 8.76%	(18) 12.68%	(26) 5.66%	(27) 6.87%
Maps	(1) 0.2%	(0) 0%	(29) 6.32%	(1) 0.25%
Photographs	(39) 7.77%	(20) 14.09%	(18) 3.92%	(6) 1.53%
Separators	(47) 9.36%	(0) 0%	(14) 3.27%	(11) 3.05%
Texts	(208) 41.43%	(72) 50.7%	(145) 31.59%	(179) 45.55%
Tables	(0) 0%	(6) 4.23%	(8) 1.74%	(1) 0.25%
Menu items	(90) 17.93%	(0) 0%	(114) 24.84%	(7) 1.78%
Scroll arrows	(4) 0.8%	(0) 0%	(10) 2.18%	(0) 0%
Scroll areas	(2) 0.4%	(0) 0%	(0) 0%	(0) 0%
Menu areas	(2) 0.4 %	(12) 8.45%	(26) 5.66%	(143) 36.39%
Scroll boxes	(2) 0.4%	(0) 0%	(0) 0%	(0) 0%
Other types of visuals	(0) 0%	(0) 0%	(1) 0.22%	(1) 0.25%

Table 3.4 Overview of instances of verbal indication of media interaction on diverse tourist themes for the four regional websites

Homepages	Zadar region	Orkney region	Istria region	Perthshire region
Verbal indication of media interaction	(3)	(8)	(5)	(0)

with 392 base units, and to the homepage of the Orkney region website with 142 base units, can be identified. Table 3.1 reveals that all four websites predominantly make use of units with accessible rather than inaccessible elements. The homepages of the Zadar (61.75%) and Orkney (74.65%) region websites make least use of the haptic and aural activities potential of digital multimodal texts, in addition to the visual activities potential. The homepages of the Perthshire (90.59%) and Istria (77.56%) regional websites make most use of the haptic and aural activities potential of digital multimodal texts.

These initial observations, which will be refined and extended in the course of the analysis of meaning-making in sub-subsection 4.1.4 of Chapter 4 on the empirical website analysis of meaning-making, give first insights into the types of tourists which are constructed for the four regional websites. For instance, the wealth of the total of base units (502) on the Zadar region website and the higher percentage of haptically and aurally inaccessible units (38.25%) in comparison to the Perthshire region homepage makes the Zadar region homepage resemble printed tourist promotional material. Thus, more traditional print media users, rather than more interactive media users who are more actively involved in the creation of tourist meanings, are created. By contrast, the lower total number of base units (393) on the homepage of the Perthshire region website and the lower percentage of haptically and aurally inaccessible units (9.41%) in comparison to the Zadar region homepage suggests that the Perthshire region homepage targets slightly more media- interactive tourists.

Also, Tables 3.2–3.4 suggest that the types of user actions, the variety of 16 types of base units listed in the table, and instances of verbal indication of media interaction add to the complexity of tourism web pages as instances of multimodal texts themselves and their analysis. Thus, the analysis of their meaning dimensions requires a complex set of tools, as informed by insights from the diverse models introduced in Chapter 2's description of a multi-layer approach to the website analysis.

In the following chapter, Chapter 4, the focus of socio-semiotic analysis will be on the representations of the regions through tourist themes on the four homepages, as realized in verbal and graphical elements with visual activity potential; the meaning potentials that are communicated to users as cultural tourists; and the ways in which users are engaged as media actors. Sub-subsection 4.1.1 will be devoted to an analysis of the importance of thematic meanings for image construction, and representation and cultural tourist and user communication, giving an overview of diverse fields of cultural activities as thematic meanings.

4
Analysis of Meaning-Making in Tourist Websites

4.1 Tourist activities

4.1.1 Importance for representation, and cultural tourist and user communication

As shown in Table 2.13 in subsection 2.2, Chapter 2, the homepages of the four regional websites can be explored in terms of several core research questions. To recap, these relate to the importance of tourist activities as tourist themes for representation and cultural tourist and user communication, the nature of representation of tourist themes, the address of users as cultural tourists, and the involvement of users as media actors.

With regard to the importance of tourist activities as tourist themes for representation and cultural tourist and user communication, various properties of commonality, that is, salience and framing, point to the hierarchical organization of diverse tourist activities in the form of thematic meanings on the page. As Kress & van Leeuwen (2007, p. 201) remark, 'salience can create a hierarchy of importance among the elements, selecting some as more important, more worthy of attention than others'. In order to give insight into the degree of importance of thematic meanings for image construction and for users as cultural tourists and media actors, instances of salience as textual cues need to be identified. Thus, scales as models for representing the degree of importance of thematic meanings for the overall images constructed for the four regions on the four region homepages have been selected. The general rule for the relation between the degree of importance of thematic meanings for image construction and the types of thematic meanings is that the less salient a type of thematic meaning is, the lower its degree of importance for image construction. For readers to get an idea of the ways in which meanings of activities, natural heritage, history and heritage, and gastronomy thematically develop, the structures of the regional websites as hierarchies of activity, information about the region, natural heritage, experience Istria, gastronomy, and history and heritage Themes are represented in Figures A1.1–A1.19 in Appendix A. The types of thematic meanings, their degree of importance for image construction, and for cultural tourist and user communication, and instances of salience as textual cues indicating their degree of importance for image construction, and cultural tourist and user communication are shown in Figures 4.1–4.4. To recall, the layout units (L) in the figures are those shown in Figures 3.20–3.23 (cf. subsection 3.2, Chapter 3).

In sum, Figure 4.1 reveals that, on the homepage of the Zadar region website, thematic meanings on landscape, activities, cultural heritage, and gastronomy are of most importance for image construction and cultural tourist and user communication, as suggested by the above-delineated textual cues. Thematic meanings on tourist attractions and events are of less significance. Diverse bits of information on locations, travel routes, weather, sea quality, news, arrival possibilities, types of media, and accommodation, and functional meanings on language options, search information, user orientation, the role of the tourist board, and contact possibilities are of least significance, as indicated by the above-identified textual cues. By contrast, as supported by Figure 4.2, thematic meanings on natural heritage, types of media, contact, shopping, and weather information are of most importance to image construction and cultural tourist and user communication on the homepage of the Orkney region website. Less attention is devoted to types of events. Competitions, special offers, accommodation, arrival possibilities, locations, user orientation, and contact possibilities are of least importance. When it comes to the homepage of the Istria region website, as indicated by Figure 4.3, most significance is assigned to thematic meanings on natural heritage, accommodation, the social experience of the environment, types of events, and locations. By contrast, activities, user navigation, contact and weather information, functional meanings on the role of the tourist board, privacy policy, an overview of website content, language versions of the website, search information, user orientation, and types of media are of less importance for image construction and cultural tourist and media communication. Finally, Figure 4.4 reveals that, on the homepage of the Perthshire region website, equal importance is ascribed to the representation of activities, events, natural heritage, and conference tourism. Also, the presentation

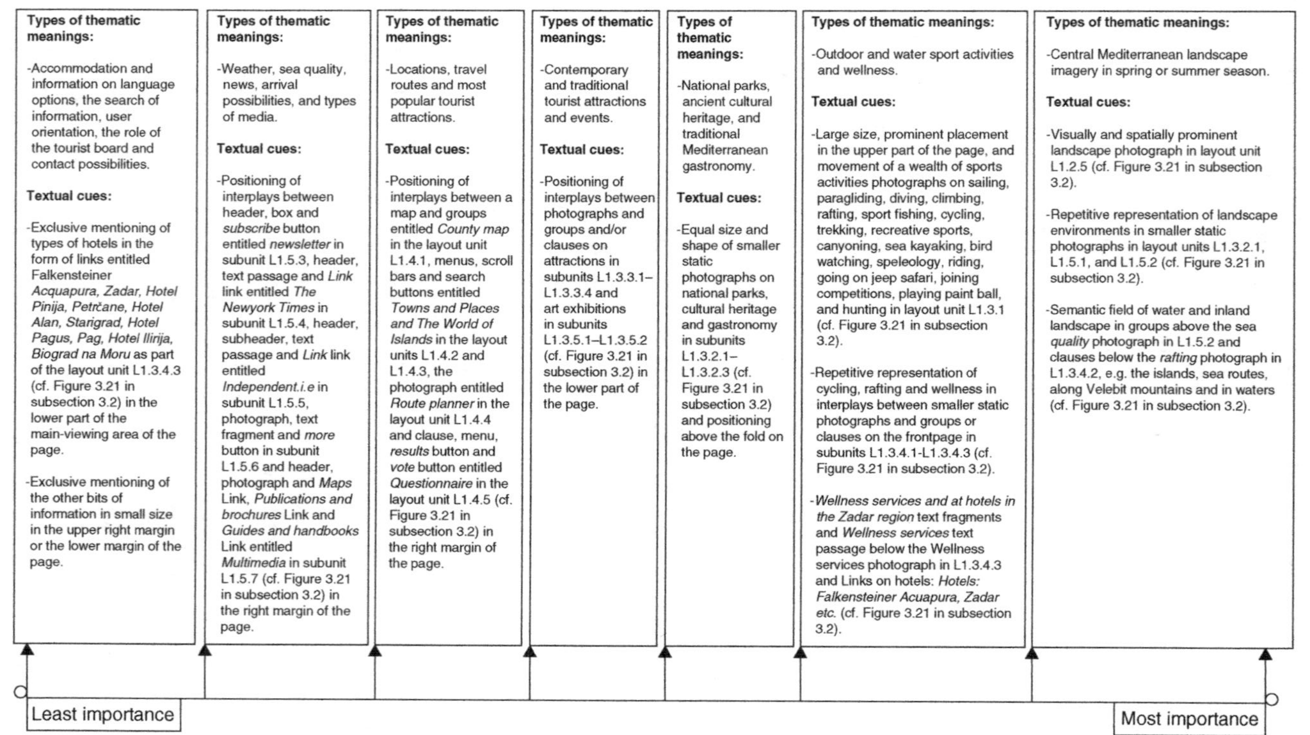

Types of thematic meanings:
-Accommodation and information on language options, the search of information, user orientation, the role of the tourist board and contact possibilities.
Textual cues:
-Exclusive mentioning of types of hotels in the form of links entitled Falkensteiner *Acquapura, Zadar, Hotel Pinija, Petrčane, Hotel Alan, Starigrad, Hotel Pagus, Pag, Hotel Ilirija, Biograd na Moru* as part of the layout unit L1.3.4.3 (cf. Figure 3.21 in subsection 3.2) in the lower part of the main-viewing area of the page.
-Exclusive mentioning of the other bits of information in small size in the upper right margin or the lower margin of the page.
Types of thematic meanings:
-Weather, sea quality, news, arrival possibilities, and types of media.
Textual cues:
-Positioning of interplays between header, box and *subscribe* button entitled *newsletter* in subunit L1.5.3, header, text passage and *Link* link entitled *The Newyork Times* in subunit L1.5.4, header, subheader, text passage and *Link* link entitled *Independent.i.e* in subunit L1.5.5, photograph, text fragment and *more* button in subunit L1.5.6 and header, photograph and *Maps* Link, *Publications and brochures* Link and *Guides and handbooks* Link entitled *Multimedia* in subunit L1.5.7 (cf. Figure 3.21 in subsection 3.2) in the right margin of the page.
Types of thematic meanings:
-Locations, travel routes and most popular tourist attractions.
Textual cues:
-Positioning of interplays between a map and groups entitled *County map* in the layout unit L1.4.1, menus, scroll bars and search buttons entitled *Towns and Places and The World of Islands* in the layout units L1.4.2 and L1.4.3, the photograph entitled *Route planner* in the layout unit L1.4.4 and clause, menu, *results* button and *vote* button entitled *Questionnaire* in the layout unit L1.4.5 (cf. Figure 3.21 in subsection 3.2) in the right margin of the page.
Types of thematic meanings:
-Contemporary and traditional tourist attractions and events.
Textual cues:
-Positioning of interplays between photographs and groups and/or clauses on attractions in subunits L1.3.3.1–L1.3.3.4 and art exhibitions in subunits L1.3.5.1–L1.3.5.2 (cf. Figure 3.21 in subsection 3.2) in the lower part of the page.
Types of thematic meanings:
-National parks, ancient cultural heritage, and traditional Mediterranean gastronomy.
Textual cues:
-Equal size and shape of smaller static photographs on national parks, cultural heritage and gastronomy in subunits L1.3.2.1–L1.3.2.3 (cf. Figure 3.21 in subsection 3.2) and positioning above the fold on the page.
Types of thematic meanings:
-Outdoor and water sport activities and wellness.
Textual cues:
-Large size, prominent placement in the upper part of the page, and movement of a wealth of sports activities photographs on sailing, paragliding, diving, climbing, rafting, sport fishing, cycling, trekking, recreative sports, canyoning, sea kayaking, bird watching, speleology, riding, going on jeep safari, joining competitions, playing paint ball, and hunting in layout unit L1.3.1 (cf. Figure 3.21 in subsection 3.2).
-Repetitive representation of cycling, rafting and wellness in interplays between smaller static photographs and groups or clauses on the frontpage in subunits L1.3.4.1-L1.3.4.3 (cf. Figure 3.21 in subsection 3.2).
-*Wellness services and at hotels in the Zadar region* text fragments and *Wellness services* text passage below the Wellness services photograph in L1.3.4.3 and Links on hotels: *Hotels: Falkensteiner Acuapura, Zadar etc.* (cf. Figure 3.21 in subsection 3.2).
Types of thematic meanings:
-Central Mediterranean landscape imagery in spring or summer season.
Textual cues:
-Visually and spatially prominent landscape photograph in layout unit L1.2.5 (cf. Figure 3.21 in subsection 3.2).
-Repetitive representation of landscape environments in smaller static photographs in layout units L1.3.2.1, L1.5.1, and L1.5.2 (cf. Figure 3.21 in subsection 3.2).
-Semantic field of water and inland landscape in groups above the sea *quality* photograph in L1.5.2 and clauses below the *rafting* photograph in L1.3.4.2, e.g. the islands, sea routes, along Velebit mountains and in waters (cf. Figure 3.21 in subsection 3.2).
Least importance
Most importance

Figure 4.1 Scale for the degree of importance of thematic meanings on the homepage of the Zadar region website

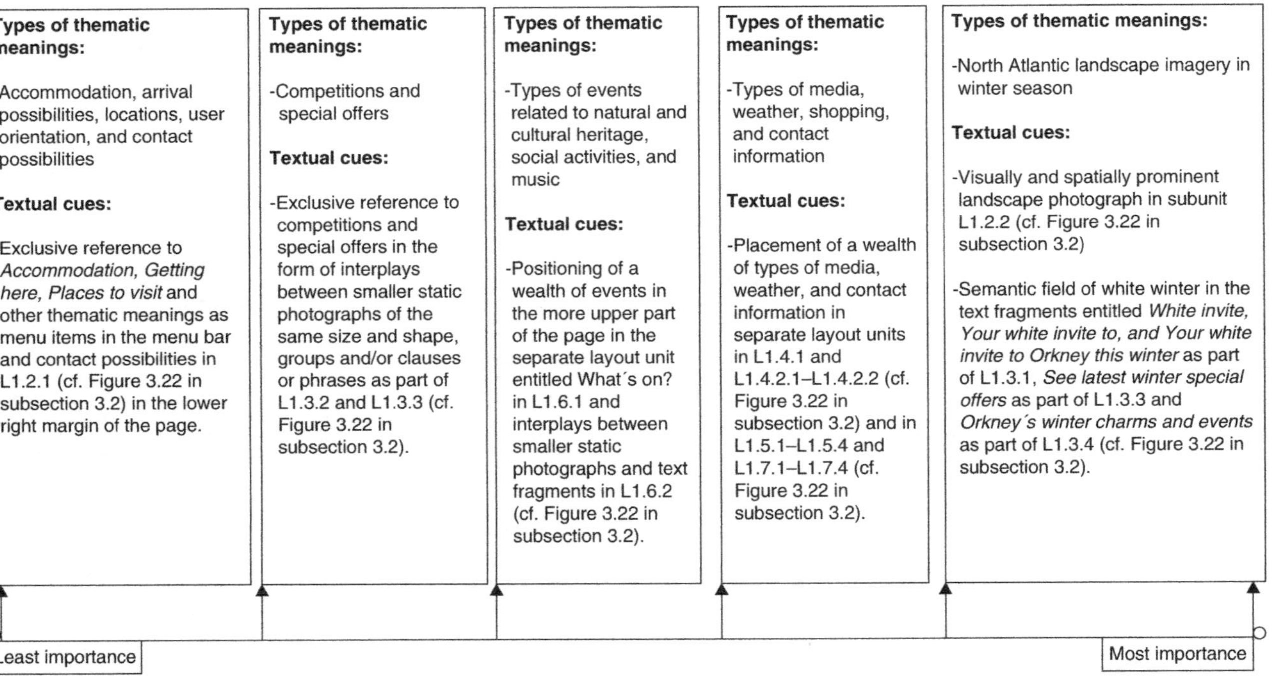

Types of thematic meanings:
-Accommodation, arrival possibilities, locations, user orientation, and contact possibilities
Textual cues:
-Exclusive reference to Accommodation, Getting here, Places to visit and other thematic meanings as menu items in the menu bar and contact possibilities in L1.2.1 (cf. Figure 3.22 in subsection 3.2) in the lower right margin of the page.
Types of thematic meanings:
-Competitions and special offers
Textual cues:
-Exclusive reference to competitions and special offers in the form of interplays between smaller static photographs of the same size and shape, groups and/or clauses or phrases as part of L1.3.2 and L1.3.3 (cf. Figure 3.22 in subsection 3.2).
Types of thematic meanings:
-Types of events related to natural and cultural heritage, social activities, and music
Textual cues:
-Positioning of a wealth of events in the more upper part of the page in the separate layout unit entitled What´s on? in L1.6.1 and interplays between smaller static photographs and text fragments in L1.6.2 (cf. Figure 3.22 in subsection 3.2).
Types of thematic meanings:
-Types of media, weather, shopping, and contact information
Textual cues:
-Placement of a wealth of types of media, weather, and contact information in separate layout units in L1.4.1 and L1.4.2.1–L1.4.2.2 (cf. Figure 3.22 in subsection 3.2) and in L1.5.1–L1.5.4 and L1.7.1–L1.7.4 (cf. Figure 3.22 in subsection 3.2).
Types of thematic meanings:
-North Atlantic landscape imagery in winter season
Textual cues:
-Visually and spatially prominent landscape photograph in subunit L1.2.2 (cf. Figure 3.22 in subsection 3.2)
-Semantic field of white winter in the text fragments entitled White invite, Your white invite to, and Your white invite to Orkney this winter as part of L1.3.1, See latest winter special offers as part of L1.3.3 and Orkney´s winter charms and events as part of L1.3.4 (cf. Figure 3.22 in subsection 3.2).
Least importance
Most importance

Figure 4.2 Scale for the degree of importance of thematic meanings on the homepage of the Orkney region website

Types of thematic meaning:	**Types of thematic meanings:**	**Types of thematic meanings:**	**Types of thematic meanings:**	**Types of thematic meanings:**	**Types of thematic meanings:**	**Types of thematic meanings:**	**Types of thematic meanings:**
-Types of media **Textual cues:** -Exclusive reference to types of media and additional information in smaller static interplays between icons and groups in the subunit L1.2.2 in the upper part of the page (cf. Figure 3.23 in subsection 3.2).	-The role of the tourist board, privacy policy, overview of website content, language version of the website, search information, user orientation and contact information, weather and user navigation on locations, natural heritage, seasonal holidays and conference tourism **Textual cues:** -Placement of the Links layout unit in L1.4.1 and L1.4.2.1–L1.4.2.6 (cf. Figure 3.23 in subsection 3.2) in the left margin of the page.	-Sport activities and wellness **Textual cues:** -Positioning of interplay between smaller static photographs of the same size and shape as part of L1.3.2.2 and as part of L1.3.2.4 in the right margin of the page (cf. Figure 3.23 in subsection 3.2).	-Locations **Textual cues:** -Large size and positioning of the interplay between *Where are we*? maps and captions in the main-viewing area in L1.6.1 and L1.6.2.1–L1.6.2.3 (cf. Figure 3.23 in subsection 3.2) in the lower part of the page -Representation of more specific information on subregions, towns of Istria region, and Istria region in relation to Croatia and neighbouring countries as signifiers of schemes of knowledge attributed to users as media actors through salience in Search Istria layout unit in L1.7.1 and L1.7.2.1–L1.7.2.2 (cf. Figure 3.23 in subsection 3.2) in the upper part of the right margin of the page.	-Types of events related to rural Mediterranean landscape, gastronomy, music and seasonal event offers **Textual cues:** -Visual and spatial prominence of the *What´s* on header and the interplay between headers, photographs, text passages and more links in L1.5.1 and L1.5.2.1.1–L1.5.2.1.2 (cf. Figure 3.23 in section 3.2). - Information on music and gastronomic manifestations, as indicated by the corresponding text fragments *Rovinj Music Festival 2009, Festival of wine, honey and home made bread, Honey Days, Promohotel* in L1.5.2.2.1–L1.5.2.2.6 (cf. Figure 3.23 in	-Social experience of sea landscape and cultural heritage environ-ment **Textual cues:** Positioning of smaller static photo-graphs in L1.2.9 in the upper part of the page (cf. Figure 3.23 in subsection 3.2).	-Accommoda tion **Textual cues:** Prominent placement of L1.2.6 in the upper part of the page and repetitive reference to accommoda tion in L1.9 in the right margin of the page (cf. Figure 3.23 in subsection 3.2).	-Sea and land landscape imagery **Textual cues:** -Large size, prominent placement in the upper part of the page and movement of landscape photographs in L1.2.4 (cf. Figure 3.23 in subsection 3.2).

Least importance → Most importance

Figure 4.3 Scale for the degree of importance of thematic meanings on the homepage of the Istria region website

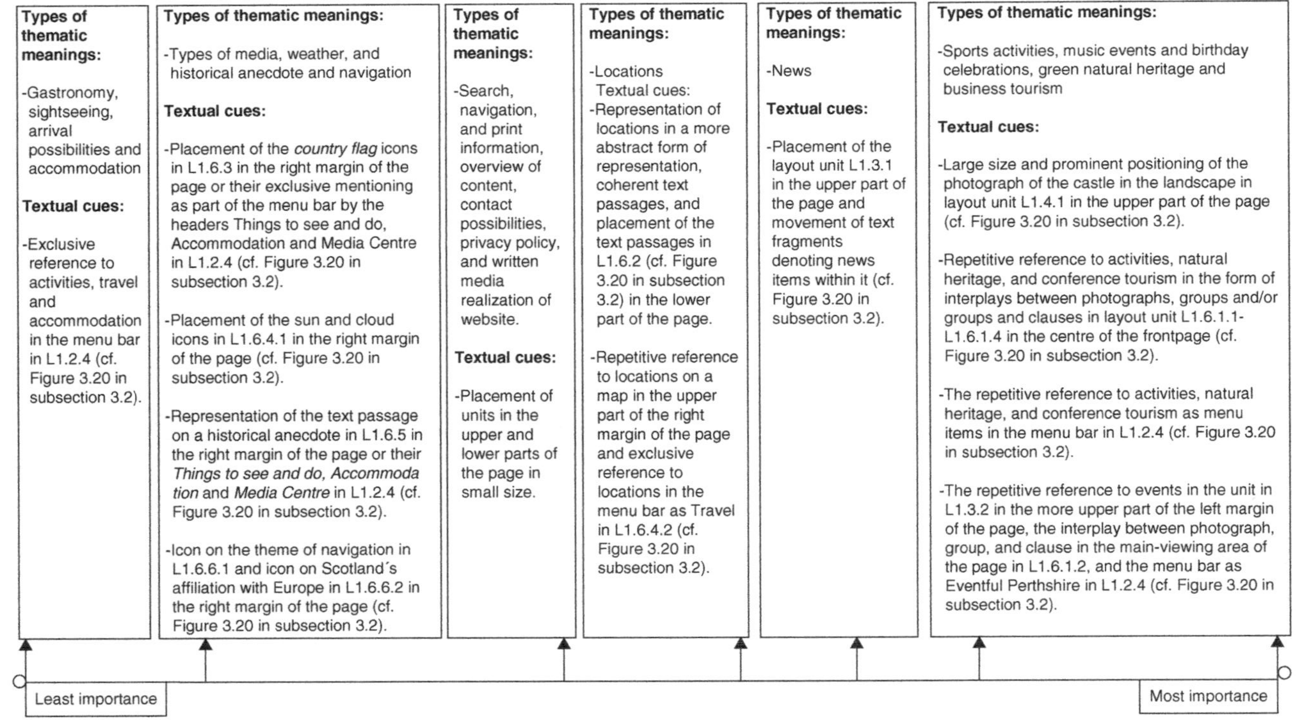

Figure 4.4 Scale for the degree of importance of thematic meanings on the homepage of the Perthshire region website

of the latest news is prioritized. Less significance, however, is assigned to the representation of locations. Thematic meanings on types of media, weather, and historical anecdotes, functional meanings on search information, navigation, print, an overview of content, contact possibilities, privacy policy, and the written media realization of the website, gastronomy, sightseeing, arrival possibilities, and accommodation are of least relevance.

4.1.2 Conventional or post-conventional tourist themes?

The experience of active holidays in the social world and media interaction in the virtual world are crucial to the ways in which the Zadar region is represented to its prospective tourists. Figure 4.5 gives an overview of statistics of experiential meanings on diverse tourist themes in clauses for the homepages of the four regional websites.

The importance of active holidays and media interaction is indicated by the predominance of narrative (66.67%) structures which can be

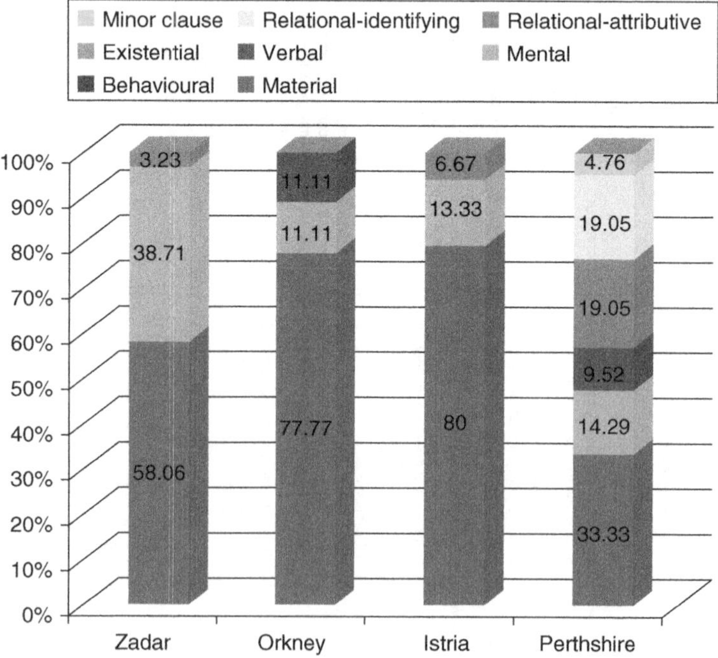

Figure 4.5 Overview of statistics of experiential meanings on diverse tourist themes in clauses for the homepages of the four regional websites

assigned to the visuals, the high frequency of material (58.06%) processes which can be assigned to the clauses, and the wealth of groups and phrases (131 instances) expressing activities. More specifically, narrative structures centre on the practice of outdoor and water sports activities by more wealthy people in Central Mediterranean landscapes and in the mountains, warm weather conditions, visits to more contemporary and unconventional tourist attractions, participation in events, arrival possibilities, travel routes, and the consultation of types of media for further information. The interpretation of the tourist attractions as contemporary and unconventional derives from intertextual knowledge that architectural sites, such as the musical pipe organs in the Zadar region, are commonly represented as natural musical instruments of contemporary construction in other texts. The identification of the sportspeople as wealthy is due to intertextual knowledge that yachts are commonly represented as types of vessels sailed by people with more stable bank accounts in other texts. The reading of the weather conditions as welcoming is due to intertextual knowledge that the wearing of short-sleeved leisure wear by people is commonly related to summer or spring seasons in other texts. In addition to the practice of sports activities and the presentation of exhibitions in civic buildings, material processes which express virtual activities can be assigned to the clauses. These actively engage users in the creation of tourist meanings around the wealth of tourist locations in the Zadar region – on a map and in menus, through user preferences of tourist themes in online forms, and through regular online reports for user information. As denoted by mental (38.71%) processes being the next most frequent type of process, space is also given to tourist highlights in the form of suggestions for holiday ideas. These include the experience of landscapes, cultural heritage sights and gastronomy, delight in sports activities, knowledge enhancement on natural heritage, and the appeal of the Zadar region as a tourist destination, in general, and tourist themes, in particular. Less attention is devoted to the portrayal of the Zadar region as a static site for the existence of tourists, natural heritage sites, gastronomic products, tourist attractions, and events. This static site relates to hunters as sportspeople, sculptures, Mediterranean seascapes, and traditional gastronomic offers, as expressed by the dearth of conceptual (33.33%) structures which can be attributed to visuals. Equally, it includes the suitability of sports infrastructure for the practice of outdoor water sports activities, as realized by relational attributive (3.23%) processes.

In contrast to the Zadar region website, thematic meanings are presented as things which simply exist on the Orkney (81.82%), Istria (75%), and Perthshire (86.67%) region websites. This is suggested by the predominance of conceptual structures and the experiential meanings expressed by the groups and phrases (39 instances on the Orkney, 41 instances on the Istria, and 13 instances on the Perthshire region websites). The representational structures which can be ascribed to the visuals and the bits of information captured by the groups experientially deal with the existence of types of events, North-Atlantic landscape and weather conditions, commercial goods and activities, and types of media on the Orkney region website. They revolve around the existence of Istrian landscape regions, weather conditions, events, locations, and accommodation on the Istria region website. Experiential meanings captured by groups and phrases add information on user navigation, holiday planning, diverse tourist themes and times, contact possibilities, and weather conditions. They refer to the existence of green landscape, weather, types of media, and locations on the Perthshire region website. Experiential meanings, as realized by groups and phrases, further relate to events, weather conditions, types of media, user navigation, and advertising.

Interestingly, this static kind of representation, as expressed by representational structures in visuals, is complemented by a more dynamic representation of thematic meanings in process types. The clear predominance of material processes on the Orkney (77.77%) and Istria (80%) region websites supports this reading. On the Orkney region website, these express encouragement to consult types of media for further information on news, weather, commercial activities such as shopping, contact possibilities, and events. On the Istria region website, these centre on participation in events and virtual activities on Istrian locations. Accordingly, limited space is given to narrative structures which can be ascribed to the visuals on the Orkney (18.18%), Istria (25%), and Perthshire (13.33%) region websites. On the Orkney region website, these focus on the participation of tourists in social, music, and sports events. On the Istria region website, they are concerned with virtual activities on locations, water sports activities, wellness, and the social experience of Istria. On the Perthshire region website, they relate to the practice of sports activities and participation in events. Equally, the Orkney (11.11%) and Istria (13.13%) region websites make less use of mental processes. In concert with verbal processes (11.11%), on the former website they deal with encouraging perception of attention-grabbing package deals and consulting types of media for further information about the region. On the latter website, mental processes relate to the perception of events as media actors and the emotional experience of events in rural areas as cultural tourists.

In contrast to the Zadar, Orkney, and Istria region websites, greater variety in the use of process types which can be assigned to the clauses can be noted on the Perthshire region website. Thus, material (33.33%) and mental (14.29%) processes interact to construe meanings in historical anecdotes, the attendance of visitor centres as sites of history and Scottish scenery, tourist activities, and expectations. By contrast, relational attributive (19.05%) and identifying (19.05%) processes interact to construe the following meanings: statistics on tourist visits as evidence for news statements, locations, arrival possibilities, the suitability of the region as a holiday destination for a wide scope of target groups, and the idealization of the pristine nature, wealth of wildlife, and aesthetic appeal of landscapes.

Moving from experiential meanings to the arguability of clauses, the Zadar and Istria region websites predominantly temper the force of verbal statements. This is achieved by the high frequency of finite clauses with modality features on the Zadar (64.52%) and Istria (42.86%) region websites. Limited or equal space is given to instances which do not allow for statements on the arguability of clauses on the Zadar (19.35%) and Istria (42.86%) region websites. This is indicated by the use of non-finite clauses. Occasionally, the Zadar (16.13%) and Istria (14.29%) region websites present propositions as indisputable facts. This is suggested by the use of tensed finite clauses.

Within finite clauses, the use of comment adjuncts or comments is restricted to the type of comment: propositional; wisdom; wise; explicitly objective in relation to holiday suggestions on the part of the tourist board on the Zadar region homepage.

In addition, Figures 4.6–4.7 give an overview of statistics of orientation, manifestation, and modality type in finite clauses.

Thus, both the Zadar and Istria region websites coincide in the predominant use of median value modality (100% on the Zadar region website and 83.33% on the Istria region website) and implicitly subjective orientation and manifestation (95% on the Zadar region website and 83.33% on the Istria region website), as expressed by modal finites. Thus, they foreground the speaker's own viewpoint. Also, both the Zadar (63.16%) and Istria (83.33%) region websites make use of readiness: ability as a type of modality in propositions about virtual activities and the practice of sports activities. In addition, the Zadar region website displays probability (36.84%) in propositions about tourist attractions, while the Istria region website uses readiness: inclination

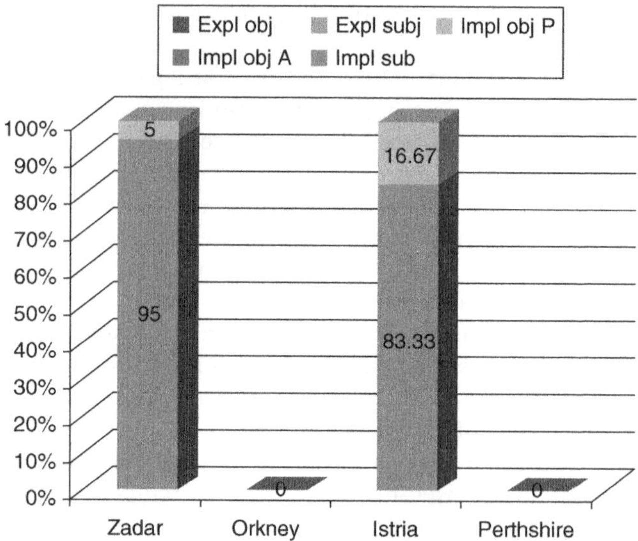

Figure 4.6 Overview of statistics of orientation and manifestation in finite clauses on diverse tourist themes for the homepages of the four regional websites

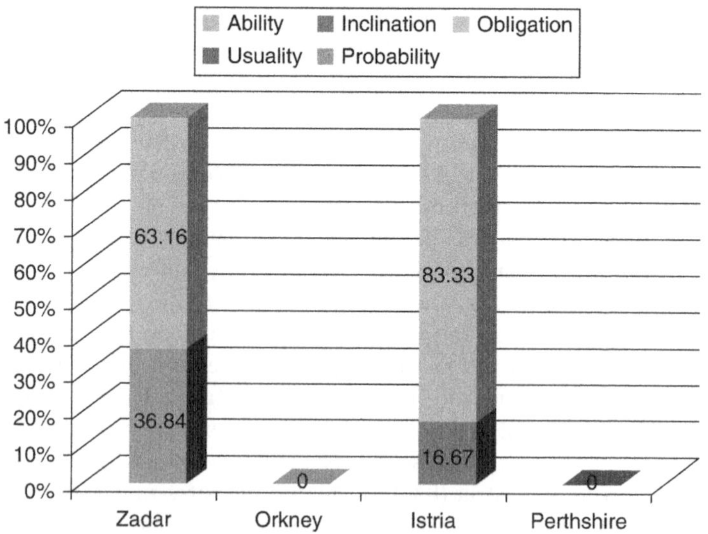

Figure 4.7 Overview of statistics of modality type in finite clauses on diverse tourist themes for the homepages of the four regional websites

(16.67%) in a proposition about the experience of rural events. By contrast, the Orkney and Perthshire region websites do not moderate the definitiness of propositions. This is suggested by the lack of finite clauses with modality features (0%). Instead, no comments can be made about the arguability of clauses. This is indicated by the predominance of non-finite clauses (88.88%) on the Orkney region websites, or, on the Perthshire region website, statements represented as facts, as realized by the high frequency of tensed finite clauses (80%). It follows from this that the Zadar and Istria region websites moderate the definitiveness of statements about activities in the virtual world and tourist activities in the social world. By contrast, the Orkney and Perthshire region websites give more space to the representation of statements about tourist activities as facts.

When it comes to types of visuals on diverse tourist themes, the Zadar (97.5%) and Istria (65.52%) region websites predominantly make use of visuals of higher-value modality. By contrast, for the Orkney region website, a similar distribution of visuals of higher- (54.55%) and lower-value (45.45%) modality can be identified. On the Perthshire region website, a predominance of visuals of lower-value modality (64.29%) can be noted. Hence, realistic representations of more conventional tourist meanings are crucial to the ways in which the Zadar and Istria region websites visually represent themselves to prospective tourists. In contrast, the Orkney and Perthshire region websites focus more on icons as simplistic representations of objects, thus stressing more post-conventional thematic meanings in types of media and the virtual activities of users as media actors.

4.1.3 Sportspeople, explorers of regions, or participants in events?

The visuals on the four regional websites predominantly offer factual information, rather than demanding that users enter into imaginary relations with the represented experiential meanings. This is suggested by the lack of direct gaze of human or quasi-human participants at users on the Orkney (0%), Istria (0%), and Perthshire (0%) region websites and the dearth of direct gaze of human participants at users on the Zadar (5%) region website. Most of the representational meanings identified in sub-subsection 4.1.2 are thus portrayed as objects for user observation and contemplation. Instances which demand users to establish an interpersonal relationship with the represented participants are limited to the representation of hunters gazing directly at users and travel routes – through the representation of children beckoning from a car – on the Zadar region website. Thus, they invite users to imagine themselves as hunters and drivers using computer programmes for planning trips between destinations.

When it comes to subjective attitude, Figure 4.8 gives an overview of statistics of realizations of subjective attitude in diverse tourist themes for the homepages of the four regional websites.

This suggests that the Orkney (83.33%), Istria (70.59%), and Perthshire (100%) region websites predominantly make use of involvement, as indicated by the use of frontal angles. In contrast, for the Zadar region website, similar distributions of involvement (56.41%) and detachment (43.59%) can be noted. Furthermore, on the Zadar and Orkney region websites, equality (84.62% on the Zadar region website, 94.44% on the Orkney region website), as indicated by eye-level angles, is privileged over viewer power (12.82% on the Zadar region website and 5.56% on the Orkney region website), as suggested by high angles, and representation power (2.56% on the Zadar region website, 0% on the Orkney

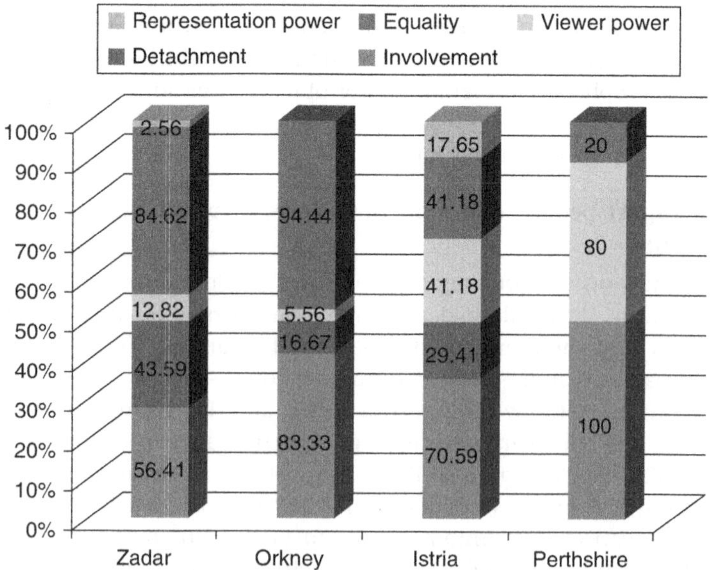

Figure 4.8 Overview of statistics of realizations of subjective attitude on diverse tourist themes for the homepages of the four regional websites

region website), as achieved by low angles. Differently, on the Istria region website, an equal distribution of viewer power (41.18%) and equality (41.18%) can be noted. Limited space is given to representation power (17.65%). On the Perthshire region website, there is a focus on viewer power (80%). Occasionally, the website makes use of equality (20%). The Zadar and Perthshire region websites further coincide in a similar distribution of impersonal (35% on the Zadar region website, 42.86% on the Perthshire region website), as suggested by long range, and social relations (47.5% on the Zadar and 42.86% on the Perthshire region website), as accomplished by medium range. On the Orkney and Istria region websites, a clearer focus on impersonal relations (54.55% on the Orkney region website and 46.67% on the Istria region website) can be observed. Fewer instances of intimate or personal relations, as indicated by close range, can be identified for the Zadar (17.5%), Orkney (36.36%), Istria (23.33%), and Perthshire (14.29%) region websites. In addition to these realizations of subjective attitude and social distance, the visuals on the four region website express objective attitude. Thus, the Zadar (100%) and Istria (72.73%) region websites exclusively or predominantly make use of maps which encode knowledge orientation. These enhance users' knowledge about the positioning of locations or regions. By contrast, on the Orkney (100%) and Perthshire (88.88%) region websites, a wealth of icons can be noted. These fulfil the semiotic function of representing diverse objects on types of media, commercial activities, contact possibilities, weather, and/or the navigation function of transferring users quickly to the corresponding internal and external web pages.

It follows from the high frequency of social and impersonal relations, the similar distribution of involvement and detachment, and the predominance of equality that users are predominantly positioned as more distant observers of diverse tourist activities and objects on the Zadar region website. Occasionally, as indicated by a map expressing objective attitude, they are constructed as learners about the positioning of tourist locations. Due to the predominant use of impersonal relations, involvement, and equality, on the Orkney region website, users are invited to look at types of events as more distant observers. At the same time, they figure as media-interactive users and perceivers of types of media, commercial activities, and contact possibilities. This is suggested by icons with a semiotic/semiotic and navigation function. On the Istria region website, the predominant use of impersonal relations and involvement, and interplays between viewer power and equality create users as landscape and activity observers. Similarly to the Zadar region website, they are further positioned as learners about the positioning of locations. This is suggested by the corresponding maps expressing knowledge orientation. The Perthshire region website positions users as observers of diverse tourist activities. This is indicated by interplays between impersonal and social relations, the predominance of viewer power, and the exclusive use of involvement. Due to the wealth of icons, it equally constructs users as perceivers, and as consumers and media actors on advertising and types of media and weather.

On all four homepages, the websites predominantly make statements and give information about the experiential meanings identified in sub-subsection 4.1.2 above, as expressed by declarative mood and encoded into the groups. Users are directly addressed or involved as cultural tourists to only a limited extent. This is demonstrated by the 90% of units with no direct address or involvement on the Zadar, 86.67% on the Orkney, 80.77% on the Istria, and 66.67% on the Perthshire region websites. On the homepage of the Zadar region website, this is represented by the involvement of users in the multimodal exchange of information on holiday suggestions, as indicated by a first person pronoun (one instance). This involvement relates to diverse tourist activities, including visiting natural heritage sites, experiencing history and heritage, and benefiting from gastronomy. These users are thus created as selectors of tourist experiences. Equally, users are directly addressed as water and outdoor sportspeople and health tourists, as suggested by second person pronouns (seven instances) and the imperative mood (two instances). On the homepage of the Orkney region website, users are addressed as guests to Orkney in the winter season, as indicated by the second person (one instance); and involved in the multimodal exchange of information on events, as indicated by encoding the first-person perspective into a header (one instance). On the homepage of the Istria region website, users figure as discoverers of the Istria region and the atmosphere created by events in rural and Mediterranean landscape environments, and holiday planners. This is indicated by the imperative mood (one instance) and second person pronouns (two instances). Also, they are involved into the multimodal exchange of information on places for tourists to visit, times to visit them, and activities to do. This is suggested by the first-person perspective encoded into headers and captions (three instances). On the homepage of the Perthshire region website, users are constructed as participants in events and satisfied tourists. In addition, they figure as tourists interested in historical anecdotes and visitors of information centres on Scottish scenery and history. This is indicated by second person pronouns (four instances) and the imperative mood (one instance).

4.1.4 Observers or dynamic and media-interactive users?

In subsection 3.2, Chapter 3, it has been suggested that the wealth of the total base units on the homepage of the Zadar region website (502 units), as indicated by Table 3.3, and the higher percentage of haptically and aurally inaccessible units (38.25%), as suggested by Table 3.1, in comparison to the Perthshire region homepage, suggests that the Zadar region homepage targets more traditional print media users, rather than more interactive media users who are more actively involved in the creation of tourist meanings. By contrast, the lower total number of base units on the homepage of the Perthshire region website (393 units), as can be seen in Table 3.3, and the lower percentage of haptically and aurally inaccessible units (9.41%), as signalled by Table 3.1, in comparison to the Zadar region homepage, suggests that the Perthshire region homepage targets slightly more media-interactive tourists.

When it comes to the variety in the use of types of base units, as supported by Table 3.3 in subsection 3.2, Chapter 3, the homepages of the Zadar (41.43%) and Orkney (50.7%) region websites predominantly devote attention to text fragments or text passages. By contrast, for the homepages of the Perthshire and Istria region websites, a similar distribution between text fragments or text passages (45.55% for the homepage of the Perthshire region website, 31.59% for the homepage of the Istria region website), on the one hand, and menu areas (36.39% for the homepage of the Perthshire region website) or menu items (24.84% for the homepage of the Istria region website), on the other hand, can be noted. Thus, the latter two websites give more space to elements of the graphical user interface which engage users as media actors than the former two websites, which predominantly make use of elements typical of static print material.

Moreover, Table 3.4 in subsection 3.2, Chapter 3 indicates that on the homepages of the Orkney (eight instances), Istria (five instances), and Zadar (three instances) region websites, media interaction is equally verbally indicated. Thus, the homepage of the Orkney region website often verbally indicates that users can become active as media actors, thus overtly constructing them as participants in business or prize contests and offers, as accomplished by: the processes win and see in the imperative mood in the November Competition Win Tait & Style scarf and the See latest winter special offers captions; enquirers and readers of and subscribers to types of print and electronic media, as suggested by the processes request, keep up to date, shop, and sign up in the imperative mood in the Request a Brochure, Keep up to date with daily news, Shop With us, and Sign up to receive special offers text fragments; and enquirers about weather and contact information, as realized by the processes check and contact in the imperative mood in the Check the local weather, and Contact Us clauses. On the homepage of the Istria region website, media interaction is equally reflected verbally, thus overtly addressing users as enquirers after information on events – as suggested by the View more events link – and geographical information on locations, regions, and countries – as suggested by the processes show, select, choose, and search in the imperative mood in the Show Croatia box, the Select a region menu, the Choose a destination menu and the Search Istria search button. On the homepage of the Zadar region website, verbal interaction with the elements, in addition to media interaction, is limited to the processes search and subscribe. These construct users as searchers for locations, communities, and islands, and subscribers to newsletters, as indicated by processes in the imperative mood. In addition, as indicated by Table 3.2, on all four homepages, more conventional types of user action abound, predominantly covering rollover and mouse click, rather than a greater variety of user actions, such as scroll or pull. Also, none of the four homepages use social media themes, such as Facebook and Twitter. Thus users are addressed as individuals rather than social actors. These initial readings can be made more detailed.

In sum, the homepages of the Perthshire and Istria region websites coincide in the following aspects: a high frequency of accessible elements (90.59% on the Perthshire region website, 77.56% on the Istria region website, as suggested by Table 3.1), a wealth of elements typical of a graphical user interface, in addition to elements which can also be found in static print material, and addressing themes on recreational tourism. To recall, as delineated in subsection 1.2, Chapter 1, lower levels of interactivity, as exemplified by the provision of more basic information on thematic meanings, and hyperlinks to further information and contact forms, can be related to the construction of more individual users as traditional print-literate tourists. By contrast, higher levels of interactivity, as illustrated by social media, such as chat rooms and discussion forums, can be linked to the creation of more contemporary, technologically-advanced, media-interactive social actors. Thus, for both pages, more medium to high levels of interactivity can be identified. This is due to the fact that in addition to hyperlinks to further information, customer support, in the form of site maps and multimedia, is offered as an example of functionality. It follows from this that on the Perthshire and Istria homepages, users are more created as contemporary media-interactive tourists for leisure and recreation purposes. On the homepage of the Orkney region website, due to the high frequency of accessible elements (74.65%), as indicated by Table 3.1, the predominant address of thematic meanings on types of media, and the high frequency of verbal indication of media interaction (eight instances), as denoted by Table 3.4, users figure as more post-conventional, technologically-versed individuals. By contrast, due to the lower frequency of accessible elements (61.75%), as indicated by Table 3.1, the address of more conventional tourist themes, and the lower level of interactivity due to hyperlinks to further information as examples of functionality, users are constructed as more traditional print-literate observers and haptic explorers of recreational tourism on the homepage of the Zadar region website.

4.1.5 Observers of tourist activities or explorers of types of media?

It follows from the analysis conducted hitherto that, in terms of the importance of thematic meanings for representation and cultural tourist and user communication, the following initial hypotheses can be confirmed: Mediterranean landscapes, sunny weather conditions, outdoor and water sports activities in Mediterranean landscapes, various artistic and religious, as well as modern and contemporary tourist attractions and events, indigenous gastronomy, and ancient history are of most importance to the Zadar region homepage; north-Atlantic landscapes, activities in these landscapes, stark weather conditions, and types of print and online media are significant to the ways in which the region is represented, and how users are addressed as cultural tourists and engaged as media actors for the Orkney region homepage; landscapes which present the Istria region as a blue-green peninsula, depict Mediterranean gourmet food and wine for bon-vivants, gastronomic and music events, and the location of Istrian tourist destinations are crucial to the Istria region homepage; green landscapes, adventure sports, music events, and activities for commercial and professional purposes, such as shopping and conference tourism, are of most importance for the Perthshire region homepage.

Equally, however, these initial hypotheses can be extended to include information on the broader categorization of thematic meanings in terms of types of thematic meanings, including conventional, recreational tourist themes, post-conventional themes on types of media, and themes related to conference tourism. Thus, the following categorizations can be identified: for the Zadar region homepage, a wealth of more conventional, recreational tourist themes, covering Central Mediterranean landscape imagery in spring or summer season, outdoor and water sports activities and health tourism, types of cultural landscapes, ancient heritage, indigenous gastronomy, and contemporary, profane, traditional, and sacred tourist attractions and events; for the Orkney region homepage, less conventional tourist themes – such as north-Atlantic landscape imagery in winter season – and more post-conventional themes revolving around print and online media; for the Istria region homepage, both more conventional, recreational tourist themes related to the holiday stay itself – covering seaside Istrian and central Istrian landscapes, their social experience, and rural, Mediterranean landscape, gastronomic and local music events – and tourist themes related to holiday planning and geographical information about the region – including accommodation and the location of Istria in relation to subregions and larger geographical units; and for the Perthshire region homepage, both conventional, recreational tourist themes – covering outdoor and adventurous sports activities, music events, towns' birthday celebrations, and green natural and cultural types of landscape – and professional tourism, that is, conference tourism and news.

The privileging of these tourist themes for the four regional websites, as initially assumed, can further be detailed in terms of patterns related to representational structures assigned to visuals, process types ascribed to clauses, and modality in clauses and visuals. When it comes to the nature of representation in visuals, the Zadar region homepage predominantly features social actions involving the above-exemplified conventional, recreational tourist themes, while for the visuals on the other three homepages, concepts are designed. These include events, weather, business, and types of media for the Orkney homepage; landscape regions, events, the location of geographical units, accommodation, and weather for the Istria region homepage; and landscapes, events, types of media, weather, and the location of geographical units for the Perthshire region website. In terms of representation, as expressed by groups, phrases, and process types, the construal of doing runs like a common thread through all four homepages, in addition to the hitherto-identified meanings involved in the construction of the importance of representation and cultural tourist and user communication. On the Zadar region homepage, this includes the practice of outdoor and water sports activities and health tourism, the representation of art exhibitions in civic buildings, and virtual activities of users on tourist locations in the region. By contrast, on the Orkney region homepage, doing involves commercial activities by users and calls for concern with weather and news. In contrast to the Zadar and Orkney region homepages, on the Istria region homepage the material world of doing encompasses user questions related to participation in events, and virtual activities on the locating of geographical units and the search for accommodation. These activities differ from those on the homepage of the Perthshire homepage, which relate to the visiting of public institutions and cultural and natural heritage sights, and historical anecdotes. Throughout, this common thread is touched upon by mental processes which construe an inner world of consciousness. On the Zadar region homepage, these processes relate to suggestions for holidays on the part of the tourist board, the enjoyment of sports activities, and attractive resources in the Zadar region as a holiday destination. On the Orkney region homepage, they are restricted to attention-grabbing package deals. On the Istria region homepage, inner activities relate to the perception and emotional experience of events. On the Perthshire homepage, they cover questions by users about fulfilling holidays, and by website producers about user knowledge about historical anecdotes.

In the above-summarized tendencies in the representations of thematic meanings, interpersonal meanings on attitude are further encoded. Contrary to what was initially assumed, the representation of statements as indisputable facts is not crucial to all four homepages. Also, differences between verbal and visual statements can be noted. Thus, when it comes to verbal statements, the Zadar and Istria region websites focus on readiness: ability and probability in reference to propositions on virtual activities, the practice of sports activities, tourist attractions, and the experience of events. By contrast, the Orkney and Perthshire region websites give more space to the portrayal of verbal statements about tourist activities as facts. They focus on realistic tourist experiences for users as media actors, thus suggesting that users can expect what is promised on the websites as cultural tourists in the social world. With regard to visual statements, realistic representations of more conventional tourist meanings are crucial to the ways in which the Zadar and Istria region websites visually represent themselves to prospective tourists. By contrast, the Orkney and Perthshire region websites focus more on icons as simplistic representations of objects, thus stressing more post-conventional thematic meanings in types of media and the virtual activities of users as media actors.

Furthermore, while it is the case that, as was initially assumed, instances of directly addressing users can be noted on all four homepages, it is equally the case that these are limited in number. In brief, on the Zadar region homepage, this relates to the involvement of users as selectors of tourist experiences, and water and outdoor sportspeople and health tourists. On the Orkney region homepage, users are addressed as guests to Orkney in the winter season and seekers of information on events. On the homepage of the Istria region website, users figure as discoverers of the Istria region and holiday planners. On the homepage of the Perthshire region website, users are constructed as participants in events and visitors of information centres on Scottish scenery and history.

Moreover, the analysis has given more insight into cultural tourist communication when it comes to the realization of the systems of contact, social distance, and subjective or objective attitude. With regard to realizations of the contact system, rather than demanding that users establish an imaginary relationship with the represented experiential meanings in visuals, these are predominantly portrayed as objects of observation and contemplation on all four homepages. This is suggested by the dearth of human or quasi-human participants directly gazing at users. Thus, as was initially assumed, all four homepages offer bits of information or make statements about the experiential meanings identified in the analysis of the nature of representation of thematic meanings. This is expressed by the declarative mood and encoded into the groups. Hence, they are presented as pieces of factual information. In terms of social distance and subjective attitude, the visuals on the four homepages predominantly create a more social or a more impersonal, rather than a more personal or intimate relationship, between users and the represented experiential meanings. This is suggested by the privileging of medium and long range over close range. Also, the Orkney, Istria, and Perthshire region websites predominantly make use of involvement, as indicated by the use of frontal angles. By contrast, for the Zadar region website, a similar distribution of involvement and detachment, as realized by oblique angles, can be noted. Furthermore, on the Zadar and Orkney region websites, equality, as indicated by an eye-level angle, is privileged over viewer power, as suggested by high angles, and representation power, as achieved by low angles. On the Istria region website, on the other hand, a similar distribution of viewer power and equality can be noted. Limited space is given to representation power. On the Perthshire region website, there is a focus on viewer power. Occasionally, the website makes use of equality. In terms of objective attitude, the Zadar and Istria region websites exclusively or predominantly make use of maps which encode knowledge orientation on the positioning of locations or regions. By contrast, on the Orkney and Pertshire region websites, a wealth of icons can be noted. These fulfil the semiotic function of representing diverse objects in types of media, commercial activities, contact possibilities, and weather, and/or the navigation function to transfer users quickly to the corresponding internal and external web pages. These constellations of social distance and attitude interact to position users as more distant observers of diverse tourist activities and objects, and learners about the positioning of tourist locations on the Zadar region homepage. Users are invited to look at types of events as more distant observers and explorers of types of media, commercial activities, and contact possibilities on the Orkney region homepage. On the Istria region homepage, users are constructed as landscape and activity observers, and learners about the positioning of locations. The Perthshire region website positions users as observers of diverse tourist activities, and perceivers and advertising consumers of and media actors on types of media and weather.

Finally, the analysis reveals that, as initially expected, the four homepages do engage users in the creation of a wealth of thematic meanings through various types of user action. More specifically, users are most actively engaged in the creation of tourist meanings in types of media, sports activities, events, green space landscape, and conference tourism through mouse click on the Perthshire homepage. The Istria region homepage offers users the possibility of activating internal and external links on sea- and landscapes and their social experience, locations which can be visited, types of events, the search for accommodation, sports activities, and conference tourism through rollover and mouse click or mouse click. The Orkney region homepage engages users less as media actors. It offers them the possibility of activating internal and external links on North-Atlantic landscape imagery and weather conditions, types of media and events, commercial activities, and contact information through rollover and mouse click or mouse click. Users are least involved as media actors on the Zadar region homepage. It predominantly offers them the possibility of activating internal and external links and buttons on sports activities, locations on a map, types of media, and inexpensive arrival possibilities through mouse clicks. Thus, on all four homepages, most types of user actions are limited to the more conventional constellations of mouse click and rollover or mouse click alone, rather than the actions of typing in, scrolling, or pulling. Equally, on none of the pages are users involved by offering them the possibility of activating links or objects on more contemporary social network platforms, such as Facebook and Twitter, and only on the Orkney region homepage can they activate audio resources. Hence, the following user profiles can be identified for the four homepages: observers, readers, and haptic explorers of conventional, recreational tourist themes (as if consulting static print material) for the Zadar region homepage; post-conventional, multimedia-literate individuals for the Orkney region homepage; slightly more dynamic, media-interactive users interacting with diverse themes for the Perthshire and Istria homepages.

After the overview of diverse tourist activities given in this chapter, the subsequent chapter will focus on walking activities as one of the four tourist activities which all four regional websites share.

4.2 Walking activities

4.2.1 Water and outdoor or adventure sports?

All four regional websites coincide in the representation of the practice of sports activities in types of landscapes or landscapes themselves. However, the websites differ in that some of them furnish the portrayal of activities in landscapes with emotional attachment, walking infrastructure, walking behaviour, and individual or team sports activities. Thus, when it comes to the statistics of representational structures on sports activities in visuals, exclusively narrative structures (100%) can be assigned to the types of visuals on the Zadar region website. These are about groups of people doing and taking pleasure in outdoor sports activities at the Mediterranean Sea and other bodies of water, and their adjacent land environment in the mountains and forests. On the Orkney region website, limited attention is devoted to narrative structures (9.52%) which can be attributed to the visuals. These deal with sports activities practiced by individuals at the seaside. To the types of visuals on the Istria region website, narrative structures on outdoor and water sports activities at the Mediterranean Sea and in green forestry can predominantly (75%) be assigned. Limited space is given to visuals to which conceptual structures on green forestry (25%) can be assigned. To the types of visuals on the Perthshire region website, narrative structures (66.67%) on the practice of outdoor and more adventurous types of sports activities in the grass landscapes, on water, and in the mountain landscape by social groups can be ascribed.

In contrast to the Zadar and Istria region websites, the Orkney region website further adds information on walking areas. This is achieved by the predominance of conceptual structures (90.48%) on vast and calm North-Atlantic landscape subregions with walking routes in the

Orkney region, which can be identified as the visuals. The identification of the landscape as calm and vast is due to intertextual knowledge that the representation of the landscape without reference to sports events – which could have revitalized the landscape and transformed it into a dynamic recreational place – is commonly coded with notions of vast and calm landscapes in other texts. The representation of vast and calm landscapes and individuals, rather than social groups, in the landscape, in turn, ties into some of the characteristic themes which have been identified for the register of tourism in subsection 1.2, Chapter 1: nirvana as the state of happiness of the individual who is conceived of as being at one with nature. While equally construing walking infrastructure, the Perthshire region website further shifts activities into the domain of rights and responsibilities guidance. This is accomplished by assigning conceptual structures (33.33%) for hands, landscapes, paths, and boots to the visuals, standing for accommodation and information facilities and responsible outdoor walking.

Thus, the Zadar and Istria regions are constructed more as paradises for outdoor and water sports enthusiasts. The Orkney region is represented as a destination for tourists seeking peace and tranquillity. The Perthshire region is constructed as an adventure recreation area for extreme sports enthusiasts with a heightened sense of environmental awareness.

When it comes to experiential meanings in groups, phrases, and clauses, Figure 4.9 gives an overview of statistics of experiential meanings for sports activities in clauses.

The activities image constructed for the Zadar region website is predicated upon the co-occurrence of outdoor sports activities, in general, and trekking, in particular, with the natural seascape and culturally-designed sports infrastructure. More specifically, this is predominantly realized by relational-attributive processes (40%), but also by material processes (28.57%) as the second most frequent, relational-identifying as the third most frequent (22.86%), and existential (8.57%) processes as the least frequent process type which can be assigned to clauses and experiential meanings expressed in groups and phrases (18 instances). Meanings revolve around encouragement to explore sea and inland landscapes of the Zadar region by practicing recreational and adventurous outdoor sports activities in attractive and peaceful landscapes, with a focus on the sea as an access point to the landscape and activities related to it – as realized by material, relational-attributive, and relational-identifying process types; and the presentation of the Zadar region landscape as abounding in nautical and diving infrastructure,

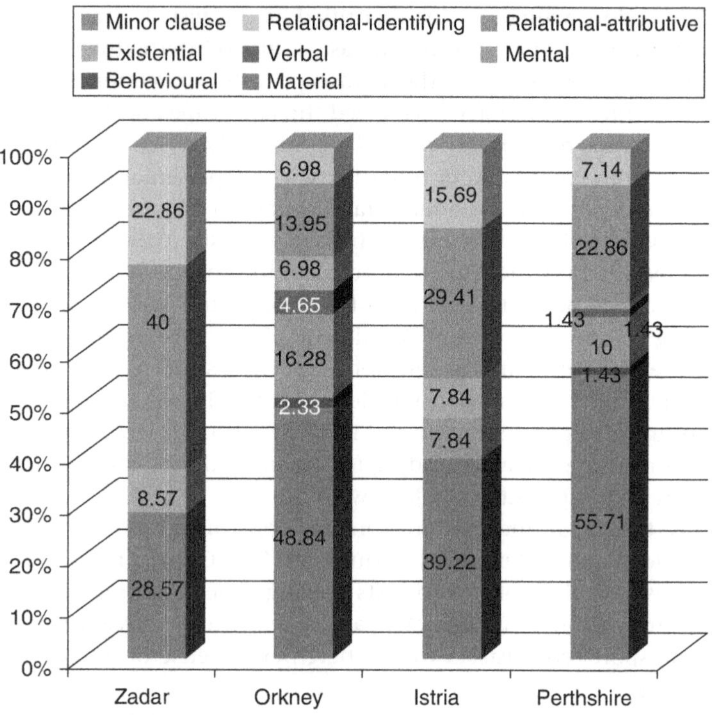

Figure 4.9 Overview of statistics of experiential meanings for sports activities in clauses for the four regional websites

maritime safety, and favourable rafting conditions – as realized by interplays between existential, relational-attributive, and relational-identifying processes. As indicated in subsection 1.2, Chapter 1, rather than being restricted to travel texts themselves, these meaning patterns are embedded in a wider social context of use: tourism communication as part of which destinations are advertised to prospective customers on the part of the website producers and tourism authorities. Moreover, the clauses on the Zadar region website predominantly give space to: the representation of degrees of popularity of trails and rafting periods, as indicated by relational-attributive and relational-identifying processes; the existence of a wealth of trails and paths, as achieved by existential and relational-attributive processes; and the specification of the trekking duration and location, as realized by relational-attributive and identifying processes. The clauses on the Zadar region website do not construe walking as a matter of saying, conscious behaviour, or the inner world of consciousness, as indicated by the lack of verbal (0%), behavioural (0%), and mental (0%) processes.

In contrast to the Zadar region website, the Orkney region website represents the practice of sports activities in the environment as a positive emotional experience and adds sources of information on it. Walking is further construed as conventionalized, environmentally-sensitive behaviour in a culturally-designed infrastructure, similarly to how it is expressed by the visuals on the Perthshire region website. For the most part, this is achieved on the Orkney region website by material processes (48.84%). These are followed by mental (16.28%), relational-attributive (13.95%), existential (6.98%), relational-identifying (6.98%), verbal (4.65%), and behavioural (2.33%) processes, and groups (five instances). More specifically, meanings accumulate around the practice of a wealth of sports activities in diverse landscapes, virtual activities by users as media actors, calls for consulting tourist promotional material for further information on sports activities, instructions on safety walking, and calls for responsible behaviour in the social world in the Orkney region. Material processes in concert with relational-attributive, relational-identifying, verbal, existential, and mental processes interact to construe these meanings. Closely tied to these activities is the inner world of consciousness of users and the conscious behaviour of users. This is achieved through reference to expectations of active holidays, in general, and positive emotions of delight and enjoyment in reference to the experience of landscape and sports activities, in particular. This is indicated by material, mental, behavioural, and relational-attributive processes. Also, more space is devoted to the existence of a variety of landscape regions for walking, types of walks, suitable walking areas, and degrees of the significance of walking in relation to the overall holiday stay. This is suggested by material, existential, relational-attributive, and relational-identifying processes.

The Istria region website differs from the hitherto-analyzed websites in that, in addition to the characterization of trails, a high level of competence for high payment is encoded into the representation of activities. This is realized by material (39.22%) as the most frequent type of process and relational-attributive (29.41%) processes as the second most frequent type of process. These are followed by relational-identifying (15.69%) processes, an equal distribution of mental (7.84%) and existential (7.84%) processes, and groups (seven instances). Thus, in general, sports is not merely constructed as an activity for leisure and adventure purposes, but also – and foremost – as a professional and complex physical activity, practiced by high profile sportspeople. This is suggested by the interplay between material, relational-attributive, mental, and existential processes. Equally, there is a focus on the benefits of sports activities in the Istria region, manifesting in the suitability of welcoming meteorological conditions and pristine landscape for the practice of sports activities. These meanings are realized by material and relational-identifying processes. Trekking, in particular, is further represented as revolving around types of walks, trekking locations and trekking duration, contact possibilities, calls for trekking advice and the characterization of trails in terms of conditions, attractiveness, positive health effects, rest facilities and accommodation. Material, existential, relational-attributive, mental and identifying processes interact to construe these meanings. Limited attention is devoted to emotions of delight and the choice of trails on the part of trekkers, as achieved by mental processes. No conscious behaviour or saying is construed, as indicated by the lack of behavioural (0%) and verbal (0%) processes.

Similarly to the Orkney region website, the Perthshire region website constructs activities as a matter of compliance with expected behaviour in a specifically-designed environment. However, it differs from the other activities' images in that it addresses a broad range of more conventional tourist activities together with adventure sports. This is predominantly accomplished by material processes (55.71%). These are followed by relational-attributive (22.86%) processes, mental (10%) processes, relational-identifying (7.14%) processes, and an equal distribution of behavioural (1.43%), existential (1.43%), and verbal (1.43%) processes, and groups (14 instances). Thus, space is predominantly given to the identification of Perthshire as an adventure-filled recreational area for the practice of diverse sports activities, and to the representation of diverse tourist activities and contact possibilities for further information. These tourist activities cover lively walking and the experience of natural heritage, cultural heritage sights, places where alcoholic beverages are produced, and sources of information on these activities, through physical contact activities in the social and the virtual world. This is realized by a series of material, relational-identifying, existential and relational-attributive processes. Also, reference is made to instructions on a code of behaviour for walkers. This relates to the definition of legal principles of freedom or entitlement and their manifestation in guidelines, the understanding of the code of behaviour, consideration of concerns for your fellow man, and the identification of the location of walkers in the environment as accepted behaviour. This is achieved through material, verbal, mental, relational-attributive, and relational-identifying processes. Moreover, importance is ascribed to the characterization of the make-up of the landscape, as accomplished by relational-attributive and relational-identifying process types. Limited attention is given to inside activities related to the delight in Scotland´s landscape and walking paths. This is realized by mental processes. Equally, limited space is devoted to the characterization of the appropriateness of treks for age – and skills – independent target groups and accommodation, rest and information facilities for walkers and cyclists. This is accomplished by relational-identifying, material, behavioural and relational-attributive processes.

With regard to the arguability of clauses, the clauses on walking activities predominantly make definite verbal statements about the experiential meanings identified above. This is suggested by the statistics of clause types on sports activities, that is, the high frequency of tensed finite clauses with an absence of modality features on the Zadar (77.14%), Istria (62.75%), and Perthshire (40%) region websites. Finite clauses with modality features are restricted to 8.57% for the Zadar, 15.69% for the Istria, and 17.14% for the Perthshire region websites. An exception to this is provided by the Orkney region website, which makes more use of finite clauses with the presence of modality features (37.21%) than tensed finite clauses (23.26%). This mostly tempers the force of the verbal statements made. In addition, non-finite clauses amount to 14.29% for the Zadar, 39.53% for the Orkney, 21.57% for the Istria and 42.86% for the Perthshire region websites. These clauses are not arguable.

Furthermore, when it comes to the statistics of value in finite clauses on sports activities, within finite clauses with modality features, an equal distribution of high (50%) and median (50%) value modality can be noted for the Zadar region website. A predominance (75%) of median value modality can be identified for the Orkney region website. The Istria and Perthshire region websites exclusively make use of median value modality (100%). These values suggest that all four regional websites make propositions which sound more assertive. Statements revolve around the popularity of trails and trekking on the Zadar, the practice of sports activities and tourist information expertise on the Perthshire, the practice of sports activities at the seaside in an environmentally responsible way on the Orkney, and trekking in diverse landscapes and tourist information on the Istria region websites. By contrast, limited attention, as on the Orkney (6.25%) region website, or no attention, as on the Zadar (0%), Istria (0%), and Perthshire region (0%) websites, is devoted to low value modality which could moderate the force of statements.

Moreover, Figure 4.10 gives an overview of statistics of orientation and manifestation in finite clauses on sports activities for the four regional websites.

It reveals that, on three of the four websites, the dominant orientation and manifestation of modality is implicitly subjective modality. This is indicated by the high frequency of modal finites on the Orkney (77.78%), Istria (75%), and Perthshire (75%) region websites. They relate to statements on trekking and Orkney as a site for various activities, types of walks and instructions on responsible walking behaviour on the Orkney region website. On the Istria region website, they deal with all-year-round sports practice, and accommodation and information facilities. On the Perthshire region website, they have to do with a wealth of widely-esteemed sports activities, walking in diverse landscape regions, walking infrastructure, the scope of the target group, and tourist information. Thus, there is a focus on the speaker's own point of view. By contrast, on the Zadar region website, more space is given to implicitly objective (66.67%) modality, as expressed by mood adjuncts, in reference to the popularity of trails among trekkers. Less attention is devoted to implicitly subjective (33.33%) modality in reference to

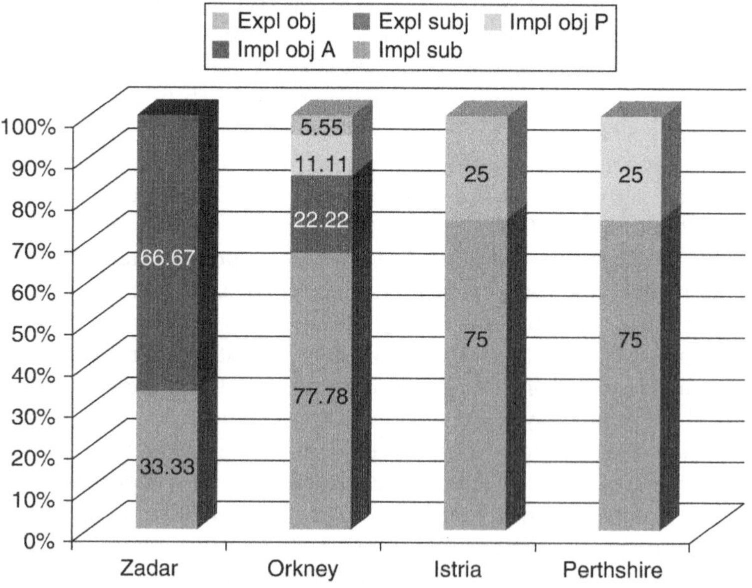

Figure 4.10 Overview of statistics of orientation and manifestation in finite clauses on sports activities for the four regional websites

statements about walking. Hence, the point of view is both subjectified, that is, presented as a subjective judgement, and objectified, that is, presented as a fact.

When it comes to types of modality, Figure 4.11 gives an overview of statistics of modality type in finite clauses on activities for the four regional websites.

Thus, the Zadar and Istria region websites make least use of kinds of modality. This is indicated by the lack of probability (0%), obligation (0%), and readiness: inclination (0%) on the Zadar, and probability (0%), usuality (0%), and readiness: inclination (0%) on the Istria region website. This is followed by the Perthshire region website, which lacks usuality (0%) and obligation (0%). By contrast, a more varied picture is presented by the Orkney region website, which uses all kinds of modality. More specifically, the clauses on the Zadar region website express both usuality (50%) and readiness: ability (50%). Statements relate to the popularity of trails among trekkers and trekking. An equal distribution of usuality (31.25%) in reference to the closeness of visitors to the sea, types of walks, and instructions on responsible outdoor walking

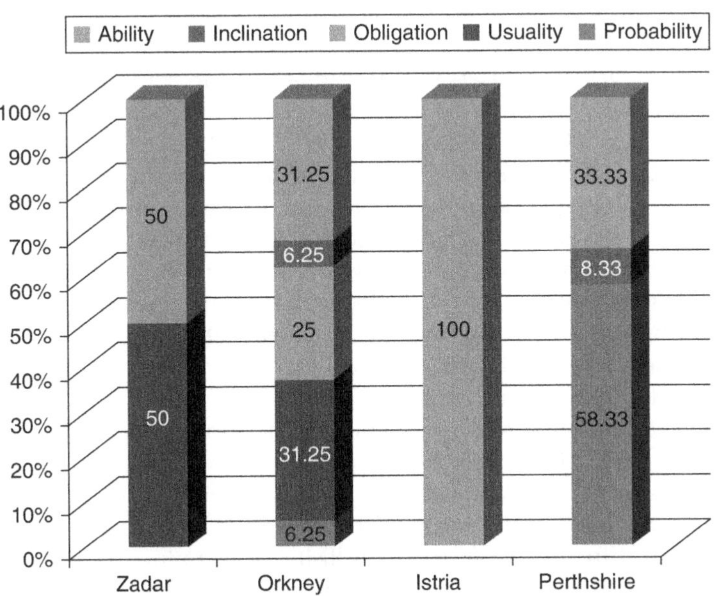

Figure 4.11 Overview of statistics of modality type in finite clauses on activities for the four regional websites

behaviour, and readiness: ability (31.25%) in reference to Orkney as a site for various activities and safe walking equipment can be noted for the Orkney region website. Equally, attention is devoted to obligation (25%) in reference to instructions on responsible outdoor walking behaviour. The Istria (100%) region website exclusively makes use of clauses expressing readiness: ability in reference to statements about all-season sports practice and the availability of accommodation and information facilities. The clauses on the Perthshire region website are dominated (58.33%) by probability in terms of type of modality in diverse propositions. These are about the wealth of widely-esteemed sports activities, walking infrastructure, the scope of the target group, the experience of facilities for the production of alcoholic beverages, and tourist information. On the Perthshire region website, less space is devoted to probability (6.25%) in reference to the choice of walking activities and readiness: inclination (6.25%) in reference to the significance of walking for the overall holiday stay on the Orkney region website, and to readiness: ability (33.33%) and inclination (8.33%) in relation to the expertise of information services staff, walking in diverse landscapes, further information sources, and the choice of types of walks.

It follows from this that the Zadar and Orkney region websites focus more on the frequency of events. In addition, the Orkney region website suggests that users should and are able to act in a certain way. The Perthshire region website indicates how probable events may be. All four regional websites express ability. Also, the Zadar (one instance) and Orkney (one instance) region websites make use of comment adjuncts expressing certainty. In this way the Zadar region website represents the popularity of trails, while the Orkney region website portrays responsible outdoor walking behaviour. The Istria (two instances) and Orkney (one instance) region websites further make use of comments expressing wisdom in reference to statements about the availability of accommodation and information facilities for advice and support, and responsible walking behaviour.

The tendency towards more definite propositions can equally be identified for visuals displayed on the four regional websites. With regard to the statistics of value for visuals on sports activities, the Zadar (100%) and Istria (100%) region websites exclusively, while the Orkney (80%) and Perthshire (66.67%) region websites predominantly use photographs as visuals of higher modality, thus making definite visual statements. At the same time, however, the Orkney and Perthshire region websites display a map on landscape regions with walking areas and icons on accommodation and information facilities, and responsible outdoor behaviour. As constituting stylized representations, these are visuals of lower modality. As mentioned in subsection 2.2, Chapter 2 on the multi-layer approach to website analysis, if users are repeatedly exposed to them, these may be perceived as more realistic than photographs due to their stereotypical simplicity.

In sum, the predominance of more definite verbal and visual statements, high and median value modality and infrequent use of types of modality, comment adjuncts and comments on all four regional websites construct more authentic tourist experiences for users as media actors. Thus, it is suggested that users can expect what is promised on the websites as cultural tourists in the social world.

4.2.2 Landscape and activity observers or lovers of dynamic sports?

In terms of contact, the statistics of realizations of the contact system on sports activities suggest that the types of visuals on all four regional websites exclusively offer factual information (100%) on the meanings which have been identified for the visuals in sub-subsection 4.2.1. This is indicated by the fact that neither of the types of visual demands an imaginary relationship with users. Thus, the represented meanings are portrayed as objects of contemplation and observation.

Most of the visuals on activities do not encode an objective attitude. Rather, as suggested by Figure 4.12, realizations of subjective attitude can be observed.

More specifically, when it comes to the statistics of realizations of subjective attitude and social distance, most photographs (84.62%) on the Zadar region website are photographed from an eye-level perspective. Users are therefore put on an equal footing with the represented participants, such as trekking travellers. Equally, the photographs are predominantly (69.23%) taken from a frontal angle, thus inviting users to take a look at the activities of represented sportspeople, rather than from an oblique angle (30.77%), positioning users as more detached from the walking routes. Most photographs position users in social relation to trekking travellers in landscapes (76.92%), as indicated by the exclusive use of medium range. Users are rarely positioned as strangers unfamiliar with the activities (23.08%) – as realized by long range – or in a powerful (7.69%) or inferior (7.69%) position to the represented activities – as realized by high angles and low angles. No instances can be identified which construct a more personal relationship with users and the represented activities (0%), as suggested by the lack of close

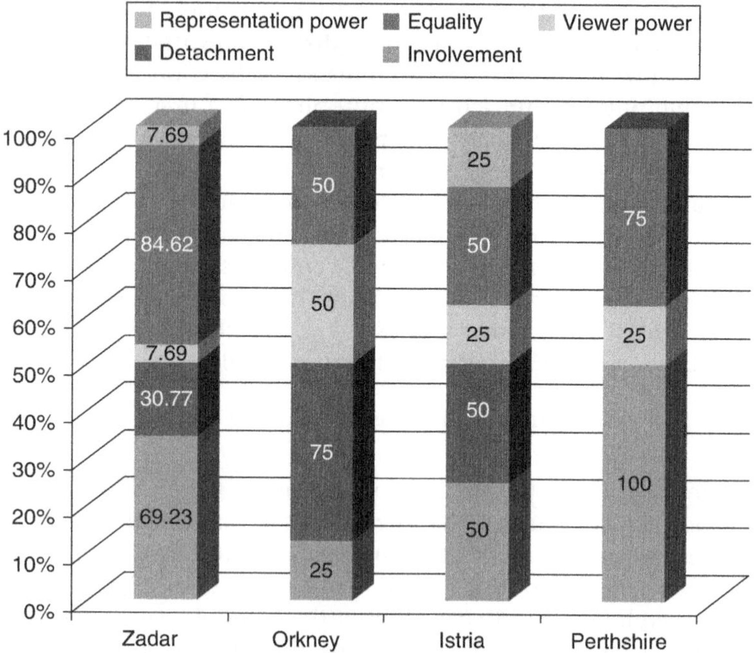

Figure 4.12 Overview of statistics of realizations of subjective attitude on sports activities for the four regional websites

range. The interaction of these realizations of social distance and subjective attitude thus creates users as more immediate observers of diverse sports activities in diverse landscape regions.

In contrast to the Zadar region website, on the Orkney region website, an equal distribution of photographs in terms of equality (50%), as realized by an eye-level angle, and viewer power (50%), as indicated by a high angle, positions users both in a more powerful and an equal power relation with the activity. Users are predominantly invited to take a closer look at the walking areas (85.71%), as indicated by close range. Also, users are positioned in a more detached way to walking (75%), as suggested by the predominant use of oblique angles. A map further encodes an objective attitude, that is, knowledge orientation on the location of geographical subregions and walking routes of Orkney (100%). This is suggested by the fact that the map can be viewed from the front and from a vertical angle, rather than the angles being manipulated so that users can view the map from the side and from above or from below. Limited cases can be noted which invite users to look at activities, as indicated by frontal angles (25%), or create a more distant relationship between users and activities, as realized by long range (14.29%). Furthermore, there are no occurrences of instances of representation power (0%) – as denoted by the lack of low angles, and social distance (0%) – as suggested by the lack of medium range. Users are thus positioned as more detached observers of landscapes and activities, and learners about the location of Orkney subregions and walking areas.

Similarly to the Zadar region website, the Istria region website predominantly puts users on an equal footing (50%) with types of sportspeople in the landscape regions and green forestry. This is realized through eye-level angles. Furthermore, it invites users to look at the activities in the landscape in both a more involved (50%) and a detached (50%) way. This is indicated by equal frequency of frontal and oblique angles. Also, it exclusively positions users in a more social relationship with the activities and landscapes. This is indicated by medium range (100%) and lack of instances of close (0%) or long (0%) range. A dearth of cases of viewer power (25%), as realized by high angles, and representation power (25%), as expressed by low angles, can be observed. Users are thus positioned as more immediate observers of landscapes and diverse sports activities in diverse landscape regions.

A privileging of eye-level angles over high angles and low angles can also be noted for the photographs on the Perthshire region website which construct an equal power relation (75%) between users and the represented sports activities. Yet, in contrast to the other websites, users are exclusively invited to take a closer look (100%) at the represented activities, boot and hand with route in the landscape, as indicated by frontal angles. Equally, they are predominantly positioned in a more personal relationship (66.67%) to the activities, walking infrastructure, and code of behaviour, as realized by close range, rather than a more impersonal relationship (33.33%), as realized by long range. With regard to attitude, two icons further encode an objective attitude (100%) towards boots, a hand, and a route in the landscape. These fulfil the semiotic function of representing accommodation and information facilities for walkers and responsible walking behaviour in the environment. As with the Orkney region website, this is expressed by the fact that the map can be viewed from the front and from a vertical angle. Hence, users are positioned as lovers of adventurous sports and invited to take notice of the walking infrastructure and responsible walking behaviour.

With regard to the units of user address as cultural tourists, and instances of user address as cultural tourists or involvement, in the units on the Zadar (92.59%) and Istria (87.5%) region websites, users are predominantly not addressed as cultural tourists. Rather, statements are made about the experiential meanings identified in the process types in sub-subsection 4.2.1. This is indicated by the exclusive use of the declarative mood in clauses and lack of direct address or involvement in groups or phrases. Accordingly, limited space is devoted to instances of user address as cultural tourists on the Zadar (7.41%) and Istria (12.5%) region websites. Thus, they are addressed as explorers of the sea and landscape regions through sports activities and searchers for peaceful landscape environments on the Zadar region website. This is suggested by the dearth of resources such as second person pronouns (one instance) and the imperative mood (three instances). On the Istria region website, the address of users as cultural tourists is limited to their address as enquirers about trekking advice by phone call, as indicated by the imperative mood (one).

In contrast to the Zadar and Istria region websites, more units which address users as cultural tourists can be noted on the Orkney (57.14%) and Perthshire (43.48%) region websites. Thus, on the Orkney region website, users are directly encouraged to become sportspeople in the Orkney region and to enquire about further information on activities, to take pleasure in walking, and to become responsible walking planners and accommodation users. This is indicated by the use of second person pronouns in the declarative mood (12 instances) and the imperative mood (three instances). Finally, on the Perthshire region website, users are directly addressed as adventurous sportspeople and multi-faceted tourists who delight in the environment, visit establishments for the production of alcoholic drinks, and understand codes of behaviour. This is accomplished by second person pronouns (13 instances), the imperative mood (ten instances) and the interrogative mood (one instance).

4.2.3 Traditional or contemporary, media-interactive users?

With regard to the statistics for units with accessible and inaccessible elements on sports activities, on the Zadar (80%), Orkney (72.73%), Istria (58.33%), and Perthshire (66.67%) region websites, a predominance of units with inaccessible elements can be noted. Accordingly, fewer units with accessible elements can be identified for the Zadar (20%), Istria (41.67%), Perthshire (33.33%), and Orkney (27.27%) region websites.

In terms of the statistics for types of user actions, the Istria region website predominantly uses rollover and mouse click (80%) and occasionally mouse click (20%); the Zadar (100%) and Orkney (100%) region websites exclusively make use of rollover and mouse click; and the Perthshire (100%) region website offers users the possibility of accessing elements exclusively through mouse click. No instances can be identified which engage users through type in (0%) or mouse click and movement (0%). More specifically, users are more actively engaged in the creation of meanings on various walking routes and areas. Thus, trekking is made a virtual activity, rather than presented as a matter of existence, as on the Istria region website. On the Zadar region website, internal links on further information on types of water and outdoor sports activities can be activated. On the Orkney region website, media interaction is realized through the possibility of activating internal and external links on walking and the virtual discovery of Orkney´s subregions and walking routes. Finally, on the Perthshire region website, users are actively involved in the creation of meanings on trekking, trekking advice, and accommodation. This is achieved by offering them the possibility of activating the corresponding internal and external links. These are about establishments providing lodgings and gastronomic offers for walkers and cyclists, types of walks and walking holidays in different landscapes as club members, outdoor skills courses, and wildlife holidays.

When it comes to the instances of verbal indication of media interaction, media interaction is made more salient on the Orkney (four instances) and Perthshire (eight instances) region websites through verbal indication. By contrast, on the Zadar (no instances) and Istria (no instances) region websites, media interaction is not equally verbally reflected. More specifically, on the Orkney region website, users are addressed as media actors for activities and walking regions. This is indicated by click, pick up, and download in the imperative mood in the clauses entitled Click on the image below, Pick up or download a map, and Click on map below. On the Perthshire region website, users are addressed as media actors for walking activities, holidays, and responsible walking behaviour. This is indicated by click, hit, find out, and complete in the imperative mood in the clauses entitled click on the links on the left hand menu, hit the link on the right, find out more by visiting www.outdooraccess-scotland.com, click on the links to the left, and complete our on-line form, the second person pronoun you in you'll find information about many more walks throughout Scotland and if you'd like to book an organised guided or self guided walking break, including baggage transfer, accommodation booking, route mapping and guidance across Scotland, and the interrogative mood in why not contact one of the walking specialists listed below? Also, as all four regional websites exclusively make use of hyperlinks to further information, rather than social media such as chat rooms and discussion forums (cf. Table 1.1 in subsection 1.2, Chapter 1), they are restricted to low levels of interactivity. Thus, on none of the four regional websites are users constructed as highly technologically advanced social actors who use online social network sites.

In sum, the following aspects suggest that a certain kind of user is constructed for the Zadar and Orkney region websites: limited engagement of users as media actors; limited salience of media interaction; limited variety in types of user actions; low levels of functionality and the address of more conventional thematic meanings. These revolve around walking, sports activities, the code of behaviour in the landscape, accommodation for walkers, walking and wildlife holidays, and walking courses. In line with the user profiles identified for the Zadar region homepage in sub-subsection 4.1.4, the kind of user can therefore be specified as follows: a more traditional tourist as a print-literate individual who observes, reads and scans through tourist promotional material. By contrast, despite low levels of interactivity and more conventional tourist meanings, more accessible elements can be identified for the Istria and Perthshire region websites than for the Zadar and Orkney region websites. Also, more salience of media interaction can be observed on the Perthshire region website. Thus, the user profiles constructed on the Perthshire and Istria region websites move more towards those identified for the Istria and Perthshire homepages in sub-subsection 4.1.4: slightly more contemporary media-interactive tourists for leisure and recreation purposes.

4.2.4 Lovers of team sports, individual landscape explorers, or dynamic all-round tourists?

To recall, the following hypotheses about the nature of representation were initially formulated: the activities' images constructed for the regions are based on water and outdoor sports activities in the Mediterranean landscape on the Zadar and Istria region websites, outdoor activities in the natural North-Atlantic environment on the Orkney region website, and adventure sports activities on the Perthshire region website.

The findings gained from the analysis of representational structures in visuals, experiential meanings in groups and phrases, and process types which can be assigned to clauses allow for the further refinement of these initial assumptions. Thus, the identification of representational structures assigned to visuals indicates that the Zadar region website focuses on the portrayal of the practice of outdoor sports activities by groups as a pleasurable social activity in diverse Mediterranean sea- and adjacent landscape regions. In contrast to the Zadar region website, the Orkney region website foregrounds the look of vast and peaceful North-Atlantic landscapes. The practice of sports activities is an individual, rather than a social, activity and does not imply notions of enjoyment. Both the Orkney and Perthshire region websites construe meanings on walking infrastructure – be it in the form of subregions as walking areas, as on the Orkney region website, or as walking lodgings, information facilities, and walking paths, as on the Perthshire region website. Similarly to the Zadar region website, doing sports is presented as a social activity in landscape regions on the Istria and Perthshire region websites. Yet, there is a stress on professional infrastructure, natural and seaside environments, and the look of green landscapes on the Istria region website. By contrast, the Perthshire region website further attaches notions of the dynamic and adventurous to activities, and constructs a more complex image of activities. In addition to sports activities in diverse landscape regions and walking infrastructure, it devotes attention to a conventionalized set of responsible walking behaviours. When it comes to the representation of activities, as achieved by groups and clauses, all the websites coincide in the representation of a wealth of types of sports activities and trekking paths. Furthermore, both the Zadar and the Istria region websites give space to the characterization of trails and trekking, be it in terms of their popularity and attractiveness, conditions and quality, rest facilities and health benefits, or trekking duration and locations. Equally, similar meanings are conveyed through the Orkney and Perthshire region websites, in that enjoyment in the landscape and sports activities, in general, and walking, in particular, are embedded in a legislative framework on responsible conduct in the environment. In addition, the Orkney, Istria, and Perthshire region websites share meanings on contact possibilities for further user information, thus construing tourism service offers. Moreover, the Zadar region website focuses on sports as a leisure activity in the natural environment. This relates to the representation of a rich sports infrastructure and landscapes, as well as the importance of the sea for sports activities and as an access point to the landscape. Less attention is devoted to the physical practice of sports activities. Similarly, the Orkney and Istria region websites give space to the practice of sports activities in the natural environment and learning about walking infrastructure in the virtual world. In addition, however, sports activities become payment for high performance on the Istria region website. Thus, users obtain more information on the benefits of sports activities as manifested in meteorological and environmental conditions and professional sports infrastructure. On the Perthshire region website, sports activities are about intense outdoor actions. Walking, sports activities and recreational areas are characterized as adventurous, lively, suitable for a broad target group, and with reference to other tourist activities. These include the experience of natural heritage, cultural sights, and production facilities for alcoholic drinks.

It follows from this that the high frequency of relational-attributive processes on the Zadar region website constitutes a more descriptive text. This construes the Zadar region as a site for trails and sports infrastructure. As suggested by less frequent use of material processes, less space is devoted to the exploration of natural, authentic, and unspoilt landscape regions through sports activities as a source of escape from notions of stressful everyday life. More closely related to this sports offer is the representation construed for the Istria region website, being more descriptive in character. This is indicated by the wealth of relational-attributive processes. In addition, however, these are fused with material processes to construe Istria as a site for the practice of professional sports. Clearly more material and less relational-attributive processes are noticeable on the Orkney and Perthshire region websites. In concert with mental processes, these construe activities in Orkney as the responsible practice and enjoyment of diverse sports activities in diverse landscapes. The Perthshire region emerges as a site for responsible engagement in diverse tourist activities, adventure, and enjoyment.

Furthermore, as expected, since it is in line with the importance of realistic representations for customer satisfaction, all four regional websites leave limited space for questioning or challenging verbal and visual propositions. This is suggested by the predominant choice of photographs as visuals of higher modality and high and median value modality, and infrequent use of modality, comment adjuncts, and comments in clauses. Users are thus offered an authentic online experience of what is waiting for them in the social world as cultural tourists. Equally, as addressed in subsection 1.2, Chapter 1, for future research, it may be interesting to see if these modality features, the predominant use of implicitly subjective orientation, and the above-identified predominance of material or relational-attributive processes types, rather than being random observations, form characteristic features of a tourist text type. However, this would require research into larger collections of tourist texts.

Moreover, with regard to the initial hypothesis formulated about cultural tourist communication, as indicated by the contact system in visuals, all four websites share offers of the above-identified factual bits of information as objects of observation, rather than demanding that users establish an imaginary relation with the represented participants. This is indicated by the lack of human or quasi-human participants gazing directly at users. The realizations of the systems of attitude and social distance further construe users as more immediate observers of diverse outdoor sports activities in diverse landscape regions on the Zadar and Istria region websites. On the Orkney region website, this is indicated by the wealth of instances of eye-level angles, frontal angles and medium range. Users are further positioned as more detached observers of landscape and activities, as realized by the equal distribution of eye-level angles and high angles and the wealth of instances of oblique angles and long range. Also, they figure as learners about the location of Orkney subregions and walking areas on the Orkney region website. This is indicated by the fact that the type of visual is a map which can be viewed from the front and from a vertical angle, rather than the angles being manipulated so that users can view the map from the side and from above or below. Also, users are invited to see and comprehend information on the walking infrastructure and responsible walking behaviour. This is indicated by close range and the possibility of perceiving icons from the front and from a vertical angle. Finally, they figure as dynamic sports-lovers on the Perthshire region website. This is suggested by the privileging or exclusive use of eye-level angles, frontal angles and close range.

In addition, when it comes to the question of addressing users as cultural tourists, as initially assumed, less space is devoted to addressing users as cultural tourists on the Zadar and Istria region websites than on the Orkney and Perthshire region websites. More specifically, limited space is devoted to the construction of users as explorers of the sea- and landscape regions through sports activities and as seekers of peaceful landscape environments on the Zadar region website. Least attention is devoted to users as enquiring about trekking advice on the Istria region website. By contrast, more space is devoted to the creation of users as active and responsible enjoyers of sports activities in diverse North-Atlantic sea and inland landscape regions interested in more detailed information on activities through consultation of resources of information on the Orkney region website. Also, users are predominantly addressed as cultural tourists on the Perthshire region website. It constructs them as energetic sportspeople practicing a wealth of adventurous outdoor activities and responsible explorers of nature, cultural sights, and production facilities for alcoholic drinks. This is realized through second person pronouns and the imperative mood.

Finally, as was initially hypothesized, none of the four websites is completely absorbed in media interaction. This is suggested by the following aspects: the dearth of frequency of accessible elements, predominantly covering internal and external links related to the semantic fields of sports activities and sports infrastructure; limited variety of types of user actions, overwhelmingly including the constellations of rollover and mouse click or mouse click, which engage users as media actors; lower levels of interactivity; and addressing more conventional tourist themes. Nevertheless, the websites differ in the degree and salience of media interaction. The Zadar and Orkney region websites make less use of accessible elements than the Istria and Perthshire region websites and lack or rarely verbally indicate media interaction. Thus, a more traditional image is developed for users as tourists whose gaze is privileged over other sense systems on the Zadar and Orkney region websites. By contrast, users are constructed as slightly more contemporary media-interactive tourists for leisure and recreation purposes on the Istria and Perthshire region websites.

It follows from the interaction of representation and cultural tourist and user communication that different tourist profiles are constructed for the four regional websites: for the Zadar region website, traditional outdoor water and team sports lovers in Central Mediterranean landscapes; for the Orkney region website, more calm-seeking, individual and environmentally sensitive North-Atlantic landscape explorers; for the Istria region website, more professional outdoor water and team sports lovers in sea and inland landscapes; and for the Perthshire region website, dynamic all-round tourists who engage in sightseeing, practice adventure sports and explore the environment with a heightened sense of responsibility.

4.3 Natural heritage

4.3.1 Mediterranean or North-Atlantic landscapes?

When it comes to the nature of representation of natural heritage, as realized by types of representational structures assigned to the visuals, for the Zadar, Istria, and Perthshire region websites, nature is constructed more as a static site for the existence of aspects of landscapes or landscape locations. This is suggested by the fact that predominantly or exclusively conceptual structures can be identified for the visuals. Thus, in terms of the statistics of representational structures on natural heritage, a wealth of conceptual structures (58.82%) on types of plantlife, valleys in mountain areas, and bodies of water, and a dearth of narrative structures (41.18%) on the behaviour of local birdlife and tourists in environmentally-protected areas can be assigned to the visuals on the Zadar region website. To most of the visuals on the Istria region website, conceptual structures (85.71%) on seaside landscapes and green forestry or places surrounded or dominated by this landscape motif can be assigned. An exception to this is presented by a visual of a sailing boat floating in the Mediterranean seascape, to which a narrative structure (14.29%) can be assigned. Types of visuals on the Perthshire region website are restricted to visuals to which conceptual structures (100%) on locations in green landscapes or landscape environments themselves, including green loch and water and mountain landscapes, can be ascribed. This is not the case with the visuals on the Orkney region website to which more narrative structures on the behaviour of local animal life (85.71%) than conceptual structures on plant life (14.29%) can be attributed. Thus, a more vivid natural heritage image is constructed for the Orkney region website.

Moving from visuals to clauses, Figure 4.13 gives an overview of the statistics of experiential meanings of natural heritage in clauses for the four regional websites.

Similarly to the nature of representation of natural heritage, as realized by types of representational structures assigned to the visuals, the representation of natural heritage as a static site for the existence of landscapes runs like a common thread through the groups, phrases, and clauses on the Zadar region website. These are predominantly devoted to the characterization of the Zadar region in terms of landscapes. Realizations of these meanings centre on relational-attributive processes (57.89%). These are followed by relational-identifying (21.05%), material (10.53%), and a similar distribution of behavioural (5.26%) and mental (5.26%) processes and groups and phrases (seven instances). No instances of existential (0%) or verbal (0%) processes can be identified. More specifically, the characterization has to do with the location and reputation of natural types of landscapes, environmentally protected areas as cultural types of landscapes and the aesthetic appeal of types of landscape. This is realized by a series of relational-attributive and identifying processes. Occasionally, the clauses elaborate on physical activities. Examples include the accessibility of landscapes by means of transport, and the creation of circumstances which trigger an increase in and development of hunting tourism, as realized by material processes, relational-identifying, and a relational-attributive process. Equally, information on the inner world of consciousness and conscious behaviour is limited. Instances involve information on knowledge

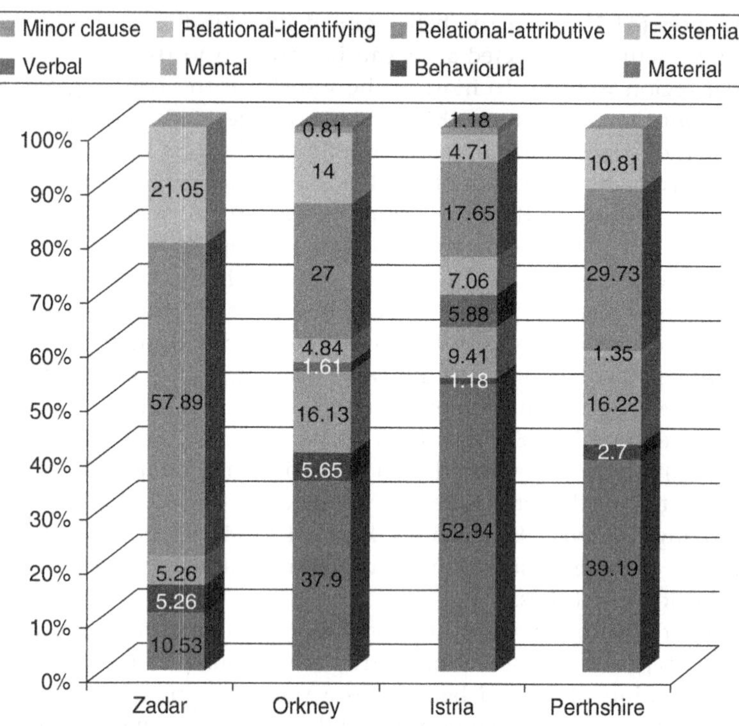

Figure 4.13 Overview of statistics of experiential meanings of natural heritage in clauses for the four regional websites

about causes for the increase of hunting tourism and the observation of birdlife in environmentally protected areas, as indicated by mental and behavioural processes.

In line with the more vivid natural heritage image constructed by the representational structures assigned to the visuals, the groups and clauses on the Orkney region website focus on animal life. These meanings are predominantly realized by a similar distribution of material (37.9%) and relational-attributive processes (27%). These are followed by mental processes (16.13%), relational-identifying processes (14%), and a similar distribution of behavioural (5.65%) and existential (4.84%) processes. The least frequently occurring process types are verbal processes (1.61%). Also, limited attention is devoted to minor clauses (0.81%) and groups (five instances). More precisely, space is given to information on the behaviour of animal and plant life, as realized by material and behavioural process types; their locations and times of availability, as indicated by relational-attributive, relational-identifying, existential, and material processes; the wealth of their existence, as suggested by existential, relational-identifying, material, and verbal processes; and the observation, experience, search, and expectance of their behaviour by tourists, as indicated by behavioural, mental, and material processes. Equally, the website characterizes plant and animal life in terms of particular features, such as look, size, and composition, as realized by relational-attributive processes; and identifies the popularity of plants and landscape and the suitability of environmental conditions for plants and animal life, as realized by relational-identifying, attributive, and mental processes. Limited cases can be noted which offer information on the consultation of types of media and guiding services for further information, as realized by material, behavioural, mental, verbal, and relational-attributive processes; and on the functions of an organization for the protection of birdlife, as realized by material, relational-attributive, and relational-identifying processes.

The groups, phrases, and clauses on the Istria region website predominantly deal with meanings revolving around environmental protection of the blue sea and green landscape. This is a motif that is carried throughout the representational structures identified for the visuals. These meanings are predominantly achieved by material processes (52.94%). Further process types relate to relational-attributive (17.65%), mental (9.41%), existential (7.06%), verbal (5.88%), relational-identifying (4.71%), and behavioural (1.18%) processes. Limited space is given to minor clauses (1.18%) and groups and phrases (seven instances). Thus, meanings on environmental protection range from the tradition of preserving seaside and inland landscapes and inhabitants, as a self-evident task, to the suitability of meteorological conditions for the production of food and drink. Furthermore, they cover examples of natural and cultural landscapes and remains, including environmentally protected areas and the fossilized remains of animals and plants dating back to prehistoric times. Finally, they culminate in the identification of environmentally protected areas as a matter of acknowledgement and calls for naming Istria an ecological tourist destination. These meanings are realized by material, relational-attributive, verbal, and existential processes. Interestingly, rather than construing physical events, material processes such as Istria has laid out its wonders in the garden of the Mediterranean, the blue Adriatic Sea washes its shores, and the towns strung like pearls along the coast further represent places in the sense of locations and the green landscape as pristine, precious, nostalgic, calm, intact, and aesthetically appealing in a metaphorical sense. Mediterranean iconography, such as sea landscapes, plants, and animal life, is portrayed as highly-esteemed, alluring, natural, and a place for public display and the aesthetic appeal of landscapes as a matter of consensus. Space is also given to information on receiving tourists with professions of kindness. This is suggested by material, existential, relational-attributive, mental, and relational-identifying processes and a minor clause. Further attention is also devoted to the exploration and perception of the environment. This refers to the discovery of Mediterranean seascapes and diverse locations by sailors and tourists participating in guided tours and the perception of signifiers of Mediterranean iconography, such as urban places, sea crafts, music, and fishermen's stories. This is realized by material, behavioural, verbal, relational-attributive, relational-identifying, and mental processes, and a minor clause.

The groups on the Perthshire region website represent nature as green natural heritage and wildlife. A similar distribution of material (39.19%) and relational-attributive (29.73%) processes, less mental (16.22%) and relational-identifying (10.81%) processes, a limited number of behavioural (2.7%) and existential (1.35%) processes, a lack of verbal (0%) processes and groups and phrases (six instances) can be noted. Thus, meanings centre on walking activities of tourists in the landscape, as realized by material and relational-attributive processes; and the behaviour of animal life and bodies of water, as achieved by material, behavioural, existential, and relational-attributive processes. Besides, the tourist's interest in information on natural heritage and service institutions as resources of further information on types of media is referred to, as achieved by material processes. Furthermore, Perthshire region is idealized as a site for nature and wildlife. In addition, emotional attachment to the landscape of users as walkers is construed. Also, the experience of the behaviour of animals is represented as delightful, noteworthy, distinctive, and absorbing, as indicated by relational-attributive, relational-identifying, and mental processes. Equally important is information on the multiple functions of aspects of landscape and their characterization. This refers to the following meanings: the function of types of woodlands as food reservoirs for animals and plants; pieces of landscapes with beneficial health effects for human beings; the make-up of the landscape as consisting of green natural and cultural types of landscapes, and bodies of water; their locations; and the representation of their wealth, their literary and public importance as a source of public events, and their aesthetic appeal and size. This is realized through a number of relational-identifying, relational-attributive, and material processes. Occasionally, mental and behavioural processes construe knowledge about typical Scottish wildlife, the unpredictability of their observation and auditory perception and the popularity of types of landscapes for animal life and tourists.

On all four regional websites, limited space is opened up for negotiating information or services. With regard to the statistics of clause types on natural heritage, this is indicated by the dearth of finite clauses with modality features on the Zadar (10.53%), Orkney (17.07%), Istria (4.76%), and Perthshire (12.16%) region websites. Equally rare are non-finite clauses on the Zadar (10.53%), Orkney (31.71%), Istria (35.71%), and Perthshire (21.62%) region websites. These clauses are therefore not arguable. Rather, a clear predominance of tensed finite clauses which portray verbal statements as indisputable facts can be noted on the Zadar (78.95%), Orkney (51.22%), Istria (59.52%), and Perthshire (66.22%) websites.

With regard to the statistics on the value of modality within finite clauses on natural heritage, the Zadar (100%) and Orkney (54.55%) region websites exclusively or predominantly make use of low rather than median or high value modality. They more strongly moderate the force of statements about arrival and bird watching possibilities on the Zadar, and exciting animal experience, plant life features, and expectations of the availability of wildlife information in the social media on the Orkney region websites. By contrast, the Istria (50%) and Perthshire (55.56%) websites display more median than low value modality. They therefore encode more strength into statements about seaside life and attractive landscape imagery on the Istria. Equally strong are statements about the emotional experience of natural and wildlife, complex walking infrastructure, the payment for events participation at information facilities, and contact possibilities for tourist information on the Perthshire region website. Infrequent use of high (13.64%) and median (31.82%) value modality can be noted in propositions about less favourable, typical, and unpredictable times and places for animal observation on the Orkney region website. Less space is given to low (25%) and high (25%) value modality in reference to statements on social activities at the sea as an established practice and the perception of Istrian locations on the Istria region website. Low (33.33%) and high (11.11%) modality in relation to the emotional experience and unpredictability of animal behaviour can be observed on the Perthshire region website.

Also, Figure 4.14 gives an overview of statistics of orientation and manifestation in finite clauses on natural heritage for the four regional websites.

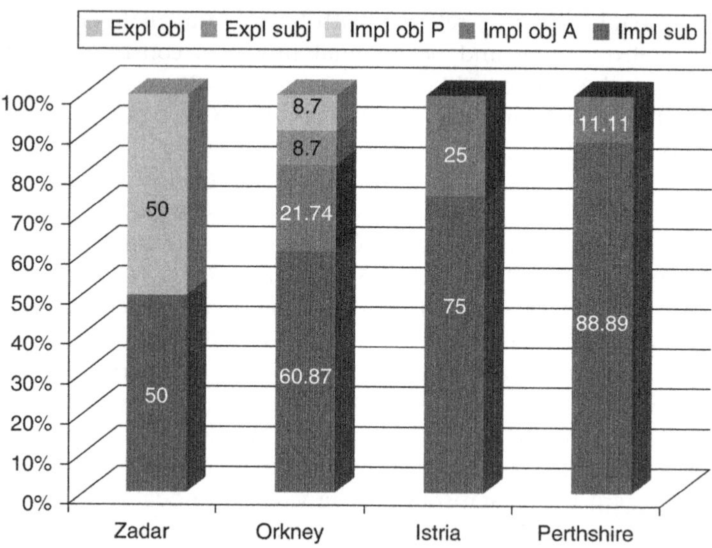

Figure 4.14 Overview of statistics of orientation and manifestation in finite clauses on natural heritage for the four regional websites

Thus, apart from the Zadar region websites, the Orkney (60.87%), Istria (75%), and Perthshire (88.89%) region websites predominantly express implicitly subjective orientation, as indicated by the frequent use of finites. The statements relate to the possibility of birdwatching and birdwatching times, exciting experience of animal life, and plant life features on the Orkney region website. On the Istria region website, propositions refer to consensus among explorers of the Mediterranean on the attractiveness of the sea and the exploration of tourist locations. On the Perthshire region website, they deal with the exploration of green natural heritage and wildlife behaviour, and tourist information. Hence, as with the representation of walking activities in sub-subsection 4.2.1, the speaker's own viewpoint is foregrounded. On the Zadar region website, both implicitly subjective orientation (50%) in reference to the possibility of birdwatching, and explicitly objective (50%) orientation in relation to arrival possibilities can be observed. This is indicated by the use of finites and relative attributive clauses. Thus, the point of view is both subjectified and objectified as a feature of the event itself. Less attention is devoted to implicitly objective orientation, as suggested by the use of adjuncts, in reference to typical times of animal observation and birth, and animal observation as a distinctive experience on the

Orkney (21.74%), social activities at the sea as an established practice on the Istria (25%), and the mythification of the behaviour of nature and wildlife on the Perthshire (11.11%) region websites. Occasionally, the Orkney region website expresses explicitly subjective orientation (8.7%) – in reference to expectations of wildlife increase and the availability of wildlife information in the social media – and explicitly objective orientation (8.7%) – in reference to tourists as objects of special attention for animal life. It follows from this that a preference for leaving implicit the source of conviction, rather than explicitly stating it, can be noted.

Figure 4.15 further gives an overview of statistics of modality type in finite clauses on natural heritage for the four regional websites.

Thus, the Orkney (77.27%), Istria (75%), and Perthshire (66.67%) region websites display more, or clearly foregrounded probability. On the Orkney region websites, this relates to statements about bird-watching possibilities, times and places, wildlife increase, the exciting experience of animal life, and features of plant life. On the Istria region website, it refers to the consensus among explorers of the Mediterranean

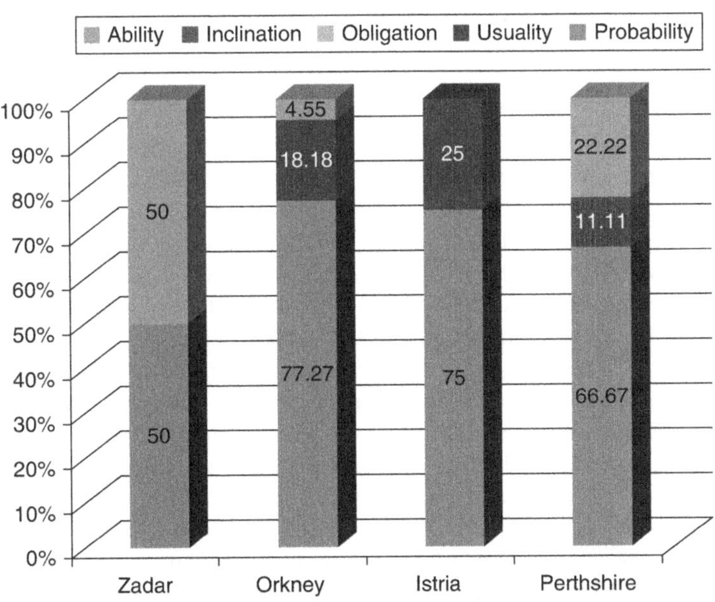

Figure 4.15 Overview of statistics of modality type in finite clauses on natural heritage for the four regional websites

on the attractiveness of the sea and the perception of locations. On the Perthshire region website, it revolves around the exploration of natural heritage and wildlife. The Zadar region website displays both an instance of probability (50%) in relation to birdwatching possibilities and readiness: ability (50%) in reference to the statement about arrival possibilities. Limited attention is devoted to the following types of modality: usuality (18.18%) in reference to animal observation and birth and readiness: ability (4.55%) in relation to the locations of animal life on the Orkney region website; usuality (25%) in relation to the statement about the closeness of social activities to the sea on the Istria region website; and usuality (11.11%) in relation to the exciting experience of animal life and readiness: ability (22.22%) in reference to tourist information on the Perthshire region website. In line with the frequent use of probability on the Orkney region website, a comment adjunct: asseverative: sure: explicitly objective can be identified. This deals with the reassurance of excitement in birdwatching activities.

All visuals on the four regional websites make definite visual statements, as suggested by the exclusive choice of photographs as visuals of higher modality (100%). As with the representation of activities, as delineated in sub-subsection 4.2.1, realistic representations are therefore at the heart of the natural heritage images constructed for the four regional websites.

4.3.2 Landscape observers or explorers?

For the visuals on the four regional websites, the contact system is predominantly – on the Zadar (94.12%) and Orkney (71.43%) websites – or exclusively – on the Istria (100%) and Perthshire (100%) region websites – realized by offers of factual information, rather than demands. This is due to the fact that a dearth of human or quasi-human participants is presented as gazing directly at users. Thus, users are not invited to enter into an imaginary relation with the representational structures assigned to the visuals in sub-subsection 4.3.1. Rather, the represented meanings are portrayed as something that is, a fact to be contemplated and observed. Exceptions to this are provided by a visual (5.88%) which demands users enter into an imaginary relation with the represented tourist on the Zadar region website, and two instances (28.57%) where animals, such as owls and seals, are portrayed as staring at users on the Orkney region website. Thus, users are invited to imagine themselves as tourists exploring environmentally protected areas in the Zadar region and to enter into an imaginary relationship with the animals in Orkney region.

In terms of the statistics of realizations of social distance on natural heritage, on the Zadar region website, a similar distribution of visuals can be noted which positions users in a more personal relationship (35.29%), as indicated by close range, and a more social relationship (47.06%), as realized by medium range. Personal relations relate to the represented Mediterranean natural products, plants, and birdlife. Social relations refer to waterfalls and lakes or bodies of water. Users are less frequently invited to adopt a more impersonal (17.65%) relationship to bays and canyons, as suggested by long range. All visuals on natural heritage on the four regional websites encode a subjective attitude. Figure 4.16 gives an overview of statistics of realizations of subjective attitude on natural heritage for the four regional websites.

Thus, on the Zadar region website, users are predominantly put on an equal footing (70.59%) with the represented Mediterranean natural products, waterfalls, lakes, bays, and birdlife, as suggested by eye-level angles, and less frequently positioned as observers (29.41%) of flowers

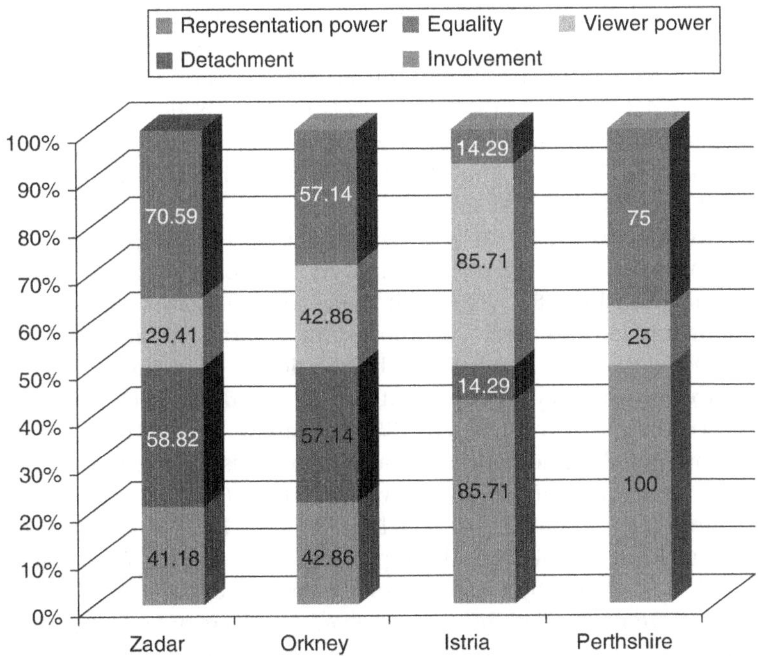

Figure 4.16 Overview of statistics of realizations of subjective attitude on natural heritage for the four regional websites

and canyons, as realized by high angles. Yet, they are not put in a less powerful position (0%) to the represented types of landscapes, as indicated by the lack of low angles. Also, a similar distribution of visuals shot from frontal and oblique angles can be noted. Thus, users are both invited to look at the represented natural products, flowers, birds, bays, and canyons, as realized by frontal angles (41.18%), and to adopt a more detached position in relation to bodies of water, birdlife, flowers and the coastal landscape (58.82%), as indicated by oblique angles. Hence, users tend to be positioned as immediate explorers or observers of a variety of landscapes, plant, and animal life from different sides.

Throughout the Orkney region website, a common thread of a similar distribution of intimacy and social distance in terms of distance, and involvement, detachment, viewer power, and equality in terms of subjective attitude can be observed. With regard to social distance, users are positioned in a more social (42.86%) or personal (57.14%) relationship to animals and plants in the landscape. This is achieved by medium and close distances. Attitude is realized both by eye-level angles which put users at an equal footing (57.14%) with the animals and plants and high angles which position them as observers (42.86%) of animals. Also, interplays between invitations to take a closer look (42.86%) at the animals and plants, as realized by frontal angles, and to observe them in a more detached way (57.14%), as realized by oblique angles, can be identified. Similarly to the Zadar region website, users thus figure both as immediate explorers and observers of the richness of plantlife and animal life from different sides.

In contrast to the Zadar and Orkney region websites, on the Istria region website, users are overwhelmingly positioned in a more impersonal relationship (85.71%) with types of landscapes, as indicated by long range, and rarely positioned in a more social relationship (14.29%) with them, as suggested by the dearth of medium range. No instances of intimacy can be identified due to the lack of close range (0%). Furthermore, most visuals (85.71%) invite users to take a look at the represented seaside and Central Istrian landscape, as expressed by frontal angles, and afford an overview of them (85.71%), as indicated by high angles. Instances of detachment from (14.29%) and an equal power relation to (14.29%) the represented experiential meanings are limited, as suggested by the dearth of oblique and eye-level angles. Users are therefore positioned more as involved observers of landscapes.

Finally, the visuals on the Perthshire region website position users more in an impersonal relationship with green landscape and places (75%), as realized by the predominant use of long range, than as users who are familiar with the represented experiential meanings (25%), as suggested by the dearth of instances of close range. They further exclusively invite users to look at the green landscape and places (100%), as realized by frontal angles. Also, users are put in a more equal power relationship with them (75%), as indicated by more frequent use of eye-level angles, rather than in a more powerful position to the represented meanings (25%), as achieved by high angles. Users are thus positioned as more distant landscape explorers.

If comparing the four regional websites in terms of units of user address as cultural tourists, the Perthshire (37.5%) and Orkney (42.86%) region websites display most units of address or involvement of users as cultural tourists. This is followed by the Istria (17.65%) region website which less frequently involves users and the Zadar (0%) region website, which does not address or involve users as cultural tourists, neither in groups and phrases, nor in clauses. Accordingly, the Zadar (100%) and Istria (82.35%) region websites make more statements about the experiential meanings identified in sub-subsection 4.3.1. This is indicated by the declarative mood and encoded into the groups and phrases. The use of statements in the declarative mood decreases on the Orkney (57.14%) and Perthshire (62.5%) region websites. Thus, on the Istria region website, the following types of users are addressed: sailors of the Mediterranean; observers and attracted visitors of and guests and travellers in Istrian towns, cities, natural, and cultural heritage sights to be guided through stories and tours; and emotional and nostalgic visitors to be received with professions of kindness. This is realized by several instances of addressing users as cultural tourists of natural heritage, that is, frequent use of second person pronouns (13 instances) and imperative mood (eight instances) and limited use of first person pronouns (two instances). Throughout, the Orkney region website directly addresses or involves users as observers of the behaviour and look of a wealth of birds and wildlife in diverse locations. Also, it addresses users as seekers of information on guiding services and types of print media on Orkney's animal and plant life and the environmentally protected areas inhabited by them. This is achieved by the imperative mood (nine instances), second person pronouns (seven instances), and a rhetorical question in interrogative mood (one instance). The Perthshire region website constructs a more versatile image of users as cultural tourists. More specifically, users are directly addressed as active walkers in domestic landscapes and perceivers of types of wildlife, plant life, and landscapes. Equally, they are mythicized as nature lovers and discoverers of the unknown with adventurous spirits. This is suggested by second (ten instances) and first (one instance) person pronouns and imperative mood (five instances).

4.3.3 Individuals or technologically skilled social actors?

When it comes to the statistics of units with accessible and inaccessible elements on natural heritage, on all four regional websites, more units with inaccessible than accessible elements can be observed, with 80% of units with inaccessible elements on the Zadar, 83.33% on the Orkney, 61.54% on the Istria, and 72.73% on the Perthshire region websites. Thus, the Istria (38.46%) and Perthshire (27.27%) region websites engage users more as media actors than the Zadar (20%) and Orkney (16.67%) region websites. Furthermore, when it comes to the statistics for types of user actions on natural heritage, the Zadar (100%) region website exclusively involves users through mouse click on internal links on general information on Zadar region and its natural heritage. By contrast, the Orkney region website exclusively (100%) engages users through rollover and mouse click on an external link providing information on an organization for the protection of birdlife. The Istria region website predominantly (70%) offers users the possibility of activating internal links on seaside and central Istrian natural and cultural types of landscapes through rollover and mouse click and less through mouse click (30%). By contrast, the Perthshire region website involves users more through mouse click (75%) and less through rollover and mouse click (25%) on internal links on natural heritage and animal life. No instances can be identified which engage users through type in (0%) or mouse click and movement (0%). On none of the websites is the possibility of users contributing actively to the construction of meanings on natural heritage made more salient by verbally indicating media interaction.

It follows from what has been delineated above that none of the four regional websites engages users as highly technically advanced social actors. Similarly to the type of user profile identified in sub-subsections 4.1.4 on diverse tourist activities and 4.2.3 on walking activities, this is supported by the following findings: the limited number of units with accessible elements, lack of salience of media interaction, less variety in types of user actions and elements to be activated, lower levels of interactivity and the address of more conventional experiential meanings. Nevertheless, due to differences in the percentage of accessible elements, the findings identified for the pages on walking activities in sub-subsection 4.2.3 can be confirmed. More traditional tourists as print-literate individuals who observe, read, and scan through tourist promotional material are addressed on the Zadar and Orkney region websites. Slightly more contemporary media-interactive tourists are constructed on the Istria and Perthshire region websites.

4.3.4 Landscape observers, travellers, eco-tourists, or adventure tourists?

In sum, initially it was assumed that the representation of natural heritage centred on the following meanings: Mediterranean landscapes on the Zadar region website; North-Atlantic landscapes on the Orkney region website; landscapes which present Istria as a blue-green peninsula on the Istria region website; and types of green landscape on the Perthshire region website. These initial assumptions can be confirmed and further detailed in terms of representational structures assigned to visuals, experiential meanings in groups and phrases, and process types assigned to clauses.

With regard to the way in which natural heritage is represented, as expressed by types of visuals, the Orkney region website focuses more on the behaviour of animal life, while the Zadar, Istria, and Perthshire region websites concentrate more on the representation of types of water and green landscapes and their locations. In addition, all groups on the four regional websites deal with types of landscapes and most encode notions of environmental protection and animal life. In terms of clauses, on the Zadar region website, there is a focus on natural and cultural types of landscapes, their location of availability and attractiveness, and stages of development of travelling for hunting purposes. The natural heritage image constructed for the Orkney region website is more complex in terms of the scope of thematic meanings. More specifically, representations revolve around the behaviour, locations, and the wealth of birds and wildlife and the exploration of their behaviour by tourists. Furthermore, plant morphology, popularity, and the suitability of the environment for plant and animal life are characterized. On the Istria region website, a semantic field of environmental protection of Istrian landscapes is construed. Closely related to this is the representation of the environment as untouched and attractive. Meanings also revolve around the exploration of landscapes, the perception of locations, and the art of music. The Perthshire region website gives more space to the behaviour of tourists in the landscape, such as walking, and the attentiveness of tourists to the landscape as a matter of interest and enjoyment. Also, it focuses on diverse functions of the landscape; the behaviour of animals in the landscape; and the representation of natural heritage in terms of the breadth of the make-up of the landscape, public events, and aesthetic appeal.

It follows from this that a more static landscape and activities-development image is constructed for the Zadar region website. The high frequency of relational-attributive processes supports this reading. By contrast, a more vivid natural heritage image, as based on animal and plant life behaviour, is created for the Orkney region website. This is suggested by the predominance of material over other process types. On the Istria region website, there is a clear focus on environmental awareness, aesthetics, and seaside activities which interact to construe natural heritage. This is indicated by a wealth of material processes. Similarly to the Orkney region website, on the Perthshire region website, a natural heritage image can be identified which is based on tourist and wildlife activities. In addition, however, nature becomes a source of public events. This is suggested by the predominance of material over other process types.

In terms of the arguability of clauses, even more pertinently than in the representation on walking activities, factuality is construed through use of more definite verbal and visual statements and fewer clauses with modality features. Thus, the initial hypothesis that the website's promises to users that the realistic tourist experiences constructed in the virtual world will be fulfilled in the social world can be confirmed.

Moving to tourist communication, as initially hypothesized, all four regional websites make use of visuals which offer information, rather than demanding users to enter into an imaginary relationship with the represented participants. More specifically, the Zadar and Orkney region websites offer factual information on aspects of landscape and animal life, while the Istria and Perthshire region websites portray types of landscapes and locations as objects for user attention and contemplation. This is indicated by the dearth or lack of the representation of human or quasi-human participants as gazing directly at users. These readings can further be complemented through the findings gained from the analysis of realizations of the systems of contact, social distance, and attitude in visuals. When it comes to the realization of the systems of social distance and attitude, the Zadar and Orkney region websites coincide in several ways: the positioning of users at both a social and a personal distance to the represented meanings; the predominant construal of equal power relations between users and the represented meanings, and occasional use of viewer power; and the creation of both involvement with and detachment from the represented meanings. Users therefore predominantly figure as being close to the represented variety of plants, animal life, and/or national parks, or as their observers from different sides. By contrast, the Istria and Perthshire region websites share the predominant positioning of users at an impersonal social distance from the represented participants and involvement with the represented types of landscapes. Yet, while users figure as involved observers of landscapes on the Istria region website, as suggested by the predominant use of high angles, they are positioned as more distant landscape explorers on the Perthshire region website, as expressed by the privileging of eye-level angles.

In addition, the initial assumption – that the Zadar and Istria region websites give less, while the Orkney and Perthshire region websites give more space to the address or involvement of users as cultural tourists – can be confirmed. Thus, a lack of address of users as cultural tourists can be identified for the Zadar region website. A dearth of user address can be identified for the Istria region website. Thus, they figure as water sportspeople and nostalgic sightseeing tourists in Istrian locations and landscapes. This is indicated by the wealth of declarative mood and the dearth of second person pronouns, and interrogative and imperative mood. By contrast, the Perthshire region website more frequently addresses users as adventurous explorers and enjoyers of animal life and nature. The Orkney region website involves users as observers of the behaviour and look of animal life and seekers of information on it. This is suggested by more frequent use of second person pronouns and the imperative mood.

Finally, the hypothesis that all four regional websites engage users as media actors merely to a limited extent can be confirmed and refined in terms of information on types of user actions and thematic meanings addressed. More specifically, the Istria and Perthshire region websites engage users more as media actors than the Orkney and Zadar region websites. All types of user actions are limited to rollover and mouse click and/or mouse click. Media interaction revolves around types of landscapes and organizations for the protection of animal life. In brief, there is a dearth of variety of types of user actions and experiential meanings which can be actively created by users as media actors. Inaccessible are privileged over accessible elements. Thus, on none of the websites do users figure as technologically versed social actors.

Representation, and cultural tourist and user communication thus contribute to the construction of different tourist profiles: more detached Mediterranean landscape observers on the Zadar region website; travellers for the enjoyment of animal behaviour on the Orkney region website; eco-tourists engaging in sustainable travel to protected Mediterranean areas on the Istria region website; and wildlife and adventure tourists captivated by species of animal life and plantlife on the Perthshire region website.

4.4 History and heritage

4.4.1 Cultural heritage sights or historical events?

On none of the four regional websites is history constructed as a narrative of a series of historical events. Rather, on most of the four regional websites, the representation of history is based on a fusion of cultural heritage sights from diverse periods of art history and landscape locations. In terms of the statistics of representational structures on history and heritage in visuals on the Zadar, Orkney, and Perthshire region websites, this is indicated by the lack of narrative structures (0%) and the exclusive use of conceptual structures (100%). The use of narrative structures on the Istria region website is limited to instances of people experiencing cultural heritage (20%). Yet, the websites differ in the extent to which they prioritize the portrayal of sights and landscapes and the mechanisms which operate to construct history. These mechanisms can be referred to as 'materialization', 'naturalization', and 'institutionalization'.

Thus, history is materialized through the portrayal of art history and the architectural sophistication of a wealth of cultural heritage sights on the Zadar region website. Instances include the Roman layout of squares and streets in the old city centre, walls, towers, churches, or aspects of churches decorated in ancient Romanesque and Byzantine building styles. This is due to intertextual knowledge that curved arches are commonly coded with notions of the Romanesque, while cupolas are coded with Byzantine architectural styles in other texts. It follows from this that, rather than seeing worship or bullying users as cultural tourists into joining the church community, the portrayal of church architecture as a marvel is foregrounded. More precisely, this is indicated by a focus on the decoration of the churches with extremely elaborate altars and figures of saints, plain pillars, complicated Corinthian capitals with ornate scrolls, and marble with saints' names written on it. At the same time, however, the portrayal of heritage sights undergoes a process of naturalization. Either heritage sights are represented in their natural environment, or landscapes of geographical locations themselves, such as the Central Mediterranean Sea and adjacent landscapes, are portrayed. Similarly to the Zadar region website, heritage and nature co-occur on the Orkney region website. The representation of examples of prehistoric remains from the Neolithic period and Iron Age in North-Atlantic wild grass and sea landscapes, such as archaeological sites and religious sights, supports this observation. This is due to intertextual knowledge that stone circles and brochs are commonly referred to as dating from Neolithic period and Iron Age and as being found in North-Atlantic landscapes in other texts. In contrast to the Zadar and Orkney region websites, the Istria region website gives less space to the portrayal of sights in their natural environment. Rather, it focuses more on sights or aspects of them. These include cultural heritage sights for the representation of spectacles, and religious mosaic artefacts of Byzantine and Roman style. As users can merely see aspects of them, without knowing where they belong, these are portrayed in a more enigmatic way. This derives from intertextual knowledge that arenas for gladiator fights for public entertainment are commonly coded with notions of Roman heritage and mosaics in basilicas are commonly related to works of Byzantine art in the Istria region in other texts. Finally, in contrast to the Zadar, Orkney, and Istria region websites, history is institutionalized on the Perthshire region website. This is due to intertextual knowledge that heritage sights, such as Celtic lake dwellings, shields, and Celtic stones, are commonly presented in institutions for the public display of cultural heritage, such as visitor attractions, centres, and museums, in other texts.

The representation of history and heritage is further realized by experiential meanings which can be identified for groups and phrases, and process types which can be assigned to clauses, as suggested by Figure 4.17.

Thus, on the Zadar region website, predominantly relational-attributive (41.11%) and a wealth of material (31.11%) process types can be identified. To a limited extent, meanings are realized by relational-identifying (16.66%), verbal (5.55%), mental (3.33%) and existential (2.22%) processes. No instances of behavioural processes (0%) and a limited number of groups (six instances) can be noted. In sum, groups, phrases, and clauses interact to construe the following meanings: first, past events and the relation between the Zadar region and various cultural currents by which the region has historically been ruled; second, types of cultural heritage sights, their historical anchorage and attractiveness; third, the architectural, political, gastronomic, and religious centrality of the Zadar region. More specifically, material, verbal, relational-attributive, relational-identifying, and mental processes interact to construe meanings on cultural influences. The processes are devoted to a historical account of the transformation of the region from settlement to urban area, the reasons for Zadar

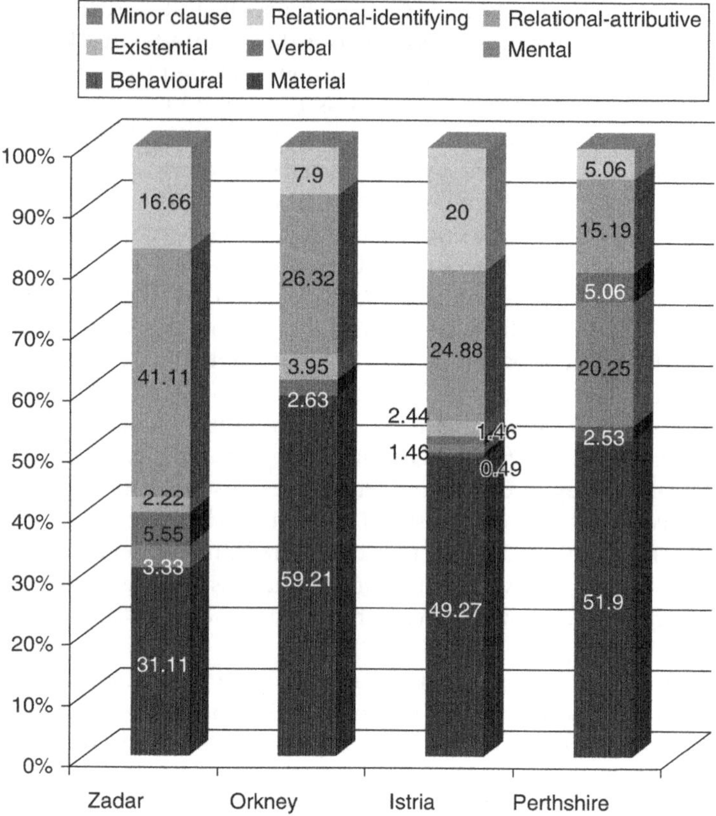

Figure 4.17 Overview of statistics of experiential meanings on history and heritage in clauses for the four regional websites

county's attractiveness for attacks, and relationships with the following cultural currents and social relations: the family relationship between representatives of the Roman Catholic Church and Croatian royalty, the coronation of Croatian royalty, Croatian rule, a Croatian-Slavic imprint of the city and its surroundings and the use of Croatian-Slavic language, Croat-Hungarian rule, tensions with Venetian rule and its temporal duration, Austrian, Italian, and Yugoslav rule, and tensions with and deconstruction of the region by groups of Serbian civilians. Equally, in terms of types of cultural heritage sights, there is a focus on the historical anchorage of heritage sights in terms of place and time, the specification of heritage sights as artistic heritage, religious heritage, and cultural heritage sights, and their characterization in terms of aesthetic appeal and architectural and interior design. This is realized by material, mental, existential, relational-attributive, and relational-identifying processes. When it comes to the centrality of the region, it is settlement life, urbanization and the architectural foundations of the city and its infrastructure, the significance of the city and surrounding places for reasons of political and religious centrality, and indigenous products that complete the historical image constructed for Istria region. This is accomplished by interplays between material, relational-attributive, and relational-identifying processes.

In contrast to the clauses on the Zadar region website, the clauses on the Orkney region focus on diverse types of events, and reference to religious and archaeological sites and their importance, and genealogy culture. This is predominantly achieved by material processes (59.21%) and a wealth of relational-attributive processes (26.32%), less by relational-identifying (7.9%), existential (3.95%), and verbal (2.63%) processes, a lack of mental (0%) and behavioural (0%) processes, and the use of groups and phrases (17 instances). Thus, as indicated by the groups and material and relational-attributive processes, types of events are historical events. These cover battles, the building of sights, the death of historic figures, and other events which mark the beginning or end of business, settlements, conflicts, and natural phenomena. The description of sites relates to the cultural influence of Norse rule in Orkney, as manifested in a wealth of remains of cultural heritage sights, inscriptions, and archaeological sites. This is accomplished by existential, relational-attributive, and relational-identifying processes. Their importance is further acknowledged by international organizations and stressed by characterizing them as kept, worth visiting, and sophisticated in terms of architecture, size, temporal stability, and religious value. This is indicated by material, relational-attributive, relational-identifying, and verbal processes. Relational-attributive, material, relational-identifying, and verbal processes trigger users' interest in history through appeals to their creativity. In terms of family history, these process types interact to construe the visit and discovery of Orkney by tourists and those seeking ancestors, virtual activities of users as media actors on family history, and the ancestral function of sites.

The Istria region website offers a description of the relationship between the region and various cultural currents by which it has been influenced, the relationships between diverse spheres of social life, the preoccupations of prehistoric people and the first settlers, and tangible and intangible heritage. This is predominantly expressed by material

(49.27%), then relational-attributive (24.88%), and relational-identifying (20%) processes, a wealth of groups (43 instances) and less frequently by existential (2.44%), mental (1.46%), verbal (1.46%), and behavioural (0.49%) processes. More precisely, meanings on the influence by diverse cultural currents relate to tensions between the first settlers and the Romans, the transition from Roman to Byzantine rule, and the acknowledgement of their importance. Also, they centre on the temporal duration and institutions of diverse rules, including Byzantine, Avar, Lombard, and Franconian rule, with a focus on the penchant for robbery of the first settlers and farmers as victims of conflicts. These meanings are realized by diverse processes, including material, mental, verbal, relational-attributive, and relational-identifying processes. At the same time, in interplays between material and relational-attributive processes, meanings are transferred into the religious, political, and economic spheres of social life. This is achieved through reference to the relationship between representatives of the profane and the sacred sphere, religious oppressions, and military missions led by Christians as contributions to economic growth of towns; the political reaction of towns to foreign rule, as implying loss of autonomy; the economic interests of Venetian rule, and destruction of heritage; and the reaction of towns to political autonomy from foreign rule, as manifesting in economic development such as food trade. Moreover, the preoccupation of prehistoric people and the first settlers is described as manifesting in the discovery of sophisticated cutting tools and animal relicts, religious practices, hunting, fieldwork, and the manufacture of clayware. This is achieved by material, behavioural, mental, relational-attributive, and relational-identifying processes. When it comes to intangible and tangible heritage, users obtain information on voices as intangible heritage and the suitability of the landscape for cultural heritage sights as tangible heritage; the formation of nautical, cultural, artistic, military, civil, and religious sights; public institutions and estates as keepers of history with their anchorage in terms of time and/or place and/or events; the infrastructural and economic development of Istria by the Romans; the popularity of stone as a building material for Roman settlements; the possession of estates by representatives of the military and political domains; and the archaeological make-up and location of fortification settlements, cultural heritage sights, and places. These signifiers of meaning are realized by the corresponding groups and diverse process types, including material, existential, verbal, relational-attributive, and relational-identifying processes.

On the Perthshire region website, diverse tourist activities are construed; historical events, figures, habits, and sights interact to culturalize and mythify the landscape region; and history is revived through imagination. This is predominantly realized by material (51.9%) processes, a similar distribution of mental (20.25%) and relational-attributive (15.19%) processes, less frequently by verbal (5.06%), relational-identifying (5.06%) and behavioural (2.53%) processes, and a limited number of groups (six instances). The website does not make use of existential (0%) processes. More specifically, there is a stress on the wealth of possible tourist activities in Perthshire in a more general way and visiting public places on cultural heritage as one of the variety of activities. This is achieved by material, mental, and relational-attributive processes. Furthermore, users are encouraged to revive history in their mental images, as indicated by behavioural and mental processes. As part of users' mental imagery, military, religious, royal, literary, and cultural heritage sights and the production of alcoholic beverages are constructed as reviving historical events, anecdotes, and the history of electricity generation for factory purposes. Royal, military, and literary figures are created as travellers through landscape and givers of heritage. Material, mental, relational-attributive, and relational-identifying processes realize these meanings. Events revolve around the following meanings: religious movements, the birth of religious figures, the building of places for reading literary and artistic works, social customs and military defence, seismic events through reference to the location of faults and their susceptibilities for earth tremors, archaeological discoveries, the influence of cultural currents and virtual activities of users as media actors for further information on events. These are realized by material, verbal, relational-attributive, relational-identifying and mental processes.

When it comes to the question of whether the hitherto-identified experiential meanings are represented more as facts, rather than creating space for their questioning in terms of believability and possibility, the analysis suggests that the clauses on history and heritage on the Zadar, Orkney, Istria, and Perthshire region websites are clearly not part of a text to be argued with. When it comes to the statistics of clause types on history and heritage, this is suggested by the low number of finite clauses with modality features amounting to 4.44% on the Zadar, 1.32% on the Orkney, 3.9% on the Istria, and 12.66% on the Perthshire region websites. Rather, a high percentage of tensed finite clauses expressing definite verbal statements can be identified. This amounts to 85.56% for the Zadar, 85.53% for the Orkney, 82.44% for the Istria, and 60.76% for the Perthshire region website. Furthermore, no comments can be made about the arguability of clauses on the

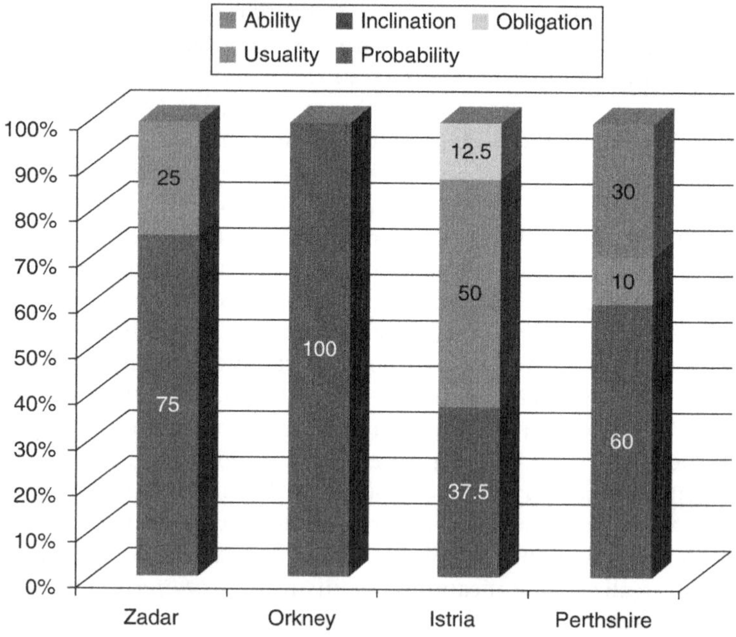

Figure 4.18 Overview of statistics of modality type in finite clauses on history and heritage for the four regional websites

Zadar (10%), Orkney (13.16%), Istria (13.66%) and Perthshire (26.58%) region websites.

Figure 4.18 further gives an overview of statistics of modality type in finite clauses on history and heritage for the four regional websites.

Within finite clauses with modality features on the Zadar region website, predominant use of low value modality (75%) and probability (75%) in the proposition about sightseeing possibilities can be noted. Limited space is given to high value modality (25%) and usuality (25%) in the proposition about conflict history. Values and types of modality on the Orkney region website are restricted to low value modality (100%) and probability (100%) in a proposition about nostalgia. The Istria and Perthshire region websites show slightly more variety in the use of realizations of modality. On the Istria region website, an equal distribution of high value modality (50%) in propositions about urbanization and Illyrian and Slavic cultural influences and median (50%) value modality in propositions about settlement construction, the identification of the first settlers, the economic development of the region, and the existence of heritage sights can be noted. Furthermore, a similar distribution of probability (37.5%) in reference to settlement construction, settlers, and urbanization, and usuality (50%) in relation to the settling of the Slavs in towns, the presence of the first settlers in literary works, the infrastructure, and the defendable positioning of towns in conflicts can be observed. By contrast, obligation (12.5%) is restricted to one instance, which deals with heritage sights. Unlike the other three websites, on the Perthshire region website, a tendency towards median value modality (90%) and probability (60%) can be identified. This refers to statements about creative and educative holidays, the desirability of storytelling on the part of the tourist board, and the exploration of history in users' mental images. Less attention is devoted to readiness: ability (30%), low value modality (10%), and usuality (10%) in propositions about the narrativization of historical and seismic events.

Moreover, Figure 4.19 gives an overview of statistics of orientation and manifestation in finite clauses on history and heritage for the four regional websites.

It reveals that, while the Zadar (75%), Orkney (100%), and Perthshire (100%) region websites use more or exclusively finites, thus expressing implicitly subjective orientation, the Istria (75%) region website

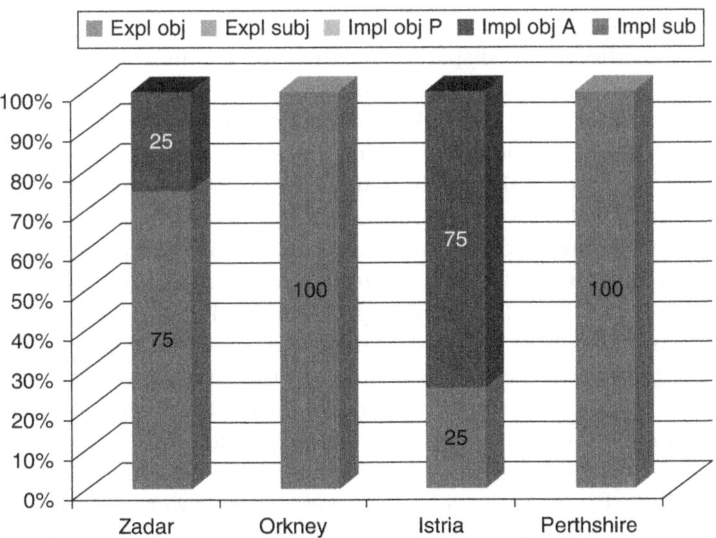

Figure 4.19 Overview of statistics of orientation and manifestation in finite clauses on history and heritage for the four regional websites

privileges implicitly objective over implicitly subjective orientation (25%). As with the orientations in the sub-subsection 4.2.1 on walking activities and 4.3.1 on natural heritage, the subjective point of view is thus more prominent.

The hitherto-identified focus on definite verbal statements and higher value modality in clauses in concert with a lack of comment adjuncts which could have expressed attitude and the exclusive use of photographs as visuals of higher (100%) modality on all four regional websites repeatedly constructs propositions as indisputable facts, rather than giving more space to their questioning and challenging.

4.4.2 Observers of landscapes and sights, or explorers of public institutions?

When it comes to realizations of the contact system on history and heritage, for all four regional websites, it is exclusively offers (100%) that can be identified. This is suggested by the fact that in none of the visuals are human or quasi-human participants portrayed as gazing directly at users. Thus, users do not enter into an imaginary relation with the experiential meanings identified in the representational structures assigned to the visuals in subsection 4.1. Rather, similarly to the visuals on activities and natural heritage in sub-subsections 4.2.2 and 4.3.2, these are portrayed as pieces of factual information for observation and contemplation.

None of the visuals displayed on the four regional websites express an objective attitude. Rather, realizations of subjective attitude and social distance can be noted. With regard to the statistics of realizations of social distance, these reveal that the visuals on the Zadar region website predominantly position users in an impersonal relationship with landscape locations and sights (53.85%), as realized by long range. Occasionally, they are put in a more social relationship with the represented meanings (30.77%), as indicated by medium range. Rarely, they are invited to adopt a more personal relationship with landscape locations and sights (15.39%), as indicated by close range. Figure 4.20 further gives an overview of statistics of orientation and manifestation in finite clauses on history and heritage for the four regional websites.

Thus, most visuals on the Zadar region website put users at an equal footing with the landscapes and sights in the landscape (38.46%) as cultural tourists, as realized by eye-level angles. Fewer instances can be identified which put users in a less powerful position than the landscapes and sights (26.92%), as suggested by low angles, or in a more powerful position than the represented sights and landscapes (34.62%),

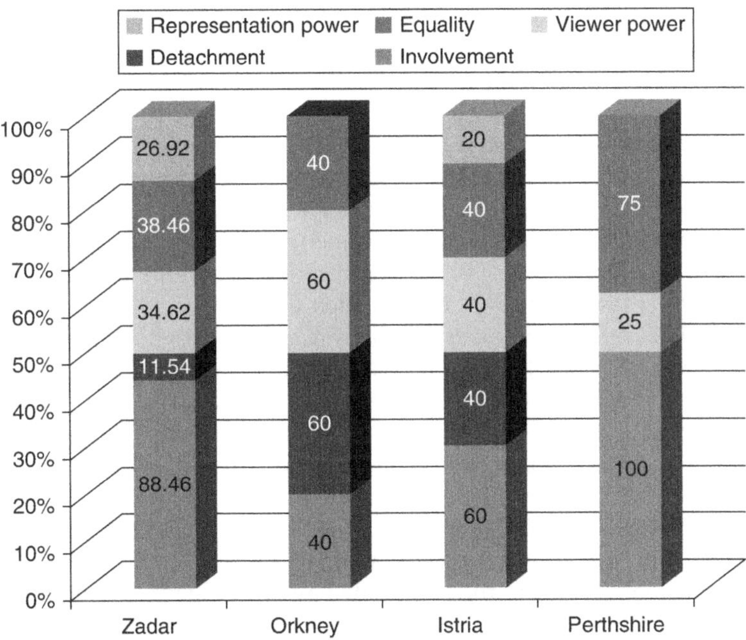

Figure 4.20 Overview of statistics of realizations of subjective attitude on history and heritage on activities for the four regional websites

as realized by high angles. Equally, users are predominantly invited to look at the landscapes and sights (88.46%), as realized by frontal angles, and less often positioned in a more detached way (11.54%), as indicated by oblique angles. There is therefore a tendency towards constructing users more as strangers getting an idea of and observing the architectural look of cultural sights in the landscape or the natural look of the Central Mediterranean landscapes of the Zadar region's surroundings.

On the Orkney region website, a similar distribution of the realizations of social distance both positions users in a social relationship with the represented remains (60%), as realized by medium range, and in a more impersonal relationship with the represented church and archaeological sites (40%), as suggested by long range. In terms of attitude, users are both invited to look at the sites in a more involved (40%) and in a more detached way (60%), as realized by interplays between oblique and frontal angles. Also, they are put both at an equal footing with the cultural remains (40%) and as their observers (60%), as indicated by eye-level angles and high angles. No instances can be identified which position users in a more personal (0%) or less powerful (0%) relationship with the represented sites and sights, as indicated by the lack of close range and low angles. Users thus figure as more immediate explorers of the archaeological sites represented, or their more detached observers.

By contrast, on the Istria region website, there is a clear privileging of a more personal relationship between users and the represented aspects of cultural heritage sights (80%), as suggested by close range. Also, a similar distribution of involvement (60%), as realized by frontal angles, and detachment (40%), as indicated by oblique angles, can be noted. Users are further positioned such a way as to perceive the sites and sights as their onlookers (40%), as realized by high angles, or their more immediate explorers in the landscape (40%), as indicated by eye-level angles. Rarely are users positioned in a less powerful (20%) or more impersonal (20%) relation to the represented meanings, as indicated by the dearth of low angles and long ranges. Hence, users are invited to take a closer look at aspects of cultural heritage, without knowing to which sights they belong.

Finally, on the Perthshire region website, users are exclusively invited to take a look (100%) at the represented aspects of sights in public institutions for the storage and display of heritage or at the represented locations, as indicated by frontal angles. Predominantly, they are put at an equal footing with them (75%), as achieved by eye-level angles. Also, they are positioned in a social relationship (50%), as accomplished by medium ranges, rather than a personal (25%) or impersonal (25%) relation to them, as suggested by the less frequent use of close and long ranges. Users are thus constructed as visitors who are interested in engaging with the cultural artifacts in public institutions for the display of cultural heritage, rather than being their detached explorers in the landscape.

When it comes to the units of user address as cultural tourists on history and heritage, the Zadar (0%) and Istria (1.59%) region websites do not or, to a very limited extent, display units which directly address users as cultural tourists exploring history and heritage. Rather, the Zadar (100%) and Istria (98.41%) region websites make statements about the experiential meanings identified in the groups, phrases and process types assigned to the clauses in sub-subsection 4.4.1. This is indicated by the exclusive or predominant use of the declarative mood. By contrast, the Orkney (33.33%) and Perthshire (44.44%) region websites occasionally, or more strongly, engage users as cultural tourists, in addition to making statements about experiential meanings. This is suggested by the declarative mood on the Orkney (66.67%) and Perthshire (55.56%) region websites.

Thus, in terms of instances and types of user address as cultural tourists on history and heritage, on the Istria region website, the address of users is restricted to their involvement in the multimodal exchange of information on cultural artifacts and sights of history. This is indicated by a first person plural pronoun (one instance). On the Orkney region website, users are involved in the multimodal exchange of information on cultural heritage. This is suggested by a first person plural pronoun (one). Also, they are directly addressed as visitors of a natural harbour and as home and ancestor seekers. This is indicated by a second person pronoun (one instance) and imperative mood (one instance). They are thus constructed as explorers of maritime and family history. On the Perthshire region website, a versatile image is constructed of users as sightseeing tourists. Instances of second person pronouns (16 instances) are privileged over instances of first person pronouns (nine instances) and imperative mood (six instances). In a more general way, users are directly addressed as selectors from a variety of tourist activities in the social and the virtual world, explorers of public institutions for the storage and display of cultural heritage sights and artifacts, natural attractions, and family history for knowledge, creativity, and enjoyment purposes. This is indicated by the imperative mood and second person pronouns. In a more specific way, they are drawn into the multimodal exchange of information on history and heritage as prospective tourists and are addressed as imaginative revivers of artistic and military past events. This is suggested by first and second person pronouns and the imperative mood. Or, in line with the mythification of history identified in the analysis of the nature of representation of history and heritage in sub-subsection 4.4.1, they are addressed as listeners to narratives and perceivers of ghosts and industrial heritage. This is realized by a series of second person pronouns and the imperative mood.

4.4.3 Observers or social media actors?

With regard to the degree of media interaction, the Istria region website engages users most as media actors if relating units with accessible (41.74%) to units with inaccessible elements (58.26%). This is followed by the Perthshire region website, with 26.67% units with accessible and 73.33% units with inaccessible elements; the Orkney region website with 22.22% units with accessible and 77.77% units with inaccessible elements; and the Zadar region website, with 16% units with accessible and 84% units with inaccessible elements. The Istria region website predominantly offers users the possibility of activating links on cultural heritage sights, stages in the history of the Istria region, and an international organization for the protection of cultural heritage sights through rollover and mouse click (95.83%) and, occasionally, through mouse click (4.17%). The Perthshire region website offers them the possibility of activating links on past events and cultural heritage sights through rollover and mouse click (50%) and mouse click (50%). On the Orkney region website, users can exclusively activate links on heritage sights and genealogy culture through rollover and mouse click (100%). On the Zadar region website, users can exclusively activate links on general information about the region, history, and cultural heritage sights through mouse click (100%). No instances can be identified which engage users through type in (0%) or mouse click and movement (0%).

Furthermore, when it comes to instances of verbal indication of media interaction, on the Istria and Perthshire region websites, a restricted number of instances (one per website) can be identified which overtly signal media interaction, thus additionally obscuring users' role as media actors. More precisely, users are addressed as seekers of information on cultural heritage sights, as indicated by find out in the imperative mood in Find out more about the Euphrasian Basilica on the Istria region website, and search in the imperative mood in Search the visitscotland.com database for information on the historic attractions and museums mentioned above and details of others in the area on the Perthshire region website.

In brief, media interaction is limited on all four regional websites. The websites exclusively offer the possibility of media interaction with links on more conventional tourist themes, thus displaying lower levels of interactivity. There is a lack of further elements and meanings which could have been presented on the four websites. Examples may include videos representing historical documentaries and contact forms to be filled in by users as media actors to obtain more information on their family history or historical timelines to be activated by users as media actors to obtain more information on regional history. Thus, the findings gained from the analysis of users as media actors on walking activities and natural heritage in sub-subsections 4.2.3 and 4.3.3 can be confirmed. On none of the four websites is a more technologically skilled social actor created. The higher degree and salience of media interaction on the Istria and Perthshire in comparison to the Zadar and Orkney region websites repeatedly positions users as slightly more contemporary media-interactive users on the former two websites.

4.4.4 Explorers of sights, or learners about or participants in the mythification of history?

Initially, it was hypothesized that the nature of representation revolved around the following meanings: monuments and ancient history on the Zadar and Istria region websites; prehistoric remains in North-Atlantic landscapes on the Orkney region website; and sightseeing as one of several possible tourist activities in the Perthshire region, including visiting natural heritage, shopping, and benefiting from gastronomy, on the Perthshire region website.

These assumptions can be confirmed for all four regional websites. In addition, however, the analysis reveals that the websites coincide in the address of certain themes and differ in the extent to which meanings on past events and heritage sights are interwoven with other meanings and the ways in which these meanings are represented. Thus, conceptual structures on historical events are assigned to most of the visuals on the four regional websites. Thus, the look of archaeological sites, religious sights and landscapes captures users' gazes. This is indicated by the exclusive identification of conceptual structures. These relate to the materialization and naturalization of history through the portrayal of artistic and religious sights and archaeological sites of diverse periods of art history in regional landscapes, or aspects of sights and locations themselves. Equally, they deal with institutionalization, through the depiction of sights in public institutions. More specifically, these cover sights in Mediterranean Sea and adjacent landscapes or locations on the Zadar region website; archaeological sites and religious sights on the Orkney region website; aspects of artistic and religious sights on the Istria region website; and sights in public institutions for the display and storage of cultural heritage and locations on the Perthshire region website.

Interestingly, while on none of the four regional websites are tensions with other cultural currents in the form of battles or fights conveyed through the photographs, they are at the heart of meanings on history construed by process types which can be assigned to the clauses. As mentioned in subsection 2.2, Chapter 2, differences between language and image have been identified. These have been related to their cognitive and communicative potential, stressing that the advantages of language manifest in the domain of semantic flexibility, while the advantages of images are related to perception and associations. Thus, users do not perceive photographs on historical conflicts. Rather, coherent text passages deal with historical conflicts, while photographs are devoted to the representation of cultural heritage sights in landscapes. One may infer from this observation that certain modes of communication, such as photographs or coherent text passages, may lend themselves to conveying certain types of meanings. In fact, in future research, the question of the relationship between taboo topics and certain modes of communication requires further investigation in larger collections of tourist promotional material. More specifically, all four regional websites have in common that they address events and heritage sights. Yet, they do so to varying degrees. The groups and clauses on the Zadar and Istria region websites are predominantly devoted to the representation of cultural influences on and conflict history of the regions. In contrast to the Zadar and Istria region websites, on the Orkney and Perthshire region websites, less space is devoted to various cultural influences. Rather, more attention is given to diverse events in a more holistic way. On the Orkney region website, this covers battles, the building of sights, the death of historic figures, business developments, settlements, and natural phenomena. On the Perthshire region website, this relates to the history of electricity generation for factory purposes, religious movements, seismic events, and archaeological discoveries. In addition, the Zadar and Orkney region websites share meanings on the importance of the regions in terms of architectural and religious sights. Also, history becomes a fusion of facts and imagination on the Perthshire and Orkney region websites. On the Perthshire region website, it is based on appeals to users' imaginations through references to website producers as storytellers, historical anecdotes as denoting fame, industrial sights as sources of knowledge about electricity generation for factory purposes. Thus, historical figures and events are represented as abstruse and enigmatic. The Orkney region website appeals to users' imaginations, curiosity and nostalgic emotions. Furthermore, on the Istria region website, users obtain information on the agricultural, religious, and professional preoccupations of prehistoric people and the political, architectural, and economic reactions of towns to diverse cultural influences. Thus, due to the use of coherent text passages, rather than a timeline of past events, there is a focus on the relationships between these bits of information in a semantically more coherent way. On the Perthshire region website, in addition to diverse tourist activities, historical signifiers revolve around the landscape as a site of historical figures, including royal, military, literary, and religious figures.

It follows from this that history is constructed as a static site of heritage sights and cultural currents on the Zadar region website, as indicated by relational-attributive processes as the most frequently occurring, and material process as the second most frequent process type; a series of diverse events, sights, and genealogy culture on the Orkney region website, as supported by the clear predominance of material processes over relational-attributive as the second most frequent process type; a sequence of periods of history on the Istria region website, as suggested by the high frequency of material processes and relational-identifying as the second most frequent process type; and a story about historical figures, events, landscapes and sights on the Perthshire region website, as denoted by the clear predominance of material processes in concert with mental processes as the second most frequent process type.

Moreover, as initially assumed, realistic representations of history and heritage are constructed for all four regional websites. Similarly to the representation of natural heritage, the clear predominance of definite verbal statements, the exclusive use of definite visual statements, the dearth of modality features, and the lack of comment adjuncts and comments support this reading.

In terms of users as cultural tourists, it has been hypothesized that all visuals on the four regional websites offer factual information. This hypothesis can be confirmed. Hence, heritage sights, or aspects of them, and landscapes are portrayed as objects for user attention, observation, and admiration. This is indicated by the lack of human or quasi-human participants directly gazing at users. Furthermore, the Orkney region website positions users as more immediate explorers of a wealth of sights in North-Atlantic landscapes. This is suggested by eye-level angles and interplays between frontal and oblique angles. The Zadar region website positions users as observers of Central Mediterranean landscapes and the variety of sights in them. This is indicated by high angles and interplays between frontal angles and oblique angles. This is not the case with the Istria region website which tends to invite users to more closely experience sights and observe locations in an involved way in the natural environment. This is suggested by the predominant use of closer range, interplays at eye-level, and high angles as well as frontal and oblique angles. On the Perthshire region website, users are constructed as visitors to public institutions for the display and storage of cultural heritage sights, as achieved by the predominance of medium range, frontal angles and eye-level angles.

With regard to user address or involvement as cultural tourists in groups, phrases, and clauses, the initial hypotheses can be confirmed and further refined: the Zadar and Istria region websites exclusively or predominantly make statements about the experiential meanings identified above. This is suggested by the declarative mood and bits of information in groups. By contrast, in addition to making statements about the experiential meanings identified in the process types above, the Orkney region website directly addresses users as discoverers of family history and naval or cultural heritage sights. This is suggested by second person pronouns and the imperative mood. On the Perthshire region website, the above-delineated mythification of history through experiential meanings is equally expressed interpersonally by assigning cultural practices to users which engage various human senses: exploring historic events and sights as visitors to public institutions for the display and storage of heritage, listening to narratives, and reviving past events through users' mental images. This is indicated by a wealth of instances of the imperative mood and second person pronoun.

Finally, media interaction is less frequent than inaccessibility on all four websites, as initially hypothesized. Thus, all websites coincide in that they offer users the possibility of activating links on cultural sights or archaeological sites through rollover and mouse click or mouse click. In addition, the Orkney region website engages users as media actors on family history. The Istria and Zadar region websites involve users as media actors on regional history. The Perthshire region website offers users the possibility of contributing to meaning-making on natural attractions. Yet, less conventional elements and resources – which could have more actively engaged users in the creation of meanings on regional and family history and natural attractions – are not used further. Hence, an image of users as individual readers and observers of and scanners through tourist promotional material, rather than social actors in the social media, is constructed.

Representation, and cultural tourist and user communication thus interact to distance users as readers of the history of cultural influences and to position them as observers of sights and Mediterranean landscapes on the Zadar region website; to invite users' interested engagement with cultural and natural sites on the Orkney region website; to create educational distance where users figure as learners about periods of history on the Istria region website; and to construct users as participants in the mythification of history on the Perthshire region website.

4.5 Gastronomy

4.5.1 Traditional Mediterranean or contemporary food and drink?

When it comes to the statistics of representational structures on gastronomy in visuals, for the visuals on the Orkney (100%) and Istria (100%) region websites, exclusively, and on the Zadar (80%) region website, predominantly, conceptual structures can be identified. On the

Perthshire region website, an equal distribution between conceptual (50%) and narrative (50%) representational structures can be noted. Thus, logically, less space is devoted to narrative structures on the Zadar (20%) region website. Yet, the four regional websites differ in that the Zadar and Orkney region websites are predominantly devoted to the portrayal of local crafts and food and drink offers in a simple presentation style. More specifically, on the Zadar region website, these cover Mediterranean food and drink offers, such as seafood, alcoholic liqueur and a selection of cold meats, and a handmade, net-like fabric. This derives from intertextual knowledge that the representational structures in the visuals are coded with certain, rather than other, meanings in other texts. Thus, plain tables and less decoration are commonly presented as evoking notions of the simple. Limited attention is devoted to the manual manufacture of local crafts and the production of Mediterranean food, as realized by narrative processes. On the Orkney region website, food offers include seafood and sweet dishes. Limited space is given to types of media for planning food and drink consumption in dining establishments.

By contrast, for the Istria and Perthshire region websites, more complex food and drink images are constructed. These are informed by anthropological and marketing perspectives. On the Istria region website, this involves a wealth of more unconventional, expensive Mediterranean gourmet offers, served in a more countrylike or simple style and in more rustic and farm style eating and accommodation establishments and wine cellars. This is due to intertextual knowledge that, for instance, notions of the more rural and traditional style and more rustic and farm style eating establishments and places for storing wine are commonly attached to wooden or plain tableware, wooden casks for storing fermented juice of grapes, wooden sticks in a fireplace and a cutlery ironware covered with ashes. Equally, however, they include a festive style of food serving and festive and formal dining establishments. This is due to intertextual knowledge that no quick delivery system of alcohol, such as plastic or ceramic cups, in a fast food establishment for people in a hurry can be observed. This is commonly coded with notions of more informal social gatherings for pleasure and amusement in other texts. Rather, the following series of signifiers is commonly coded with notions of the more formal and fine: drinking vessels with more delicate (as more easily breakable) glass material and a more refined shape of glass for enjoyment; an uplifted posture of a hand holding a truffle; the dropping of a small quantity of liquid out of the neck of a bottle; and an eating establishment with a sit down option, and careful table setting with napkins and precise arrangement of cutlery and glasses on the table. The gastronomic image is further based on the relationship of Mediterranean gourmet offers to their natural environment. This encompasses the presentation of truffles on the ground and cultural types of landscapes related to grape and olive cultivation. For the Perthshire region website, both narrative structures on experiencing agricultural markets and alcoholic beverage-tasting situations, and conceptual structures on the advertising of food and drink offers in eating establishments, in general, can be identified.

Moving from visuals to groups, phrases, and clauses, the gastronomic and crafts image for the Zadar region website does not construct a convenient food society opting for processed, mass-produced food offers in a fast lifestyle. Rather, it is clearly orientated towards a traditional, natural, and healthy Mediterranean diet and way of life. This is indicated through reference to the way of food preparation and manufacture of products, their locations of origins and availability, typical food combinations, a certain dietary regime, food quality, and food consumption behaviour. Figure 4.21 gives an overview of statistics of experiential meanings on gastronomy in clauses for the four regional websites.

More specifically, experiential meanings are predominantly realized by material (55.17%) processes. This is followed by relational-attributive (27.59%) and relational-identifying (11.72%) processes. Least space is devoted to mental (2.07%), verbal (2.07%), and existential (1.38%) processes. No instances of behavioural (0%) process can be identified. Instances (19) of groups and phrases denoting gastronomic offers and crafts can be identified. Interplays between material, relational-attributive, relational-identifying and verbal processes, groups, and phrases are devoted to the portrayal of a cooked or roasted and simple way of preparing Mediterranean food offers and ingredients. These include vegetables, cold meat selections, olive oil, lamb, and cheese. Throughout, there is a particular focus on fishing as part of an established tradition and material heritage as a matter of evidence of the fishing tradition. This is followed by a series of material, relational-attributive, and relational-identifying processes which represent a certain body culture with supposedly crucial effects of slimness. They also characterize food offers and ingredients as beneficial to health and construe references to beneficial health effects of products as a matter of acknowledgement. In addition, these process types interact to present food offers as natural in terms of locations of origins, and plant and animal breeding. The gastronomy is further based on a traditional way of production and storage, and the distinctive flavour of autochthonous crafts, and Mediterranean food and traditional

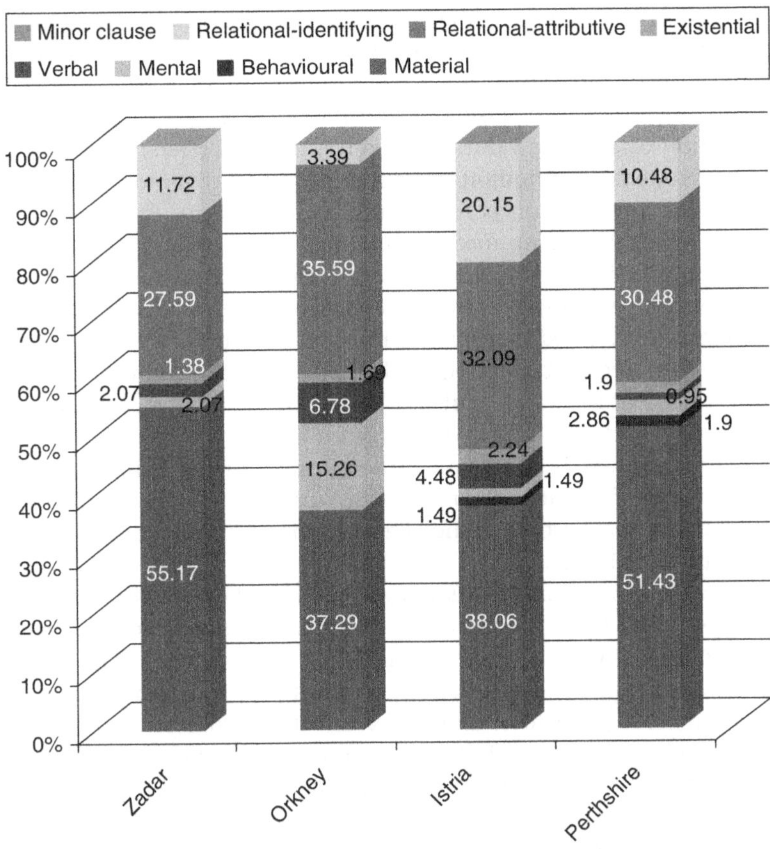

Figure 4.21 Overview of statistics of experiential meanings on gastronomy in clauses for the four regional websites

alcoholic drinks as handiworks or manufactured goods. Sophistication in terms of production phases of crafts and food offers and their marketing, the existence of a wealth of presentation techniques, and forms of products are also crucial to the gastronomic image created for Istria region. These meanings are realized by relational-attributive, verbal, existential, material and relational-identifying processes. Equally, space is given to the compatibility of food and drink offers with one another and typical courses of serving, as accomplished by material and relational-attributive processes. Reference is made to natural, public, and educational locations and diverse times of the availability of craft and public food as a matter of observation. These meanings are realized by material, mental, existential, and relational-attributive processes. A wide scope of public acknowledgement of the quality and popularity of products, product origins, and the wealth of olive trees is construed. In this context, there is a stress on the attribution of precious values to products through reference to the history of product consumption by famous royal and governmental figures. Also, food consumption is represented as a delightful activity. Diverse process types, including material, mental, verbal, relational-attributive and relational-identifying processes, interact to construe these meanings. Occasionally, users learn about their purpose as gifts or souvenirs. The meanings created through the interaction of process types assigned to clauses are equally reflected in the experiential meanings of groups. These represent food and drink as a matter of the art of eating and style of cooking, and food and drink consumption as an artful and refined activity. Also there is a focus on autochthonous offers. This is suggested by examples of Mediterranean food and drink which are referred to in concert with local products and their specific origins in Zadar region in prepositional phrases.

The gastronomic and crafts image on the Orkney region website is not predicated upon Mediterranean food and drink offers as a matter of culinary art in which users with a sense of body culture take pleasure. By contrast, the clauses and groups interact to transfer the preoccupation with plain food and drink into the domain of competitive restaurant business. This is indicated by a similar distribution of relational-attributive (35.59%) and material (37.29%) processes, a wealth of groups and phrases (105 instances), less mental processes (15.26%), even less verbal (6.78%), relational-identifying (3.39%) and existential (1.69%), and no behavioural (0%) processes. Thus, food and drink are conceptualized using places of food consumption, that is, diverse regional eating and commercial establishments as main reference points. This is suggested by a wealth of groups and relational-attributive and relational-identifying processes. Equally, there is a focus on the representation of local substantial and natural agricultural sea products and more refined dishes for consumers of varying degrees of cost-consciousness as food judges. This addresses food from other cultures as manufactured goods which are consumed by users as cultural tourists. Material, verbal, existential, and relational-attributive processes realize these meanings. Also, users have the possibility of performing virtual activities to obtain more information on offers for eating out, as achieved by material processes. Prominent space is further given to relational-attributive processes which, in concert with material, relational-identifying and verbal processes, characterize the reception of customers with professions of kindness, customer service and quality products as signifiers of successful holidays, and construe food assessment. Least space is given to material and mental processes which construe food consumption and the perception of the environment as a matter of recollection and enjoyment.

Similarly to the Zadar region website, but even more pertinently, on the Istria region website, the representation of food and drink is shifted into the area of Epicurean life philosophy. Both in groups and clauses, this centres on artful and dedicated food preparation of more precious, expensive, and less conventional Mediterranean offers, myths about their functions and origins, and delight in food consumption in elevated dining establishments. More precisely, these meanings are predominantly realized by material (38.06%) and relational-attributive (32.09%) processes, a wealth of groups and phrases (213 instances), less by relational-identifying (20.15%) processes, and least by verbal (4.48%), existential (2.24%), mental (1.49%), and behavioural (1.49%) processes. Material, mental, and relational-identifying processes interact to characterize Istrian food preparation as a matter of creativity and emotional attachment, and cooked food preparation, fish, and vegetables as main ingredients and wine vinegar and olive oil as main seasoning. Also, they address eating as an enjoyable and selective activity featuring precious gastronomic offers. Particular attention is devoted to truffles as a more unconventional and expensive food offer. The evaluation of truffles as gourmet food is represented as a matter of consensus among gastronomic experts. As indicated by material, relational-attributive, and relational-identifying processes, they are described in terms of particular features, their quality is positively appreciated, and their preferred eating situations in upscale dining establishments are stressed. More specifically, the groups on more rural and rustic and fine and formal eating establishments, locations and phone numbers as sole contact details give more insight into the nature of representation of Istrian gastronomy. This is tied to more upscale and traditional sit-down dining establishments for higher income tourists seeking refined enjoyment and investing more time in dining. Due emphasis is further placed on the portrayal of wine. Thus, evidence is given about the history of wine transportation through reference to myths about wine cultivation. Natural features and exhausting labour are identified as signifiers of high quality wine sorts through reference to protagonists in myths as tellers of quality wine. Types of wine are described in terms of look, taste and composition, with reference to their wide scope of esteem. These meanings are grammaticalised by material, verbal, existential, and relational-attributive and identifying processes. Importance is also ascribed to the representation of olive oil as a multifunctional asset. Various process types, covering material, mental, verbal, behavioural, existential, relational-attributive and relational-identifying processes, interact to construe these meanings. This asset manifests in its distinctive flavour, compatibility with other gastronomic offers, beneficial health effects, and enjoyability of its consumption. It culminates in the shifting of olive oil and semantically related lexis, including olive tree and olive branch, into the domain of the religious and precious values and Greek and Roman origins. This is achieved through reference to myths as accounts of the development of the olive tree, famous historic literary figures and their works praising olive oil, and olive and clay jug mills as material evidence of the production sites for olive oil. Finally, Istrian gastronomy is construed as a product of conflictual and diverse cultural influences, with consumers of diverse social classes and inhabitants in a series of material, existential, relational-attributive, and identifying processes.

In contrast to the Zadar, Orkney, and Istria region websites, on the Perthshire region website, meanings are organized around tourist attractions, in general, and shopping, gastronomy and events, in particular. The preoccupation with food and drink is developed as a commercial and leisure activity. More specifically, material (51.43%) processes prevail. They are followed by less frequent use of relational-attributive (30.48%) processes, a limited number of groups and phrases (12 instances), and least frequent use of relational-identifying (10.48%), mental (2.86%), behavioural (1.9%), verbal (0.95%), and existential (1.9%) processes. In addition to construing gastronomy as one of many tourist attractions in groups, they deal with the virtual activities of users as media actors on shopping, places for the production of alcoholic beverage, dining establishments, and entertainment in material and mental processes. Furthermore, shopping is represented as the selling and buying of a wealth of cheap local crafts and discounted items at agricultural selling places and places where objects of great and artistic value can be bought as a social business. Also, the Perthshire region website portrays shopping as a health promoting activity to improve the buyer's state of mind, and an indispensible prerequisite for a complete holiday stay. These meanings are accomplished by material, relational-attributive and relational-identifying processes. When it comes to gastronomy, prominent place is devoted to the exploration of gastronomic offers through tastings, fruit picking, and visiting production facilities, with a stress on natural origins and suitable weather conditions.

In this context, the importance of fruit production, and alcoholic beverages and their production facilities is drawn upon. This is achieved by interplays between material, behavioural, verbal, relational-attributive and relational-identifying processes. The website further represents the quality of modern gastronomy and gastronomic expertise through reference to competitive measures, such as customer service, contests, demonstration of gastronomic skills, and press reviews. Material, mental, relational-attributive, and relational-identifying processes interact to construe these meanings. With regard to events, the Perthshire region is constructed as a site for a wealth of more festive and formal events, concert festivities, and music performance. There is a focus on music places as signifiers of new cultural orientations as a matter of enjoyment. This is accomplished by material, mental, existential, relational-attributive, relational-identifying, and existential processes.

As in the clauses on walking activities, natural heritage, and history and heritage, the clauses on gastronomy continue with the predominant representation of verbal propositions as things which simply are. With regard to the statistics of clause types on gastronomy, this is indicated by the frequent use of tensed finite clauses on the Zadar (80%), Orkney (52.54%), Istria (75.37%), and Perthshire (51.43%) region websites. Clauses which are not arguable [on the Zadar (9.66%), on the Orkney (40.68%), on the Istria (12.69%), and on the Perthshire 43.81%)] are less frequent, as indicated by the frequency of non-finite clauses. Least attention is devoted to finite clauses with modality features, covering 10.34% on the Zadar, 6.78% on the Orkney, 11.94% on the Istria, and 4.76% on the Perthshire region websites.

More specifically, intermediate degrees between positive and negative polarity are expressed by a varied use of types of modality on the Zadar region website. Figure 4.22 gives an overview of statistics of modality type in finite clauses on gastronomy for the four regional websites.

Thus, these cover obligation (33.33%) in reference to food tasting, alcoholic beverages, and food storage; readiness: ability (26.67%) in reference to local foods' and crafts' availability and olive tree cultivation in production facilities; usuality (20%) in reference to typical food preparation and the compatibility of crafts to clothing; and probability (20%) in reference to the enjoyment and supposed health effects of Mediterranean food and the identification of crafts as mementos. When it comes to the statistics of value in finite clauses, the website further predominantly makes use of median value modality (40%) in statements about local crafts' and foods' availability, and olive tree cultivation in production facilities. This is followed by high value modality (26.67%)

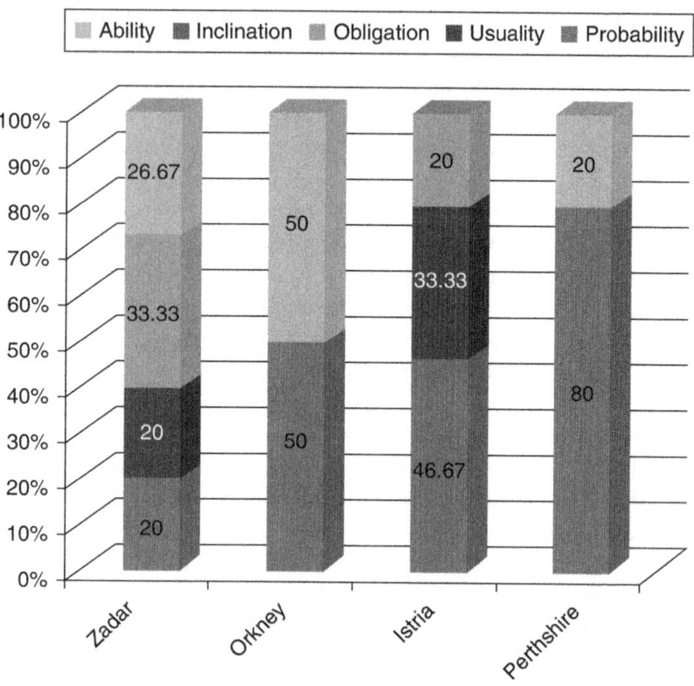

Figure 4.22 Overview of statistics of modality type in finite clauses on gastronomy for the four regional websites

and low value modality (33.33%). High value modality can be identified for propositions about local food tasting, alcoholic beverages, and instructions on food storage. Low value modality relates to propositions about the enjoyment and supposed health effects of Mediterranean food, the identification of crafts as mementos, and the compatibility of lace with clothing. On the Orkney region website, median value modality (75%) can be identified for propositions about food service marketing. These revolve around customer service and quality products as signifiers of successful holidays, online food shopping and virtual activities for further information on dining establishments, and food offers. Low value modality (25%) is restricted to a statement on food enjoyment. Also, an equal distribution of probability (50%) in reference to statements about food service and quality and delightful food consumption and readiness: ability (50%) in propositions about online food shopping and other virtual activities can be noted. On the Istria region website, the distribution of types of modality ranges from probability (46.67%) in relation to statements about cultural influences on the cuisine, cooked and roasted food preparation, and its presentation as noteworthy and distinctive; over usuality (33.33%) in reference to statements about creative food preparation and the enjoyment of typical Mediterranean ingredients as noteworthy activities; to obligation (20%) in reference to propositions about the creative preparation of refined food. A clear privileging of high value modality (53.34%) is noticeable. This relates to propositions about the creative preparation and enjoyment of food and the cultural diversity of Istrian cuisine in favour of median (26.67%) and low (20%) value modality in reference to statements about cooked and roasted food preparation, the classification of truffles by gastronomic experts as the ultimate refined food and the cultural origins of gastronomic offers. On the Perthshire region website, types of modality are limited to probability (80%) in reference to statements about the public availability of agricultural products and types of events as the most frequent type and readiness: ability (20%) in reference to service facilities for further information as the least frequent type. A privileging of median (60%) over low (40%) and high (0%) value modality can be noted in propositions about the public availability of local products, types of events, and service facilities for further information.

Finally, Figure 4.23 gives an overview of statistics of orientation and manifestation in finite clauses on gastronomy for the four regional websites.

It reveals that the Zadar (80%) and Orkney (100%) region websites predominantly or exclusively make use of the implicitly subjective type, as expressed by the frequent use of finites. By contrast, a similar distribution of implicitly subjective (38.89%) and implicitly objective (44.44%) orientation can be identified for the Istria region website, as expressed by modal finites and mood adjuncts. Similarly, the Perthshire region website gives space both to implicitly subjective (40%) and implicitly objective (50%) orientation and manifestation. For two of the websites, the findings gained from the analysis of the clauses on walking activities, natural heritage and history and heritage can thus be confirmed. The subjective viewpoint is foregrounded. No use of comment adjuncts can be noted for the Zadar and Orkney region websites. This is not the case with the Istria region website. The website makes use of the types propositional: asseverative: natural: implicitly objective (one instance), propositional: asseverative: natural: explicitly objective (one instance) and speech-functional: validity: implicitly objective (one instance) in

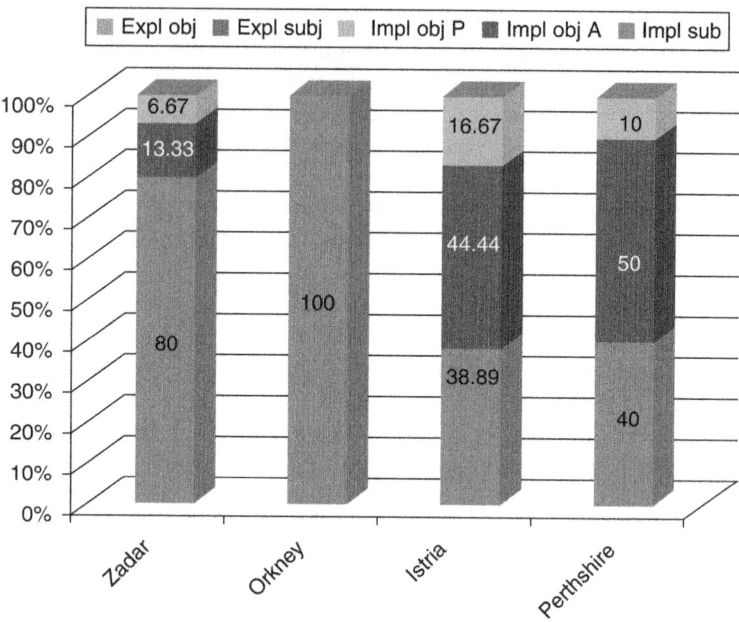

Figure 4.23 Overview of statistics of orientation and manifestation in finite clauses on gastronomy for the four regional websites

reference to statements about Mediterranean food ingredients, quality wine, and the cultivation of olives. Thus, Mediterranean food and drink offers and olive cultivation are represented as essential aspects of Istrian cuisine and self-evident activities of an 'Istrian way of life'. For the Perthshire region website, the following types of comment adjuncts can be identified: propositional: asseverative: obvious: implicitly objective (one instance), propositional: qualificative: prediction: explicitly objective and propositional: qualificative: predication: implicitly objective (two instances) and propositional: presumption: implicitly objective (two instances). These relate to the availability of commercial entities, the wealth and esteemed quality of gastronomic offers and the representation of alcoholic beverages as crucial to Perthshire's gastronomic image as self-evident.

It follows from the above-described predominance of definite verbal statements, median or high value modality, limited use of comment adjuncts and comments in clauses, and exclusive use of photographs as visuals of higher modality (100%) on all four regional websites that more realistic food, drink, and crafts images are constructed for the regional websites.

4.5.2 Admirers of Mediterranean or North-Atlantic food and drink?

In terms of contact, none of the visuals on the four websites present human or quasi-human participants as gazing directly at users; thus no imaginary relationship is established with them. Instead, all of them (100%) offer factual information that has been identified in the analysis of the representational structures assigned to the visuals in sub-subsection 4.5.1. Thus, they are represented as objects of contemplation.

In terms of attitude, the visuals represent photographs which encode a subjective attitude or advertising banners and photographs on eating out guides which encode an objective attitude. Thus, with regard to the statistics of realizations of objective attitude on gastronomy, rather than functioning as knowledge orientation (0%) or action orientation (0%), the advertising banners fulfil the navigation function to route visitors to the official eating and drinking site of Scotland's national tourism organization and the communication function to promote food and drink in Scotland as a part of tourism on the Perthshire (100%) region website. Similarly, on the Orkney (100%) region website, the photograph of a guide to eating out semiotically represents the planning of food and drink consumption in dining establishments, while simultaneously offering users the possibility of activating the photograph. A click on the photograph leads to the opening of a PDF document showing the guide to eating out.

When it comes to subjective attitude and social distance, on all four regional websites, users are exclusively or predominantly positioned in more personal relation to the represented meanings. When it comes to the statistics of realizations of social distance, this is suggested by predominant use of close range – be it in relation to local Mediterranean food and drink offers and fabrics, as on the Zadar (100%) region website; food and drink offers, as on the Orkney (83.33%) region website; more unconventional and expensive Mediterranean gourmet offers and traditional and more refined dining and accommodation establishments, as on the Istria (60%) region website; and the advertising of food and drink in Scotland, in general, and an alcoholic beverage tasting situation, in particular, as on the Perthshire (75%) region website. Less frequently, users are positioned in a more social position in relation to eating and accommodation establishments, food and drink offers and cultural types of landscapes for grape and olive cultivation on the

Istria (40%) region website and types of media for planning food and drink consumption in dining establishments (16.67%) on the Orkney region website. This is suggested by medium range. Less space is given to a more impersonal relationship with Perth's farmers' market on the Perthshire (25%) region website, as realized by long range.

Furthermore, the statistics of realizations of subjective attitude on gastronomy in Figure 4.24 suggest that most websites predominantly involve users with the represented meanings by the privileging of frontal over oblique angles on the Zadar (80%), the Orkney (100%), and the Istria (80%) region websites. An exception to this is provided by the Perthshire region website where an equal distribution of frontal (50%) and oblique angles (50%) can be observed.

Finally, the Zadar (80%) and Orkney (80%) region websites predominantly position users in such a way that they can afford an overview of the represented offers, their manufacture, and agricultural markets as

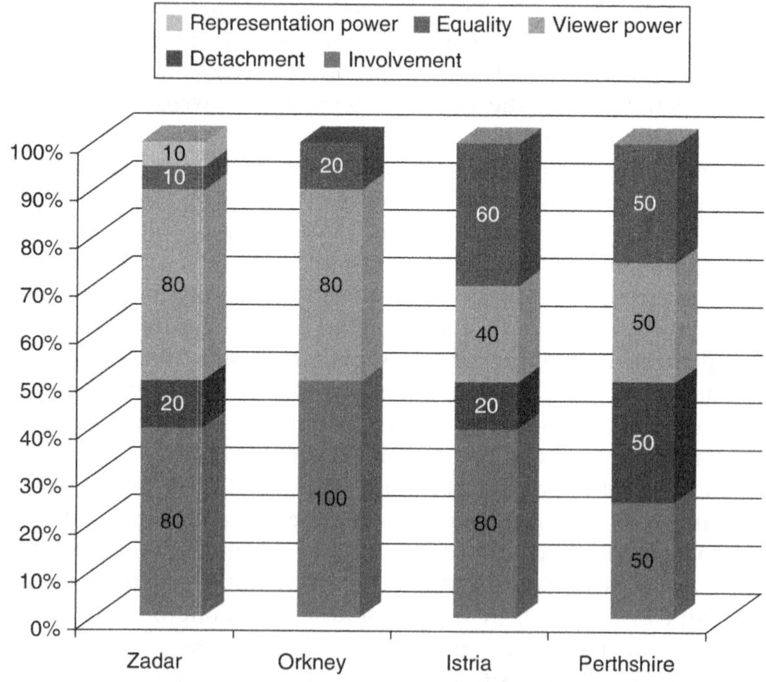

Figure 4.24 Overview of statistics of realizations of subjective attitude on gastronomy on activities for the four regional websites

observers, as indicated by the predominant use of high angles. By contrast, the Istria region website overwhelmingly puts users on an equal footing with the represented Mediterranean gourmet offers, traditional dining and accommodation establishments, and cultural types of grape and wine cultivation (60%). This is suggested by eye-level angles. For the Perthshire region website, an equal distribution between viewer power in relation to agricultural markets (50%) and equality in relation to alcoholic beverage tasting (50%) can be identified.

These choices of camera angle and size of frame position users in certain ways. Thus, they are invited to become interested in the look of food ingredients, dishes, and local crafts on all four regional websites. In addition, they are positioned as explorers of the landscapes in which food is cultivated and the establishments where gastronomic offers are served on the Istria region website. By contrast, they figure as observers of alcoholic beverage tasting and agricultural markets on the Perthshire region website.

In this sense, with regard to units of user address as cultural tourists on gastronomy, all four regional websites use more units which do not than units which do directly address or involve users as cultural tourists: 95.45% can be identified for the Zadar, 87.27% for the Orkney, 94.23% for the Istria, and 77.78% for the Perthshire region website. Accordingly, the four websites predominantly make statements about the experiential meanings identified in the process types assigned to the clauses in sub-subsection 4.5.1, as indicated by the declarative mood, or offer bits of information in groups and phrases. Limited space is devoted to directly addressing users as cultural tourists on the Zadar (4.55%), Orkney (12.73%), Istria (5.77%), and Perthshire (22.22%) region websites.

Thus, on the Zadar region website, instances of addressing users as cultural tourists on gastronomy are limited to a clause which draws them into the multimodal exchange of information on the promotion of a certain type of body culture. This is achieved by a first person plural pronoun (one instance). Users therefore figure as health-conscious food consumers.

The Istria region website gives space to clauses which address users as gourmet food enjoyers whose gustatory and olfactory sense systems are affected, and food nostalgists. This is suggested by second person pronouns (four instances) in the declarative mood. Also, users are involved in the multimodal exchange of information on the historical and cultural function of the olive tree and myths about wine cultivation. More specifically, they are aligned with the perception of olive oil as an asset and wine as quality wine. Furthermore, they are involved as enquirers about the conceptualization of Istrian gastronomy as being marked by diverse cultural currents and social groups of food consumers. This is realized by first person plural pronouns (two instances) in the declarative mood, the interrogative mood (seven instances) and a persuasive comment adjunct in the imperative mood (one instance). Thus, users are constructed as food bon vivants of an Epicurean type and more active participants in the construction of gastronomic myths and cultural influences on gastronomy.

In contrast to the Zadar region website, the clauses on the Orkney region website involve users as demanding judges of gastronomic offers and service and product quality, and online food shoppers. Moreover, users are addressed as tasters who take pleasure in more refined food and alcoholic beverages, and altruistic and nostalgic consumers of substantial, natural agricultural and sea products. These meanings are realized by the interrogative (two instances) and imperative (12 instances) moods and first (two instances) and second person (seven instances) pronouns. Users are thus created as more contemporary food customers and experimental food tasters in competitive markets.

Finally, the Perthshire region website refers to users as travellers for both leisure and commercial purposes. Thus, they are addressed as amused and social buyers in excess, or compulsive shoppers in a wealth of cheap shops, social tasters of enjoyable agricultural food and alcoholic beverages, visitors to gastronomic markets and production facilities, fruit gatherers, and participants in events. This is realized by frequent use of the imperative mood (11 instances) and second person pronouns (six instances) and a dearth of the interrogative mood (one instance).

4.5.3 Individual or technologically advanced social actors?

In terms of the statistics of units with accessible and inaccessible elements on gastronomy, the Zadar region website engages users least (12.12%) and has a higher percentage of units with inaccessible elements (87.88%). This is followed by an increase of units with accessible elements (31.82%) on the Perthshire region website in relation to inaccessible elements (68.18%). By contrast, for the Orkney region website, more accessible (68.52%) than inaccessible (31.48%) elements can be identified. Users are most engaged on the Istria region website, with 75.21% of units with accessible elements and 24.79% with inaccessible elements.

Moreover, in terms of types of user actions, the Zadar region website exclusively makes use of instances of mouse click (100%). Users can activate internal links dealing with further information on food and drink offers and autochthonous crafts. Also, the possibility of users becoming active as media actors is not verbally indicated. Thus, on the Zadar region website, users figure as more traditional readers of or scanners through tourist promotional text passages. On the Orkney region website, types of user actions cover instances of rollover and mouse click (97.37%) and mouse click (2.63%) on gastronomy. More specifically, media interaction is made more salient through verbal indication (one instance). This is indicated by click in the imperative mood in click here to download guide. Users are offered the possibility of activating a wealth of external links and a guide. Thus, they are addressed as media actors on dining establishments, in addition to admirers of food and drink offers and skimmers of text passages. On the Istria region website, types of user actions embrace rollover and mouse click (88.64%), mouse click (10.23%), and type in (1.14%). Users have the possibility of contributing to the construction of meanings on a range of dining establishments through activation of external links, and on Istrian gastronomy through activation of internal links, thus becoming more media active. Media interaction is equally verbally indicated (one instance). This is indicated by search in the imperative mood. Hence, the website engages users as seekers of additional information on Istrian gastronomy and selectors of places of food and drink, while simultaneously privileging the user's sight through visuals and text passages. On the Perthshire region website, users can activate elements through rollover and mouse click (71.43%) and mouse click (28.57%). No instances can be identified which engage users through mouse click and movement (0%). As with the Orkney and Istria region websites, the possibility of users interacting with elements as media actors is equally verbally suggested (11 instances). This is indicated by select, click, check and search in imperative mood in select Perthshire from the 'search by area' drop down menu (four times), click here to search the visitscotland.com database for shopping, check the box for Scotland at Work, search the visitscotland.com database for whisky distilleries, click the link to search the database for a list of eating out establishments, click here to search the visitscotland.com database for eating and drinking establishments, don't forget to check the events database for a list of what's happening and where and click here to search the visitscotland.com database for information on entertainment. Users have the further possibility of activating external links and advertising banners. These more actively engage them as media actors on a set of commercial, leisure, and food activities. At the same time, they construct users as advertising consumers as well as readers of tourist texts and observers of visuals.

4.5.4 Food and drink connoisseurs or consumers?

In terms of the nature of representation, as initially assumed, food and drink and local crafts are represented as revolving around indigenous seafood and craft offers on the Zadar region website; food and drink from local sources on the Orkney region website; refined Mediterranean food and wine for users as food bon vivants on the Istria region website; and benefiting from food and drink as one of many possible activities in the Perthshire region, such as shopping and participating in events, on the Perthshire region website. At the same time, however, if taking a look at the visuals, groups, phrases and clauses in a more detailed way, there is more to the nature of representations of food, drink, and crafts construed for the four regions.

Thus, all four regional websites are dominated by conceptual structures which can be assigned to the visuals. Yet, while the Zadar and Orkney region websites focus on the portrayal of simple local food and drink products and crafts, the gastronomic images constructed for the Istria and Perthshire region websites are more complex, in that they are based on aspects of a food anthropology and food marketing. On the Istria region website, these include natural food cultivation, and traditional preparation and consumption of Mediterranean gourmet food in both rustic and formal places. On the Perthshire region website, they cover the advertising of food and drink offers, in general, and alcoholic beverage tasting in places for their production or agricultural food selling places, in particular. These food and drink images are further complemented by a more varied image, as accomplished by groups, phrases and process types which can be attributed to clauses. Thus, all four regional websites are coded with notions of quality and enjoyment or tastiness. Furthermore, the Orkney and Perthshire region websites shift the preoccupation with local and foreign food offers and drink and crafts into the domain of business activities. By contrast, the Zadar and Istria region websites are preoccupied with the presentation of traditional Mediterranean cuisine. At the same time, however, the four regional websites differ in terms of gastronomic images. On the Zadar region website, a gastronomic image is constructed which is based on a traditional, natural, and healthy Mediterranean diet, culinary tradition, and way of life, as indicated by a clear predominance of material processes. Thus, autochthonous and high quality food and drink consumption is predominantly construed as an artful, precious, and refined activity and one that outlines distinctiveness of flavour and make-up and wide scope of popularity. In addition, the image draws on a range of eating establishments, a cooked or roasted and simple way of

Mediterranean food preparation, and traditional production methods and food storage. Space is further given to the compatibility of food and drink offers with one another, their beneficial health effects and a slim body culture, and their places and times of availability. Throughout, there is a focus on fishing and olive cultivation as established practices. On the Orkney region website, gastronomy becomes a matter of competitive restaurant business, as predominantly achieved by a similar distribution of material and relational-attributive processes. More specifically, there is a focus on a range of eating establishments and the preoccupation with food and drink as a business activity. This revolves around service quality promises by producers for substantial and natural sea-farmed products and more refined consumers of varying degrees of cost consciousness. On the Istria region website, gastronomy is steeped in the area of Epicurean life philosophy, as achieved by a similar distribution of material and relational-attributive processes. More precisely, a gastronomic image is construed which is based on dining establishments for gourmet cuisine influenced by diverse cultural currents. Food preparation is further represented as a highly sophisticated and creative task and food consumption as a matter of refined enjoyment. Due emphasis is placed on the study of aspects of wine and winemaking and grapevine and olive growing as significant and established practices for gastronomic, religious, and health reasons. On the Perthshire region website, a co-occurrence between benefiting from food and drink offers, on the one hand, and other tourist activities, on the other hand, contributes to the representation of eating and drinking as a commercial and leisure activity. This is predominantly accomplished by material processes. Thus, meanings on gastronomy cover fruit production, agricultural markets and selling places, and alcoholic beverages and places of their production. Meanings on other tourist activities relate to sightseeing, business activities in commercial establishments, social entertainment activities of a more festive and formal type, and music entertainment.

Furthermore, as was initially hypothesized, the findings gained from the analysis of modality in the walking activities, natural heritage and history, and heritage subsections can equally be confirmed for the arguability of clauses on gastronomy. Realistic representations in the virtual world are promised to users.

Moving from representation to cultural tourist communication, the initially-formulated hypothesis that the visuals on the websites do not demand users to enter into an imaginary relationship with them can be confirmed. Rather, they offer factual information on the experiential meanings identified in sub-subsection 4.5.1 as objects of user observation and contemplation. This is due to the lack of human or quasi-human participants whose gazes cross with users'. In addition, with regard to social distance and attitude, users are constructed as admirers or close observers of Mediterranean and North-Atlantic food and drink offers and local crafts on the four regional websites. This is achieved by directing the user to look closely at these products, as indicated by close range, frontal angles and high angles. At the same time, on the Istria region website, users figure as more immediate explorers or observers of landscapes for food and drink cultivation. This is achieved by medium range, frontal angles and eye-level angles. On the Perthshire region website, users are further positioned as more distant observers of places of food and drink availability, as suggested by long range, frontal angles and high angles. Also, they are positioned as close observers of alcoholic drink tasting situations, as realized by close range, oblique angles and eye-level angles.

The hypotheses that limited direct address of users as cultural tourists can be noted for the Zadar and more direct address can be observed for the Perthshire region website can be confirmed. Yet, the hypotheses that limited direct address can be noted for the Istria region and more direct address obtains for the Orkney region website cannot be confirmed for thematic meanings on food and drink. More specifically, the Zadar and Orkney region websites focus more on statements about experiential meanings identified in the process types in sub-subsection 4.5.1. This is suggested by predominant use of the declarative mood. Equally, they give least or less space to the involvement or address of users as cultural tourists. On the Zadar region website, instances are limited to their inclusion as health-conscious food consumers, as accomplished by the interrogative mood. On the Orkney region website, examples include their address as food customers and social enjoyers of both refined and substantial food, as achieved by the imperative mood and second person pronouns. By contrast, more or most attention is devoted to the address of users as cultural tourists on the Istria and Perthshire region websites. This is suggested by the wealth of instances of imperative and interrogative moods and first and second person pronouns. Thus, the Istria region website addresses users as Mediterranean food bon vivants and curious learners about myths on Mediterranean gourmet food and their cultural influences. The Perthshire region website addresses users as business customers in the sense of social consumers of products, explorers of places for food and drink selling and production, and participants in events.

Finally, in terms of user communication, the hypothesis that, to a limited extent, users are engaged as media actors on all four regional websites can be confirmed for the Zadar and Perthshire region websites, but not for the Orkney and Istria region websites. More precisely, while the former two websites offer more units with inaccessible than accessible elements, on the latter two websites, the situation is reversed. Yet, the type of user constructed for the four regional websites is still one who can be regarded as an individual and less a technologically versed user than a technologically advanced social actor. This is suggested by several aspects: less variety of types of user actions, covering rollover and mouse click or mouse click; and the lack of elements capturing more post-conventional thematic meanings, such as cooking competition videos or feedback forms to be filled in by dining establishment visitors. Yet, differences in thematic meanings contribute to the construction of different user profiles. Thus, the Zadar region website conceives of users as more traditional readers of and scanners through tourist promotional material. This is indicated by the exclusive possibility of activating links on more general information on food and drink and the region. The Orkney and the Istria region websites create users both as traditional perceivers of tourist promotional material, as if reading static material, and virtual selectors of food and drink and places of their consumption and cultivation. On the Orkney region website, this is expressed by links to eating establishments, and types of media on food and drink. On the Istria region website, this is suggested by links to food and drink offers, dining and accommodation establishments, and cultural types of landscapes. The Perthshire region website construes users as readers and observers of tourist texts, culturally active tourists, in general, and consumers of food and drink advertising campaigns, in particular. This is achieved by links to activities, shopping, dining establishments, and entertainment, and by advertising banners on eating in Scotland.

It follows from the interplay between representation and cultural tourist and user communication that users figure as more traditional Mediterranean food and drink connoisseurs experiencing food anthropology as an Epicurean life philosophy on the Zadar and Istria region websites. By contrast, on the Orkney and Perthshire region websites, they are created as more contemporary food and drink consumers for commercial and leisure purposes whose expectations need to be fulfilled in a competitive food business market.

5 Conclusion

5.1 Main findings

This book has been devoted to the analysis of the ways in which meaning is made in multimodal texts through case studies of Croatian and Scottish tourism websites. First insights into meaning-making in tourism texts have suggested that meaning-making is an active and complex process. Meanings are constructed through the development of meaning dimensions of verbal and graphical elements on the basis of the following parameters: prominent perceptual features of elements which are represented on web pages, as indicated by salience and framing; users' knowledge (genre, intertextual, and cultural) of which meanings are commonly assigned to which constellations of elements in other texts; and types of user actions. Accordingly, tourism websites constitute dynamic texts. It follows from this that tourism websites fulfil the communicative purposes of *representation* and *cultural tourist* and *user communication*. More specifically, tourism web pages as meaning potentials in the virtual world *represent* diverse thematic meanings, as captured by diverse elements and resources. These can be thought of as tourist activities practiced by users as *cultural tourists* in the social world. At the same time, the user's role as a cultural tourist is conflated with their role as a media actor. More precisely, users ascribe meanings to elements on tourism web pages as *media actors* through various types of user actions.

These initial insights into meaning-making have raised four core research questions: To what extent are cultural fields of tourist activities as tourist themes important for the images constructed for the regions, and for users as cultural tourists and media actors? Which thematic meanings are represented and in what ways are they represented? In what ways are users addressed or involved as cultural tourists? In what ways are users engaged as media actors? In response, the theories of systemic functional linguistics and social semiotics have served as starting points for reflecting on and exploring these research questions. This leads us to the role and power of the distinct kinds of analyses set out. In terms of the validity of the results of these kinds of analyses, it needs to be said that the graphs used in the empirical website analysis have not been subjected to standard significance tests, that is, various statistical methods to check whether the results are statistically valid. This would have gone beyond the scope of this book. Nevertheless, the results demonstrate how the different kinds of analysis performed can work to pull apart the communicative stances of websites.

In brief, the empirical analysis of websites has given insight into the functioning of multimodal texts as well as the cultural dimensions of interplays between semiotic resources in multimodal texts; that is, how representation and cultural tourist and user communication interact to construct different tourist profiles. The analysis has proved that the complex analytical toolkit developed in Chapter 2 led to the identification of tourist profiles. With regard to the degree of importance of thematic meanings for representation and cultural tourist and user communication, empirical analysis has suggested that the salience, framing, and positioning of layout units tells us more about the degree of importance of thematic meanings for representation and cultural tourist and user communication. When it comes to representation, empirical analysis has revealed that representational structures assigned to visuals, groups, phrases, and process types assigned to clauses, clause types, the value of modality in finite clauses and visuals, and the type and orientation of modality in finite clauses gives insight into the nature of representation of tourist activities. In terms of cultural tourist communication, empirical analysis has indicated that the system of contact in visuals tells us something about whether images either demand something from users if human or quasi-human participants are represented as gazing at the user, or offer something to users if there is an absence of gaze at the user. Furthermore, the analysis has revealed that the interaction of the systems of attitude and social distance in visuals gives insight into users' different types of personal relations to the experiential meanings expressed by the visuals. Also, it has suggested that the choice of mood in clauses gives insight into the different types of tourists which are addressed or involved, and the different activities which are practiced. Finally, in terms of user communication, the analysis has revealed that the accessibility of elements, the variety in the use of types of user actions, the degree of salience of media interaction, and the address of thematic meanings tell us more about the types of users constructed as media actors. In addition, as a by-product of the analysis, future research into larger collections of travel texts may explore whether the repetitive occurrence of certain process types to construe certain meanings and modality features are more random observations or characteristic features of tourism websites as travel texts.

The core research questions, in turn, have allowed for the formulation of initial hypotheses, most of which have been confirmed and complemented by more detailed discoveries. More specifically, the analysis of the homepages has revealed that the following thematic meanings are of most importance for representation and cultural tourist and user communication on the four regional websites: landscapes, activities, cultural heritage, and gastronomy on the Zadar region website; landscapes, types of media, contact, shopping, and weather information on the Orkney region website; landscapes, accommodation, the social experience of the environment, types of events, and locations on the Istria region website; and activities, events, natural heritage, and conference tourism on the Perthshire region website.

Furthermore, the nature of representation of activities, in general, and walking, in particular, as realized by representational structures assigned to visuals, groups, phrases, and process types assigned to clauses, clause types, the value of modality in finite clauses and visuals, and the type and orientation of modality in finite clauses, has been identified. The findings have revealed that, on the Zadar and Istria region websites, the representation of activities is based on the following meaning patterns: the portrayal of a wealth of outdoor sports activities as an enjoyable social activity in a variety of Mediterranean sea- and adjacent landscapes under welcoming weather conditions; rich sports and trekking infrastructure; and a wealth of trekking paths and their characterization in terms of popularity, attractiveness, conditions and quality, beneficial health effects, trekking duration, and locations. In addition, the Istria region website places due emphasis on notions of professionalism through reference to the possibility of high quality and all-season training for professional sportspeople in an untouched landscape environment. By contrast, on the Orkney region website, there is a focus on the look of the vast and calm North-Atlantic landscape; the location of subregions for walking; the social and virtual experience of the practice of diverse sports activities; the wealth of walking paths; the importance for walking for the overall holiday stay; and safety instructions on responsible behaviour in the environment. The Perthshire region website constructs a more complex image of activities for Perthshire. It does so by presenting more dynamic and adventurous sports activities in various attractive or popular landscapes and recreational areas as one of several possible tourist activities in Perthshire. At the same time, it presents walking infrastructure in terms of paths, housing, information services, and responsible behaviour in the environment. All four regional websites tend to construct more realistic tourist experiences for users as media actors, rather than creating space for argument and negotiation. Thus, they suggest that the potential customer expectation of what is promised on the websites to users as media actors in the virtual world is satisfied for users as cultural tourists in the social world. Also, as a by-product of the analysis, the repetitive occurrence of certain process types to construe certain meanings and modality features may point to characteristic features of tourism websites as travel texts. These cover the following findings: a more descriptive nature of texts on walking and sports infrastructure on some websites, as realized by the predominance of relational-attributive processes on the Zadar region website or interplays between relational-attributive and material processes on the Istria region website; the stressing of the practice of sports activities on other websites, as indicated by the wealth of material processes on the Orkney and Perthshire region websites; and the focus on the speaker's own point of view, as suggested by the predominant use of implicitly subjective modality in terms of the orientation of modality on most of the websites. Thus, future research into larger collections of travel texts may explore whether these findings are more random observations or can be seen as a characteristic feature of the register or text type *travel texts*.

When it comes to cultural tourist communication, as indicated by the system of contact in visuals, none of the four regional websites asks users to enter into an imaginary relationship with the represented meanings, but offers factual information on the above-delineated bits of information on the nature of representation of activities. Differences and similarities between the websites can be noted with regard to meanings construed through the interaction of the systems of attitude and social distance in visuals and mood in clauses. Thus, the Zadar and Istria region websites construct users as sports-lovers in diverse, calm sea- and landscape regions. The Orkney region website addresses users as active and responsible sportspeople taking pleasure in diverse North-Atlantic sea- and landscapes and walking subregions in a more involved way, or observing them in a more detached way. The Perthshire region website involves users as more versatile tourists in the sense of dynamic and responsible sportspeople undertaking more adventurous outdoor activities, nature-lovers, and explorers of cultural sights and gastronomic production facilities.

Due to less accessibility of elements through media interaction, less variety in the use of elements and types of user actions, limited salience of media interaction and the representation of more conventional thematic meanings on sports activities and sports infrastructure, all four regional websites construct users as more traditional activity-seeking tourists and less contemporary activity-creating social actors in terms of user communication.

Natural heritage is further represented as revolving around the existence of plantlife and the location and appeal of landscapes, environmental protection awareness, and the touristic concept of hunting tourism on the Zadar region website. On the Orkney region website, natural heritage is portrayed as covering plant and animal life, and their behaviour, features, habitats, and observation by tourists. The Istria region website concentrates more on the protection of the natural environment, in general, and the seascape, in particular, its exploration by visitors, and the representation of natural heritage as pristine and attractive. The Perthshire region website outlines walking activities and the importance of the landscape as an attractive site for animals, tourists, and public events.

As with thematic meanings on activities and walking, realistic representations of natural heritage can be confirmed for the four regional websites. Also, bits of factual information on the above-delineated meanings are offered to users as objects for observation on all four regional websites. Users are further positioned as animal- and landscape-lovers or close observers of landscapes on the Zadar and Orkney region websites. They are constructed more as distant landscape observers or explorers on the Istria and Perthshire region websites. Also, the Istria region website addresses users as emotional and nostalgic travellers through Mediterranean sea- and adjacent landscapes and locations, and visitors of cultural heritage sights. By contrast, the Orkney region website involves them as explorers of animal behaviour and diverse sources of information on this. The Perthshire region website addresses users as explorers and enjoyers of animal life and nature, and dynamic walkers in green landscapes.

As with the thematic meanings on activities, users are presented more as individual and less technologically versed, rather than more technologically skilled social media actors. More specifically, media interaction is limited to types of landscapes and organizations for the protection of animal life.

Moving to history and heritage, there are repetitive patterns on all four regional websites which revolve around the portrayal of a wealth of events and important, widely known, and attractive cultural heritage sights, artefacts, and/or geographical locations. At the same time, the four regional websites differ in their representation of history and heritage. Thus, history and heritage are depicted as encompassing religious sights in the Mediterranean landscape and their anchorage in terms of time and place information, tensions with other cultural currents, the history of settlement development, and the political, artistic, and cultural significance of the region on the Zadar region website. The Orkney region website captures a wider scope of historical events. These cover thematic meanings on tensions, the construction of sights, the death of figures, business activities, settlements and natural phenomena, and Orkney as a site of family history. In addition to embedding the portrayal of history in calls for users' imagination, curiosity, and nostalgia, the website stresses the architecture of heritage sights. Similarly to the Zadar region website, the architectural construction of the region and cultural influences on and conflict history of the region are equally the topic of history and heritage, as portrayed on the Istria region website. In addition, however, users obtain information on historical contexts and inhabitants through reference to the reactions of towns to diverse cultural influences and the preoccupations of prehistoric people. History and heritage are introduced in concert with other thematic meanings, such as natural heritage and shopping, and presented as important and glorious on the Perthshire region website. More specifically, the history and heritage image constructed is based on diverse types of heritage sights, the significance of the landscape as a site of historical figures, and diverse historical events, with a particular focus on seismic events. Also, gastronomic offers are represented as revivers of history; and, similarly to the Orkney region website, appeals to users' imaginations – which contribute to the construction of historical figures and events as abstruse and enigmatic – can be identified. Similar to the thematic meanings on walking activities, the choice of process types to construe certain meanings may point to characteristic features of tourism websites and complement the characteristic lexical items, principles, and themes which construe the register of tourism. This was introduced in subsection 1.2, Chapter 1. Again, the occurrence of several text functions can be noted. Thus, the Perthshire region website is more about storytelling, as suggested by the frequent use of material and mental processes. The Zadar region website represents more descriptive texts, as expressed by the wealth of relational-attributive processes. The Orkney and Istria region websites combine descriptive with narrative features, as achieved by both material and relational-attributive or relational-identifying processes. Similar to the thematic meanings on walking activities, thematic meanings on history and heritage, as realized by these process types, are represented as indisputable facts.

Cultural tourist communication is repeatedly realized through reference to bits of factual information as objects for user observation on all four regional websites. Furthermore, the Zadar and Orkney region websites create users as both immediate explorers or observers of the look of sights in landscapes, while the Istria and Perthshire region websites construct users more as close explorers of landscapes, or public institutions for the display and storage of cultural heritage sights. The Orkney region website further address users as explorers of family history and cultural heritage sights. The Perthshire region website additionally involves users as participants in the mythification of history.

While, similarly to thematic meanings on activities and natural heritage, a traditional image for users as less technologically advanced readers of and scanners through tourist promotional material is construed in terms of user communication on history and heritage, differences between thematic meanings captured by accessible elements can be observed for the four regional websites. The Istria and Zadar region websites focus more on regional history. The Orkney region website gives space to family history. The Perthshire region website deals with natural attractions. All websites coincide in that they offer users the possibility of interacting with links on cultural heritage sights or archaeological sites.

When it comes to the nature of representation of gastronomy, on the Zadar and Istria region websites, food becomes a matter of refined and health-conscious enjoyment of traditional food and drink offers. On the Zadar region website, this is supported by the following signifiers of gastronomy: artful, precious, and refined consumption of indigenous and high quality food, drink, and crafts, with a focus on seafood, characteristics of food in terms of flavour, make-up and popularity, eating establishments, cooked or roasted and simple Mediterranean food preparation, simple presentation styles of crafts, the compatibility of food and drink offers with one another and their beneficial health effects, and local and public places of availability of offers. On the Istria region website, attention is devoted to the following signifiers: more rustic and formal dining establishments for culturally diverse gourmet cuisine, sophistication and creativity in food preparation, enjoyment of food consumption, high quality wine and olive cultivation as established practices, and the positive appreciation of the multifunctional role of olives for gastronomic, health, and religious reasons. These signifiers of gastronomy differ from the Orkney and Perthshire region websites which focus more on food and crafts businesses. Thus, the Orkney region website outlines the preoccupation with both refined and more substantial, local food and food from other cultures as a business activity, and gives more space to a range of eating establishments. The Perthshire region website deals more with the representation of food and drink consumption as one of several commercial and entertainment activities. Thus, there is a focus on the following meanings: fruit production, agricultural markets, and local selling points of crafts and gastronomic offers; alcoholic beverages and their places of production and consumption; the advertising of food and drink consumption in Scotland; shopping in commercial establishments; and a wealth of more festive and formal nightlife entertainment options. The websites predominantly focus on the representation of propositions about gastronomy as pieces of factual information. It follows from this that, rather than 'coming into crisis', naturalism is flourishing as an integral part of tourism representations on activities, natural heritage, history and heritage, and gastronomy.

Cultural tourist communication is further accomplished by factual information on the above-delineated bits of information as objects of user observation and attention on all four regional websites. In addition, the Zadar, Orkney, and Istria region websites position users more as admirers of Mediterranean and North-Atlantic gastronomic offers and crafts. Moreover, the hitherto-identified tendency to highlight food enjoyment for an elevated consumption group on the Zadar region website, and food business for customers on the Orkney region websites is equally reflected in the address of users as cultural tourists. Thus, the Zadar region website involves users as explorers of slim body culture, while the Orkney region website addresses users as social food enjoyers and judges of food quality. The Perthshire region website affords users an overview of places of food and drink availability and alcoholic drink tasting situations, and addresses users as business customers and explorers of places of food and drink availability and production. The Istria region website invites users to become Mediterranean food *bon vivants*, curious learners about myths on Istria's culturally diverse cuisine and more immediate explorers of landscapes for food and drink cultivation.

Similarly to thematic meanings on activities, natural heritage and history and heritage, the limited space devoted to users as media actors contributes to their construction more as individual and less technically versed users than technological advanced social actors. Yet, differences between the four websites can be identified in terms of thematic meanings addressed, as indicated by the corresponding links and advertising banners. These contribute to the construction of the following user profiles: traditional types of tourists as observers of and scanners through tourist promotional material on local food, drink, and crafts on the Zadar region website; both traditional tourists and virtual selectors of food and drink and places of their consumption and cultivation on the Orkney and Istria region websites; and culturally active tourists and consumers of food and drink advertising campaigns, in addition to traditional observers of tourist promotional material, on the Perthshire region website.

5.2 What next?

The above-delineated findings trigger a series of questions and point to directions for future research on the functioning of meaning-making in promotional texts for scientific, business, and didactic purposes. With regard to scientific purposes, does meaning-making, as explored in promotional websites, generally function through the interaction of representation and cultural tourist and user communication? For instance, one may assume that other socio-cultural contexts, such as the advertising of coffee specialties, function in a similar way. Coffee products and consumers may be represented on websites. Due to genre, intertextual and cultural knowledge, in the social world, coffee drinkers can be thought of as cultural actors in the sense of people who live their private live as careerists, but also indulge in coffee drinks as part of their enjoyment phases in coffee breaks. In the virtual world, users may figure as media actors in the sense of online coffee shoppers who activate corresponding internal and external links or virtual explorers of coffee preparation with new coffee machines who perceive corresponding coffee videos. Moreover, as noted in subsection 2.1, Chapter 2, future research may benefit from studies into the actual reception of web pages by users, using eye tracking as a methodology. Also, particularly when it comes to the meanings captured by intertextual knowledge on thematic meanings, as introduced in subsection 2.2, Chapter 2, research may gain insights from knowledge of the specialized field language. This may give more detailed insights into the nature of representation of thematic meanings. When it comes to business purposes, the analysis of tourism web pages may usefully be complemented by information from the tourist offices and website marketeers responsible for the web pages. A comparison of the above-summarized findings with strategies for the tourist regions may give insight into whether the investigated web pages live up to their intended communicative purposes, as reflected by the replies of the producers. A further question may be: To what extent do web pages exploit their media and interactivity potential? While the findings have pointed to limited exploitation, the updated web page versions of the Zadar region website, for instance, make more use of social media. These offer the possibility of exchanging ideas and creating media content through social media networks, such as Facebook or Twitter. Thus, the creative media agency of users as social actors represents a further strand of future research. Multimodal, rather than monomodal, elements, and their representational and communicative functions may further be of use as resources for the design of websites by website producers and marketeers. Thus, awareness of and knowledge about resources which are used to represent destinations, and address users as cultural tourists and involve them as media actors may enable tourist boards and website designers to design websites for specific target groups. Besides, as suggested in subsection 1.1, Chapter 1, multimodal discourse analysis of hypertexts may be useful for didactic purposes in teaching and learning contexts. More specifically, it may enhance students' writing and literacy achievements, in general, and the acquisition of cultural knowledge and promotion of critical thinking of second language learners – in this work, of Scottish and Croatian – in particular. It follows from this that the study of multimodal texts through representation and cultural tourist and user communication has various uses. It may well be applied to diverse socio-cultural contexts and across text types. It may usefully be complemented by research from diverse disciplines. In brief, it emerges as an innovative and as yet open-ended research field.

Appendices

Appendix A: Navigation and layout

A1. The Zadar region website

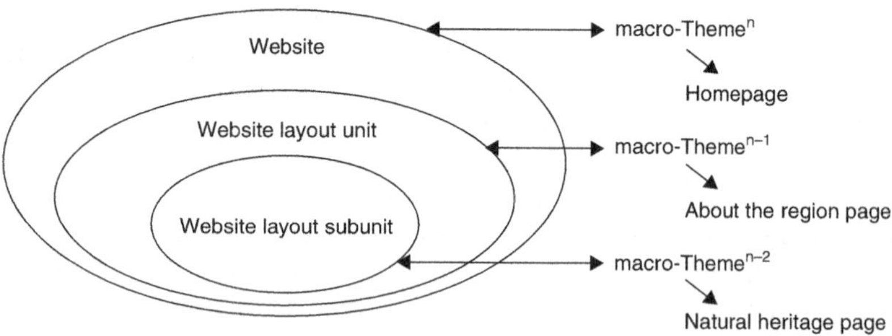

Figure A1.1 Structure of the Zadar region website as a hierarchy of information about the region themes

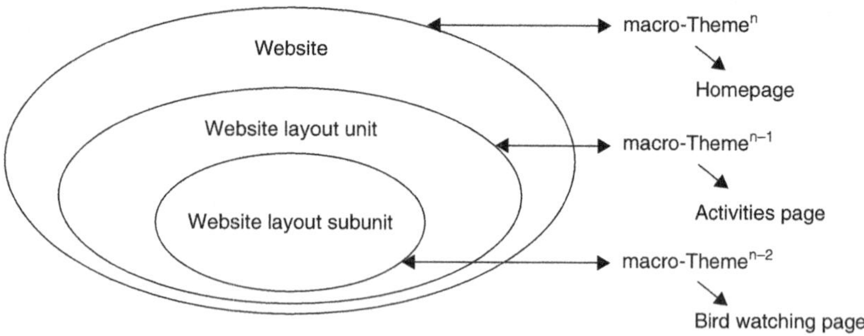

Figure A1.2 Structure of the Zadar region website as a hierarchy of activity themes

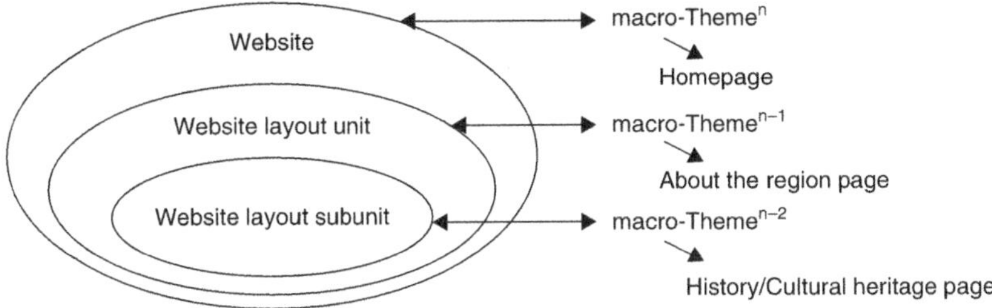

Figure A1.3 Structure of the Zadar region website as a hierarchy of information about the region themes, different figure

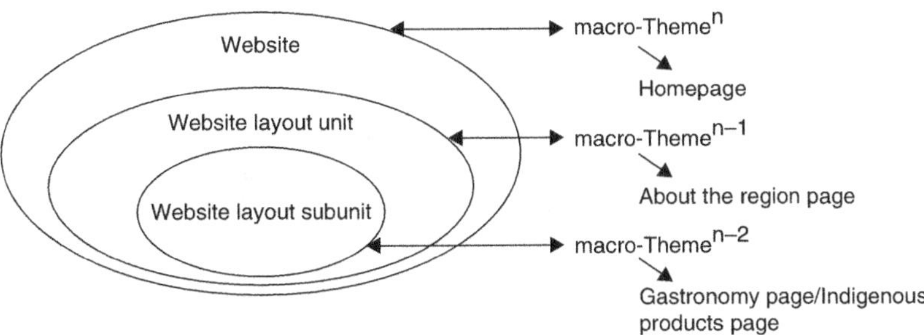

Figure A1.4 Structure of the Zadar region website as a hierarchy of gastronomy themes

A2. The Orkney region website

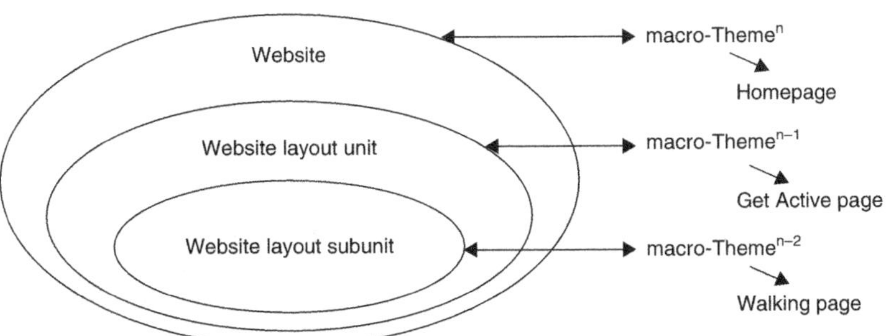

Figure A1.5 Structure of the Orkney region website as a hierarchy of activity themes

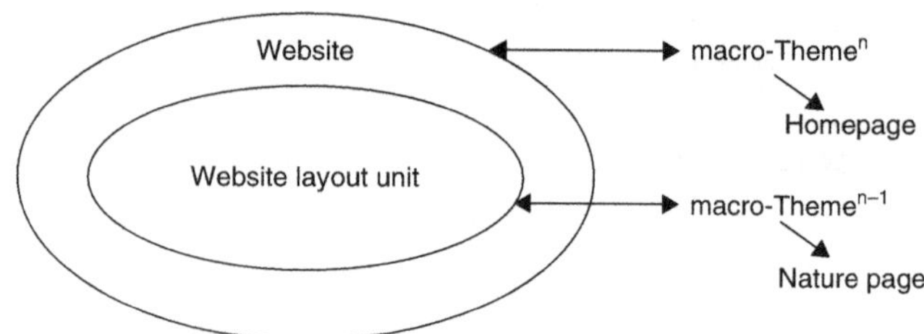

Figure A1.6 Structure of the Orkney region website as a hierarchy of natural heritage themes

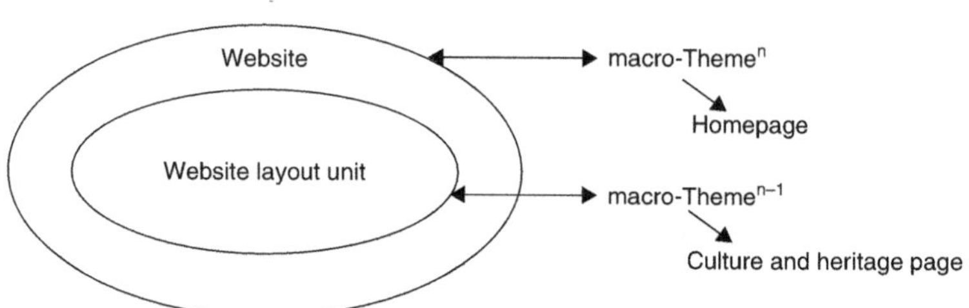

Figure A1.7 Structure of the Orkney region website as a hierarchy of history and heritage themes

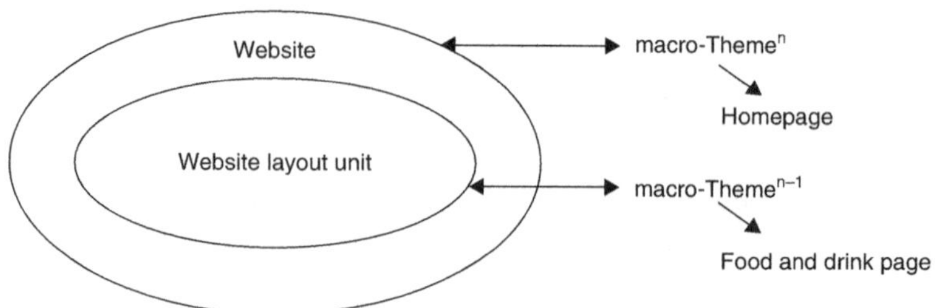

Figure A1.8 Structure of the Orkney region website as a hierarchy of gastronomy themes

A3. The Istria region website

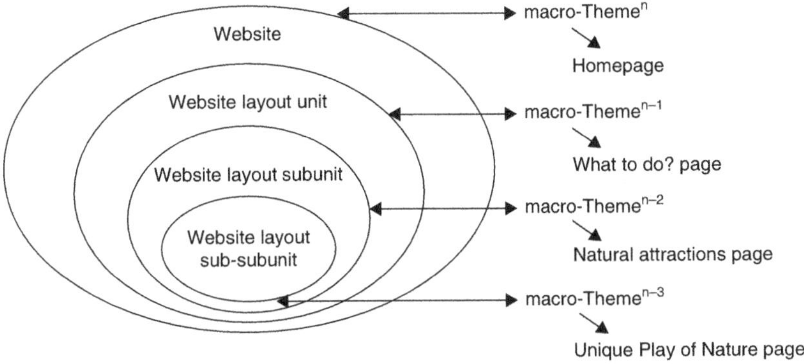

Figure A1.9 Structure of the Istria region website as a hierarchy of activity themes

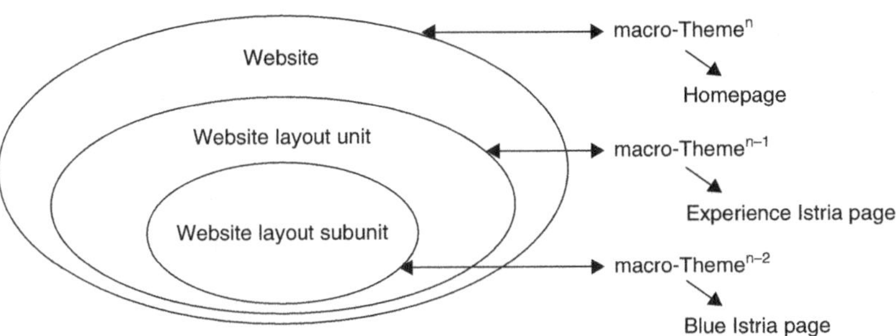

Figure A1.10 Structure of the Istria region website as a hierarchy of experience Istria themes

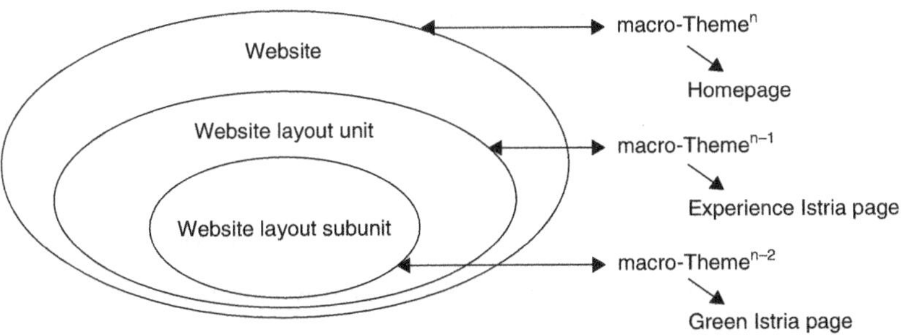

Figure A1.11 Structure of the Istria region website as a hierarchy of experience Istria themes, different figure

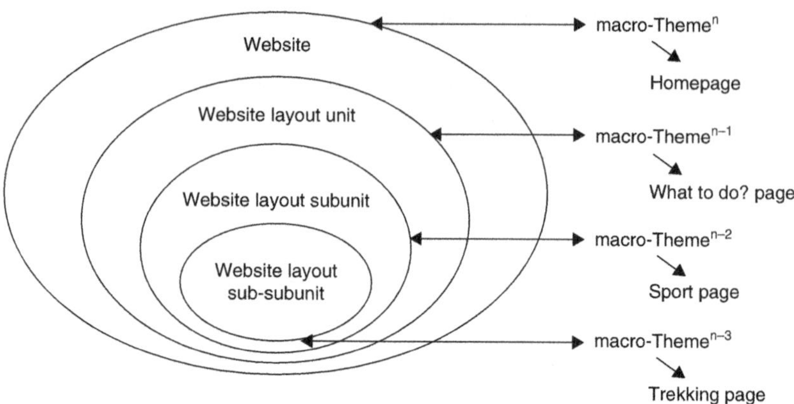

Figure A1.12 Structure of the Istria region website as a hierarchy of activity themes

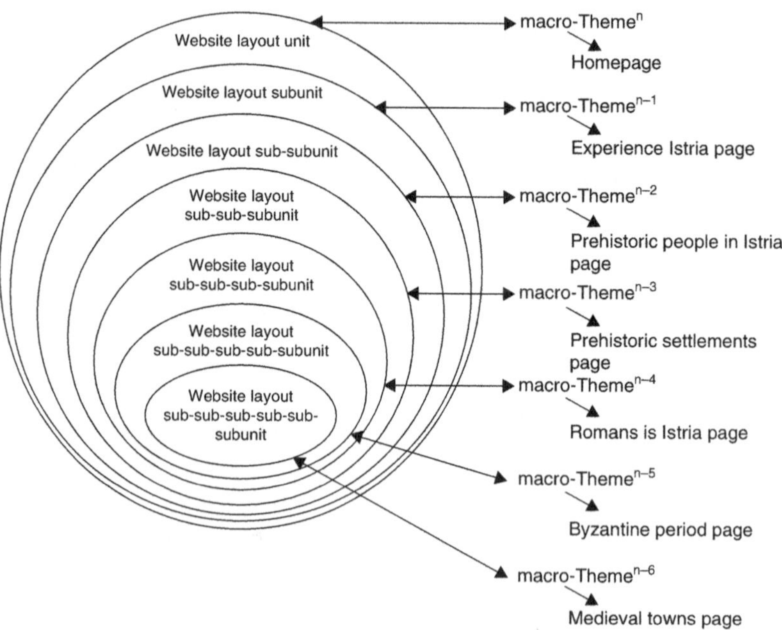

Figure A1.13 Structure of the Istria region website as a hierarchy of history and heritage themes

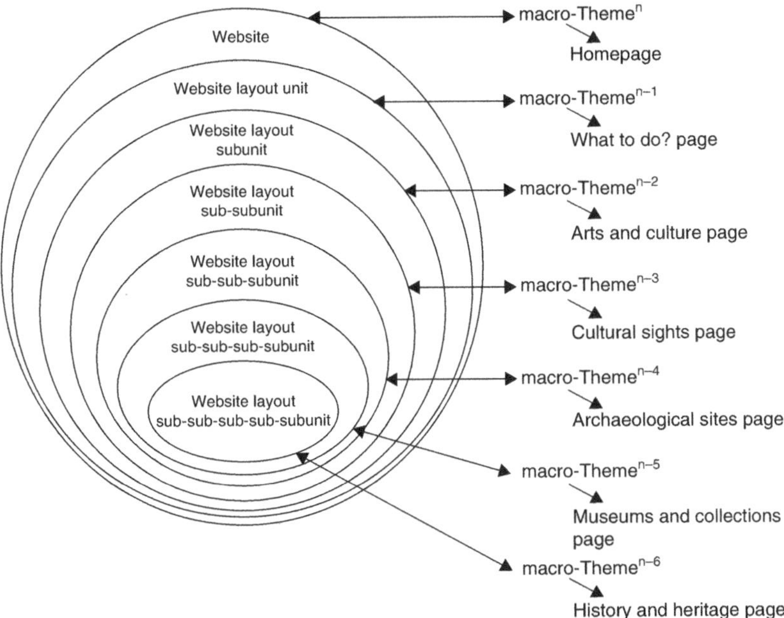

Figure A1.14 Structure of the Istria region website as a hierarchy of history and heritage themes, different figure

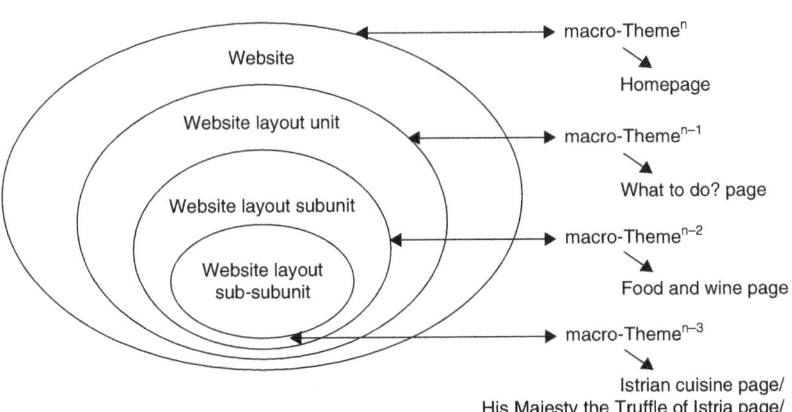

Figure A1.15 Structure of the Istria region website as a hierarchy of activity themes

A4. The Perthshire region website

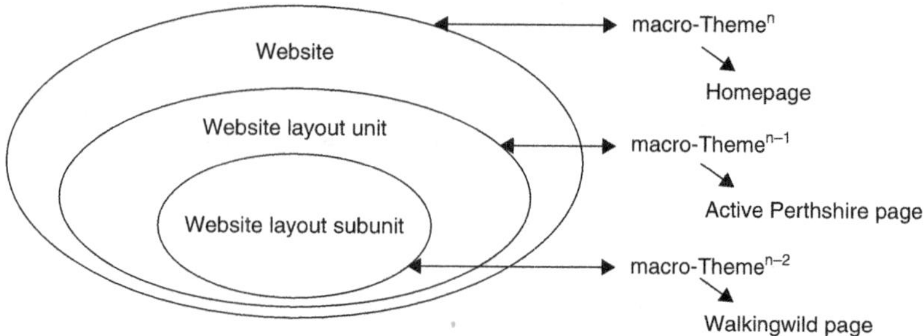

Figure A1.16 Structure of the Perthshire region website as a hierarchy of activity themes

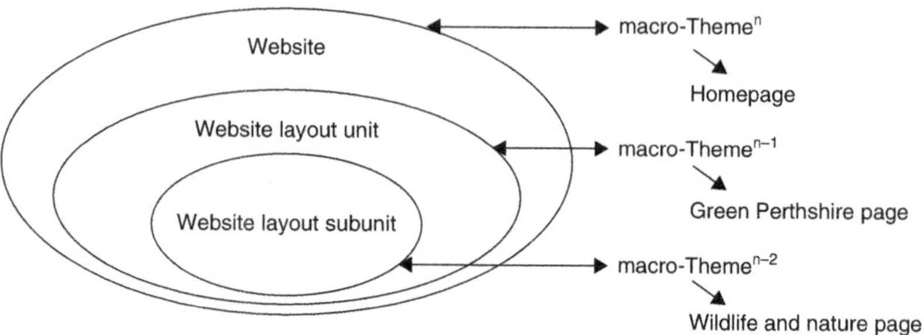

Figure A1.17 Structure of the Perthshire region website as a hierarchy of natural heritage themes

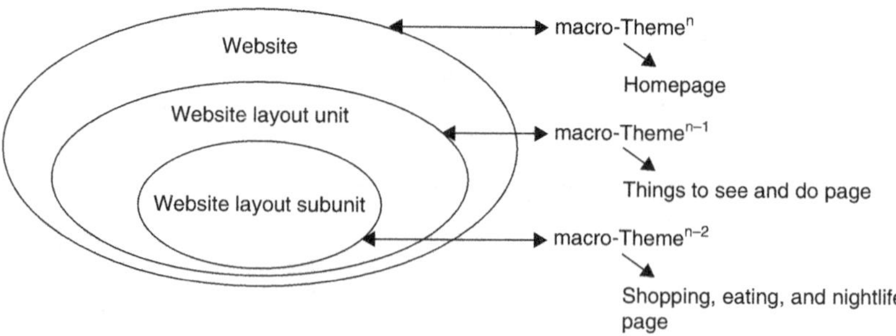

Figure A1.18 Structure of the Perthshire region website as a hierarchy of gastronomy themes

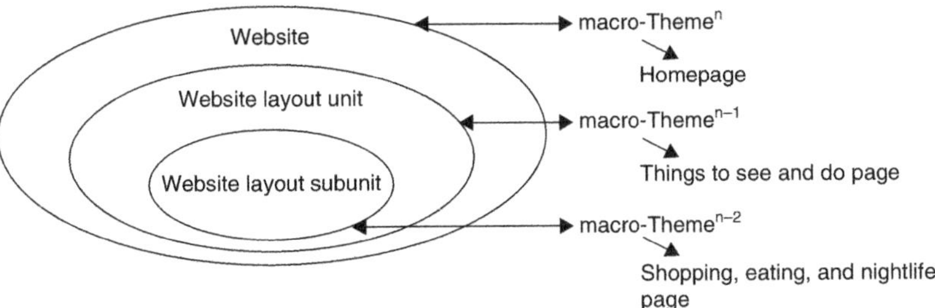

Figure A1.19 Structure of the Perthshire region website as a hierarchy of activities themes

Appendix B: Base Elements

B1. Homepage of the Zadar county website

Table A1.1 Base units of the homepage of the Zadar county website

U001 Bl coloured, haptically and aurally inaccessible
U002 T Hrvatski, responding to mouse click
U003 S vertical, haptically and aurally inaccessible
U004 T English, responding to mouse click
U005 S vertical, haptically and aurally inaccessible
U006 T Deutsch, responding to mouse click
U007 S vertical, haptically and aurally inaccessible
U008 T Français, responding to mouse click
U009 S vertical, haptically and aurally inaccessible
U010 T Italiano, responding to mouse click
U011 T Zadar Region, responding to mouse click
U012 B search, responding to type in
U013 T Google TM, haptically and aurally inaccessible
U014 T Custom Search, haptically and aurally inaccessible
U015 I magnifier, responding to mouse click
U016 S vertical, responding to mouse click
U017 MEI home, responding to mouse click
U018 S vertical, haptically and aurally inaccessible
U019 MEI about the region, responding to mouse click
U020 S vertical, haptically and aurally inaccessible
U021 MEI destinations, responding to mouse click
U022 S vertical, haptically and aurally inaccessible
U023 MEI accommodation, responding to mouse click
U024 S vertical, haptically and aurally inaccessible
U025 MEI activities, responding to mouse click
U026 S vertical, haptically and aurally inaccessible
U027 MEI attractions, responding to mouse click
U028 S vertical, haptically and aurally inaccessible
U029 MEI arrival, responding to mouse click
U030 P landscape, haptically and aurally inaccessible
U031 P sailing, moving, responding to mouse click
U032 B rounded, semirectangle, responding to mouse click
U033 T Activities, responding to mouse click
U034 I arrows, responding to mouse click
U035 B coloured, haptically and aurally inaccessible
U036 S vertical, haptically and aurally inaccessible
U037 T Activities, haptically and aurally inaccessible
U038 T sailing, haptically and aurally inaccessible
U039 T more, responding to mouse click
U040 I arrows, responding to mouse click
U041 P sailing, moving, responding to mouse click
U042 B rounded, semirectangle, responding to mouse click
U043 T Activities, responding to mouse click
U044 I arrows, responding to mouse click
U045 B coloured, haptically and aurally inaccessible
U046 S vertical, haptically and aurally inaccessible
U047 T Activities, haptically and aurally inaccessible
U048 T sailing, haptically and aurally inaccessible
U049 T more, responding to mouse click
U050 I arrows, responding to

mouse click

U051 P paragliding, moving, responding to mouse click

U052 B coloured, semirectangle, responding to mouse click

U053 T Activities, responding to mouse click

U054 I arrows, responding to mouse click

U055 B coloured, haptically and aurally inaccessible

U056 S vertical, haptically and aurally inaccessible

U057 T Activities, haptically and aurally inaccessible

U058 T paragliding, haptically and aurally inaccessible

U059 T more, responding to mouse click

U060 I arrows, responding to mouse click

U061 P diving, moving, responding to mouse click

U062 B coloured, semirectangle, responding to mouse click

U063 T Activities, responding to mouse click

U064 I arrows, responding to mouse click

U065 B coloured, haptically and aurally inaccessible

U066 S vertical, haptically and aurally inaccessible

U067 T Activities, haptically and aurally inaccessible

U068 T diving, haptically and aurally inaccessible

U069 T more, responding to mouse click

U070 I arrows, responding to mouse click

U071 P diving, moving, responding to mouse click

U072 B coloured, semirectangle, responding to mouse click

U073 T Activities, responding to mouse click

U074 I arrows, responding to mouse click

U075 B coloured, haptically and aurally inaccessible

U076 S vertical, haptically and aurally inaccessible

U077 T Activities, haptically and aurally inaccessible

U078 T diving, haptically and aurally inaccessible

U079 T more, responding to mouse click

U080 I arrows, responding to mouse click

U081 P climbing, moving, responding to mouse click

U082 B coloured, semirectangle, responding to mouse click

U083 T Activities, responding to mouse click

U084 I arrows, responding to mouse click

U085 B coloured, haptically and aurally inaccessible

U086 S vertical, haptically and aurally inaccessible

U087 T Activities, haptically and aurally inaccessible

U088 T climbing, haptically and aurally inaccessible

U089 T more, responding to mouse click

U090 I arrows, responding to mouse click

U091 P climbing, moving, responding to mouse click

U092 B coloured, semirectangle, responding to mouse click

U093 T Activities, responding to mouse click

U094 I arrows, responding to mouse click

U095 B coloured, haptically and aurally inaccessible

U096 S vertical, haptically and aurally inaccessible

U097 T Activities, haptically and aurally inaccessible

U098 T climbing, haptically and aurally inaccessible

U099 T more, responding to mouse click

U100 I arrows, responding to mouse click

(continued)

Table A1.1 Continued

U101 P rafting, moving, responding to mouse click	U118 T rafting, haptically and aurally inaccessible	U135 B coloured, haptically and aurally inaccessible
U102 B coloured, semirectangle, responding to mouse click	U119 T more, responding to mouse click	U136 S vertical, haptically and aurally inaccessible
U103 T Activities, responding to mouse click	U120 I arrows, responding to mouse click	U137 T Activities, haptically and aurally inaccessible
U104 I arrows, responding to mouse click	U121 P sport fishing, moving, responding to mouse click	U138 T cycling, haptically and aurally inaccessible
U105 B coloured, haptically and aurally inaccessible	U122 B coloured, semirectangle, responding to mouse click	U139 T more, responding to mouse click
U106 S vertical, haptically and aurally inaccessible	U123 T Activities, responding to mouse click	U140 I arrows, responding to mouse click
U107 T Activities, haptically and aurally inaccessible	U124 I arrows, responding to mouse click	U141 P trekking and mountain-bike trail maps, moving, responding to mouse click
U108 T rafting, haptically and aurally inaccessible	U125 B coloured, haptically and aurally inaccessible	U142 B coloured, semirectangle, responding to mouse click
U109 T more, responding to mouse click	U126 S vertical, haptically and aurally inaccessible	U143 T Activities, responding to mouse click
U110 I arrows, responding to mouse click	U127 T Activities, haptically and aurally inaccessible	U144 I arrows, responding to mouse click
U111 P rafting, moving, responding to mouse click	U128 T sport fishing, haptically and aurally inaccessible	U145 B coloured, haptically and aurally inaccessible
U112 B coloured, semirectangle, responding to mouse click	U129 T more, responding to mouse click	U146 S vertical, haptically and aurally inaccessible
U113 T Activities, responding to mouse click	U130 I arrows, responding to mouse click	U147 T Activities, haptically and aurally inaccessible
U114 I arrows, responding to mouse click	U131 P cycling, moving, responding to mouse click	U148 T recreational sports, haptically and aurally inaccessible
U115 B coloured, haptically and aurally inaccessible	U132 B coloured, semirectangle, responding to mouse click	U149 T more, responding to mouse click
U116 S vertical, haptically and aurally inaccessible	U133 T Activities, responding to mouse click	U150 I arrows, responding to mouse click
U117 T Activities, haptically and aurally inaccessible	U134 I arrows, responding to mouse click	

U151 P recreational sports, moving, responding to mouse click

U152 B coloured, semirectangle, responding to mouse click

U153 T Activities, responding to mouse click

U154 I arrows, responding to mouse click

U155 B coloured, haptically and aurally inaccessible

U156 S vertical, haptically and aurally inaccessible

U157 T Activities, haptically and aurally inaccessible

U158 T recreational sports, haptically and aurally inaccessible

U159 T more, responding to mouse click

U160 I arrows, responding to mouse click

U161 P canyoning, moving, responding to mouse click

U162 B coloured, semirectangle, responding to mouse click

U163 T Activities, responding to mouse click

U164 I arrows, responding to mouse click

U165 B coloured, haptically and aurally inaccessible

U166 S vertical, haptically and aurally inaccessible

U167 T Activities, haptically and aurally inaccessible

U168 T canyoning, haptically and aurally inaccessible

U169 T more, responding to mouse click

U170 I arrows, responding to mouse click

U171 P seakayak, moving, responding to mouse click

U172 B coloured, semirectangle, responding to mouse click

U173 T Activities, responding to mouse click

U174 I arrows, responding to mouse click

U175 B coloured, haptically and aurally inaccessible

U176 S vertical, haptically and aurally inaccessible

U177 T Activities, haptically and aurally inaccessible

U178 T sea kayak, haptically and aurally inaccessible

U179 T more, responding to mouse click

U180 I arrows, responding to mouse click

U181 P bird watching, moving, responding to mouse click

U182 B coloured, semirectangle, responding to mouse click

U183 T Activities, responding to mouse click

U184 I arrows, responding to mouse click

U185 B coloured, haptically and aurally inaccessible

U186 S vertical, haptically and aurally inaccessible

U187 T Activities, haptically and aurally inaccessible

U188 T bird watching, haptically and aurally inaccessible

U189 T more, responding to mouse click

U190 I arrows, responding to mouse click

U191 P riding, moving, responding to mouse click

U192 B coloured, semirectangle, responding to mouse click

U193 T Activities, responding to mouse click

U194 I arrows, responding to mouse click

U195 B coloured, haptically and aurally inaccessible

U196 S vertical, haptically and aurally inaccessible

U197 T Activities, haptically and aurally inaccessible

U198 T riding, haptically and aurally inaccessible

U199 T more, responding to mouse click

U200 I arrows, responding to mouse click

(continued)

Table A1.1 Continued

U201 P jeep safari, moving, responding to mouse click

U202 B coloured, semirectangle, responding to mouse click

U203 T Activities, responding to mouse click

U204 I arrows, responding to mouse click

U205 B coloured, haptically and aurally inaccessible

U206 S vertical, haptically and aurally inaccessible

U207 T Activities, haptically and aurally inaccessible

U208 T jeep safari, haptically and aurally inaccessible

U209 T more, responding to mouse click

U210 I arrows, responding to mouse click

U211 P competitions, moving, responding to mouse click

U212 B coloured, semirectangle, responding to mouse click

U213 T Activities, responding to mouse click

U214 I arrows, responding to mouse click

U215 B coloured, haptically and aurally inaccessible

U216 S vertical, haptically and aurally inaccessible

U217 T Activities, haptically and aurally inaccessible

U218 T competitions, haptically and aurally inaccessible

U219 T more, responding to mouse click

U220 I arrows, responding to mouse click

U221 P paintball, moving, responding to mouse click

U222 B coloured, semirectangle, responding to mouse click

U223 T Activities, responding to mouse click

U224 I arrows, responding to mouse click

U225 B coloured, haptically and aurally inaccessible

U226 S vertical, haptically and aurally inaccessible

U227 T Activities, haptically and aurally inaccessible

U228 T paintball, haptically and aurally inaccessible

U229 T more, responding to mouse click

U230 I arrows, responding to mouse click

U231 P hunt, moving, responding to mouse click

U232 B coloured, semirectangle, responding to mouse click

U233 T Activities, responding to mouse click

U234 I arrows, responding to mouse click

U235 B coloured, haptically and aurally inaccessible

U236 S vertical, haptically and aurally inaccessible

U237 T Activities, haptically and aurally inaccessible

U238 T diving, haptically and aurally inaccessible

U239 T more, responding to mouse click

U240 I arrows, responding to mouse click

U241 S vertical, haptically and aurally inaccessible

U242 T We Recommend, haptically and aurally inaccessible

U243 P national parks, haptically and aurally inaccessible

U244 T Visit, haptically and aurally inaccessible

U245 T more, responding to rollover and mouse click

U246 P cities´ sightseeing, haptically and aurally inaccessible

U247 T Historical, haptically and aurally inaccessible

U248 T more, responding to rollover and mouse click

U249 P cuisine specialties, haptically and aurally inaccessible

U250 T Autochthonous, haptically and aurally inaccessible

U251 T more, responding to

rollover and mouse click	U266 T City Galleria, haptically and aurally inaccessible	U280 T Hotels, haptically and aurally inaccessible
U252 S vertical, haptically and aurally inaccessible	U267 T A place, haptically and aurally inaccessible	U281 T Falkensteiner, responding to rollover and mouse click
U253 T Highlights, haptically and aurally inaccessible	U268 P City Galleria, haptically and aurally inaccessible	U282 S vertical, haptically and aurally inaccessible
U254 P Greeting the Sun, haptically and aurally inaccessible	U269 T paragraph, haptically and aurally inaccessible	U283 T Events, haptically and aurally inaccessible
U255 T Greeting the Sun, haptically and aurally inaccessible	U270 S vertical, haptically and aurally inaccessible	U284 P Events, haptically and aurally inaccessible
U256 T The newest, haptically and aurally inaccessible	U271 T Active Holidays, haptically and aurally inaccessible	U285 T September, haptically and aurally inaccessible
U257 T more, responding to rollover and mouse click	U272 P cycling destination, haptically and aurally inaccessible	U286 T City Lodge, haptically and aurally inaccessible
U258 P Sea Organ, haptically and aurally inaccessible	U273 T paragraph, haptically and aurally inaccessible	U287 T Selection, haptically and aurally inaccessible
U259 T Sea Organ, haptically and aurally inaccessible	U274 P Activities, haptically and aurally inaccessible	U288 T 1. Selection, haptically and aurally inaccessible
U260 T Unique, haptically and aurally inaccessible	U275 T paragraph, haptically and aurally inaccessible	U289 T City Lodge, haptically and aurally inaccessible
U261 T more, responding to rollover and mouse click	U276 T more, responding to rollover and mouse click	U290 T August, haptically and aurally inaccessible
U262 P Gold and Silver, haptically and aurally inaccessible	U277 P Wellness Services, haptically and aurally inaccessible	U291 T 2. Selection, haptically and aurally inaccessible
U263 T Gold and Silver, haptically and aurally inaccessible	U278 T Wellness Services, haptically and aurally inaccessible	U292 T City Lodge, haptically and aurally inaccessible
U264 T Permanent, haptically and aurally inaccessible	U279 T paragraph, haptically and aurally inaccessible	U293 T September, haptically and aurally inaccessible
U265 T more, responding to rollover and mouse click		

(continued)

Table A1.1 Continued

U294 P Zadar Sea, haptically and aurally inaccessible
U295 T 23. October, haptically and aurally inaccessible
U296 T Zadar, haptically and aurally inaccessible
U297 T paragraph, haptically and aurally inaccessible
U298 G vertical, haptically and aurally inaccessible
U299 S vertical, haptically and aurally inaccessible
U300 T County Map, haptically and aurally inaccessible
U301 M County Map, responding to mouse click
U302 D, responding to mouse click
U303 T 1, responding to mouse click
U304 D, responding to mouse click
U305 T2, responding to mouse click
U306 D, responding to mouse click
U307 T3, responding to mouse click
U308 D, responding to mouse click
U309 T4, responding to mouse click
U310 D, responding to mouse click
U311 T5, responding to mouse click
U312 T 1, haptically and aurally inaccessible
U313 S vertical, haptically and aurally inaccessible
U314 T Zadar, responding to rollover and mouse click
U315 T 2, haptically and aurally inaccessible
U316 S vertical, haptically and aurally inaccessible
U317 T Kornati, responding to rollover and mouse click
U318 T 3, haptically and aurally inaccessible
U319 S vertical, haptically and aurally inaccessible
U320 T Telašćica, responding to rollover and mouse click
U321 T 4, haptically and aurally inaccessible
U322 S vertical, haptically and aurally inaccessible
U323 T Velebit, responding to rollover and mouse click
U324 S vertical, haptically and aurally inaccessible
U325 T Towns and, haptically and aurally inaccessible
U326 B white, responding to type in
U327 MA white, responding to mouse click
U328 MEI Banj, responding to mouse click
U329 MEI Barotul, responding to mouse click
U330 MEI Benkovac, responding to mouse click
U331 MEI Bibinje, responding to mouse click
U332 MEI Biograd, responding to mouse click
U333 MEI Bozava, responding to mouse click
U334 MEI Brbinj, responding to mouse click
U335 MEI Brgulje, responding to mouse click
U336 MEI Caska, responding to mouse click
U337 MEI Dinjiska, responding to mouse click
U338 MEI Dobropoljana, responding to mouse click
U339 MEI Gracac, responding to mouse click
U340 MEI Ist, responding to mouse click
U341 MEI Iz, responding to mouse click
U342 MEI Kali, responding to mouse click
U343 MEI Karin, responding to mouse click
U344 MEI Kolan, responding to mouse click
U345 MEI Kosljun, responding to mouse click
U346 MEI Kraj, responding to mouse click
U347 MEI Kukljica, responding to mouse click
U348 MEI Luka, responding to mouse click

U349 MEI Lukoran, responding to mouse click

U350 MEI Mandre, responding to mouse click

U351 MEI Maslenica, responding to mouse click

U352 MEI Viskovici, responding to mouse click

U353 MEI Molat, responding to mouse click

U354 MEI Mrljane, responding to mouse click

U355 MEI Nevidjane, responding to mouse click

U356 MEI Nin, responding to mouse click

U357 MEI Novigrad, responding to mouse click

U358 MEI Obrovac, responding to mouse click

U359 MEI Olib, responding to mouse click

U360 MEI Osljak, responding to mouse click

U361 MEI Pag, responding to mouse click

U362 MEI Pakostane, responding to mouse click

U363 MEI Pasman, responding to mouse click

U364 MEI Petrcane, responding to mouse click

U365 MEI Poljana, responding to mouse click

U366 MEI Posedarje, responding to mouse click

U367 MEI Povljana, responding to mouse click

U368 MEI Preko, responding to mouse click

U369 MEI Premuda Privlaka, responding to mouse click

U370 MEI Razanac, responding to mouse click

U371 MEI Rivanj, responding to mouse click

U372 MEI Rovanjska, responding to mouse click

U373 MEI Sali, responding to mouse click

U374 MEI Savar, responding to mouse click

U375 MEI Seline, responding to mouse click

U376 MEI Sestrunj, responding to mouse click

U377 MEI Silba, responding to mouse click

U378 MEI Simuni, responding to mouse click

U379 MEI Smokvica, responding to mouse click

U380 MEI Soline, responding to mouse click

U381 MEI Starigrad Paklenica, responding to mouse click

U382 MEI Sukosan, responding to mouse click

U383 MEI Sutomiscica, responding to mouse click

U384 MEI Sv. Filip I Jakov, responding to mouse click

U385 MEI Sveti Petar, responding to mouse click

U386 MEI Tkon, responding to mouse click

U387 MEI Tribanj, responding to mouse click

U388 MEI Turanj, responding to mouse click

U389 MEI Ugljan, responding to mouse click

U390 MEI Ugrinic, responding to mouse click

U391 MEI Veli Izr, responding to mouse click

U392 MEI Veli Rat – Verunic, responding to mouse click

U393 MEI Velika Rava, responding to mouse click

U394 MEI Vinjerac, responding to mouse click

U395 MEI Vir Vlasici, responding to mouse click

U396 MEI Vrgada, responding to mouse click

U397 MEI Zadar, responding to mouse click

U398 MEI Zaglav, responding to mouse click

U399 MEI Zapuntel, responding to mouse click

U400 MEI Zaton, responding to mouse click

U401 MEI Zdrelac, responding to mouse click

U402 MEI Zman, responding to mouse click

(continued)

Table A1.1 Continued

U403 MEI Zverinac, responding to mouse click
U404 SCAR grey, responding to rollover and mouse click
U405 SCA grey, responding to rollover and mouse click
U406 SCB grey, responding to mouse click and movement
U407 SCAR arrow, responding to rollover and mouse click
U408 B coloured, responding to mouse click
U409 T search, responding to mouse click
U410 S vertical, haptically and aurally inaccessible
U411 T The World, haptically and aurally inaccessible
U412 B white, responding to type in
U413 MA white, responding to mouse click
U414 T Dugi Otok, responding to mouse click
U415 T Ist, responding to mouse click
U416 T Iz, responding to mouse click
U417 T Kornat, responding to mouse click
U418 T Molat, responding to mouse click
U419 T Olib, responding to mouse click
U420 T Osljak, responding to mouse click
U421 T Pag, responding to mouse click
U422 T Pasman, responding to mouse click
U423 T Premuda, responding to mouse click
U424 T Rava, responding to mouse click
U425 T Rivanj, responding to mouse click
U426 T Sestrunj, responding to mouse click
U427 T Silba, responding to mouse click
U428 T Ugljan, responding to mouse click
U429 T Vir, responding to mouse click
U430 T Vrgada, responding to mouse click
U431 T Zverinac, responding to mouse click
U432 SCAR grey, responding to rollover and mouse click
U433 SCA grey, responding to rollover and mouse click
U434 SCB grey, responding to mouse click and movement
U435 SCAR grey, responding to rollover and mouse click
U436 B coloured, responding to mouse click
U437 T search, responding to mouse click
U438 S vertical, haptically and aurally inaccessible
U439 T Routeplaner [sic.], haptically and aurally inaccessible
U440 P Routeplaner [sic.], responding to mouse click
U441 S vertical, haptically and aurally inaccessible
U442 T Questionnaire, haptically and aurally inaccessible
U443 T paragraph, haptically and aurally inaccessible
U444 MEI circle, responding to mouse click
U445 T nature, responding to mouse click
U446 MEI circle, responding to mouse click
U447 MEI recommendation, responding to mouse click
U448 MEI circle, responding to mouse click
U449 T cultural, responding to mouse click
U450 MEI circle, responding to mouse click
U451 T prices, responding to mouse click
U452 MEI circle, responding to mouse click
U453 T active, responding to mouse click
U454 MEI circle, responding to

mouse click

U455 T other, responding to mouse click

U456 B coloured, responding to mouse click

U457 T results, responding to mouse click

U458 B coloured, responding to mouse click

U459 T vote, responding to mouse click

U460 G vertical, haptically and aurally inaccessible

U461 T weather, haptically and aurally inaccessible

U462 P weather, responding to mouse click

U463 B coloured, responding to mouse click

U464 T www, responding to mouse click

U465 T sea quality, haptically and aurally inaccessible

U466 P sea quality, responding to mouse click

U467 B coloured, responding to mouse click

U468 T www, responding to mouse click

U469 T newsletter, haptically and aurally inaccessible

U470 B white, responding to type in

U471 B coloured, responding to mouse click

U472 T subscribe, responding to mouse click

U473 T News, haptically and aurally inaccessible

U474 T The Newyork, haptically and aurally inaccessible

U475 T paragraph, haptically and aurally inaccessible

U476 T Published, haptically and aurally inaccessible

U477 T Link, responding to rollover and mouse click

U478 T Independent, haptically and aurally inaccessible

U479 T paragraph, haptically and aurally inaccessible

U480 T paragraph, haptically and aurally inaccessible

U481 T Irish, haptically and aurally inaccessible

U482 T May, haptically and aurally inaccessible

U483 T Link, responding to rollover and mouse click

U484 P Ryanair, haptically and aurally inaccessible

U485 T Ryanair, haptically and aurally inaccessible

U486 T more, responding to rollover and mouse click

U487 T Multimedia, haptically and aurally inaccessible

U488 P Multimedia, haptically and aurally inaccessible

U489 T Maps, responding to rollover and mouse click

U490 T Publications, responding to rollover and mouse click

U491 T Guides, responding to rollover and mouse click

U492 B coloured, haptically and aurally inaccessible

U493 T about us, responding to rollover and mouse click

U494 S vertical, haptically and aurally inaccessible

U495 T contact, responding to rollover and mouse click

U496 S vertical, haptically and aurally inaccessible

U497 T home, responding to rollover and mouse click

U498 I copyright, haptically and aurally inaccessible

U499 T Zadar, haptically and aurally inaccessible

U500 T Web , haptically and aurally inaccessible

U501 T Vip-Data, responding to rollover and mouse click

U502 Bl coloured, haptically and aurally inaccessible

AB: advertising banner; B: box; Bl: block; D: drawing; G: grid; I: icon; M: map; P: photograph; S: separator; T: text; Tab: table; MEI: menu item; SCAR: scroll arrow; SCA: scroll area; MA: menu area; SCB: scroll box; V: type of visual.

B2. Homepage of the Orkney region website

Table A1.2 Base units of the homepage of the Orkney region website

U001 P landscape, background, haptically and aurally inaccessible

U002 T Orkney´ s, haptically and aurally inaccessible

U003 MA white, responding to rollover and mouse click

U004 T Home, responding to rollover and mouse click

U005 MA white, responding to rollover and mouse click

U006 T About Orkney, responding to rollover and mouse click

U007 MA white, responding to rollover and mouse click

U008 T Accommodation, responding to rollover and mouse click

U009 MA white, responding to rollover and mouse click

U010 T Getting Here, responding to rollover and mouse click

U011 MA white, responding to rollover and mouse click

U012 T Getting Around, responding to rollover and mouse click

U013 MA white, responding to rollover and mouse click

U014 T Places to Visit, responding to rollover and mouse click

U015 MA white, responding to rollover and mouse click

U016 T Get Active, responding to rollover and mouse click

U017 MA white, responding to rollover and mouse click

U018 T Nature, responding to rollover and mouse click

U019 MA white, responding to rollover and mouse click

U020 T Culture and History, responding to rollover and mouse click

U021 MA white, responding to rollover and mouse click

U022 T Food and Drink, responding to rollover and mouse click

U023 MA white, responding to rollover and mouse click

U024 T Arts and Crafts, responding to rollover and mouse click

U025 MA white, responding to rollover and mouse click

U026 T Children´ s Treasures, responding to rollover and mouse click

U027 P landscape, haptically and aurally inaccessible

U028 D card, haptically and aurally inaccessible

U029 T Your, haptically and aurally inaccessible

U030 T [illegible], haptically and aurally inaccessible

U031 D envelope, haptically and aurally inaccessible

U032 T [illegible], haptically and aurally inaccessible

U033 I flower, haptically and aurally inaccessible

U034 T Live, haptically and aurally inaccessible

U035 T visitscotland.com, haptically and aurally inaccessible

U036 Tab white, haptically and aurally inaccessible

U037 T White, responding to rollover and mouse click

U038 P White Invite, responding to mouse click

U039 T Your, responding to rollover and mouse click

U040 T Monthly, responding to rollover and mouse click

U041 P Monthly Competition, responding to mouse click

U042 T November, responding to rollover and mouse click

U043 T Special Offers, responding to rollover and mouse click

U044 P special offers, responding to mouse click

U045 T See, responding to rollover and mouse click

U046 T Northern, responding to rollover and mouse click
U047 P lights, responding to mouse click
U048 T Orkney´ s, responding to rollover and mouse click
U049 Tab white, haptically and aurally inaccessible
U050 T 2010, haptically and aurally inaccessible
U051 P Orkney, haptically and aurally inaccessible
U052 Tab coloured, haptically and aurally inaccessible
U053 I flower, haptically and aurally inaccessible
U054 T Visit, haptically and aurally inaccessible
U055 T Where, haptically and aurally inaccessible
U056 T Orkney, haptically and aurally inaccessible
U057 T visitorkney.com, haptically and aurally inaccessible
U058 T Request, responding to rollover and mouse click
U059 I English, haptically and aurally inaccessible
U060 T English, responding to rollover and mouse click
U061 I Dutch, haptically and aurally inaccessible
U062 T Dutch, responding to rollover and mouse click
U063 I French, haptically and aurally inaccessible
U064 T French, responding to rollover and mouse click
U065 I German, haptically and aurally inaccessible
U066 T German, responding to rollover and mouse click
U067 I Italian, haptically and aurally inaccessible
U068 T Italian, responding to rollover and mouse click
U069 I Norwegian, haptically and aurally inaccessible
U070 T Norwegian, responding to rollover and mouse click
U071 I Audio, haptically and aurally inaccessible
U072 T Audio, responding to rollover and mouse click
U073 Tab white, haptically and aurally inaccessible
U074 I weather, responding to mouse click
U075 T Weather, responding to rollover and mouse click
U076 T Check, responding to rollover and mouse click
U077 I News, responding to mouse click
U078 T Local, responding to rollover and mouse click
U079 T Keep, responding to rollover and mouse click
U080 I webcam, responding to mouse click
U081 T Live, responding to rollover and mouse click
U082 T Live, responding to rollover and mouse click
U083 I film, responding to mouse click
U084 T Orkney, responding to rollover and mouse click
U085 T 45, responding to rollover and mouse click
U086 Tab white, haptically and aurally inaccessible
U087 T What´s, haptically and aurally inaccessible
U088 P calendar, responding to rollover and mouse click
U089 P November, responding to rollover and mouse click
U090 B coloured, responding to rollover and mouse click
U091 T November, responding to rollover and mouse click
U092 P December, responding to rollover and mouse click
U093 B coloured, responding to rollover and mouse click
U094 T December, responding to rollover and mouse click
U095 P January, responding to rollover and mouse click
U096 B coloured, responding to rollover and mouse click
U097 T January, responding to rollover and mouse click

(continued)

Table A1.2 Continued

U098 P February, responding to rollover and mouse click	U112 T June, responding to rollover and mouse click	U126 I Free, responding to mouse click
U099 B coloured, responding to rollover and mouse click	U113 P July, responding to rollover and mouse click	U127 T Free, responding to rollover and mouse click
U100 T February, responding to rollover and mouse click	U114 B coloured, responding to rollover and mouse click	U128 T Scenic, responding to rollover and mouse click
U101 P March, responding to rollover and mouse click	U115 T July, responding to rollover and mouse click	U129 I Shop, responding to mouse click
U102 B coloured, responding to rollover and mouse click	U116 P August, responding to rollover and mouse click	U130 T Shop, responding to rollover and mouse click
U103 T March, responding to rollover and mouse click	U117 B coloured, responding to rollover and mouse click	U131 T Book, responding to rollover and mouse click
U104 P April, responding to rollover and mouse click	U118 T August, responding to rollover and mouse click	U132 I Contact, responding to mouse click
U105 B coloured, responding to rollover and mouse click	U119 P September, responding to rollover and mouse click	U133 T Contact, responding to rollover and mouse click
U106 T April, responding to rollover and mouse click	U120 B coloured, responding to rollover and mouse click	U134 T For, responding to rollover and mouse click
U107 P May, responding to rollover and mouse click	U121 T September, responding to rollover and mouse click	U135 I Monthly, responding to mouse click
U108 B coloured, responding to rollover and mouse click	U122 P October, responding to rollover and mouse click	U136 T Monthly, responding to rollover and mouse click
U109 T May, responding to rollover and mouse click	U123 B coloured, responding to rollover and mouse click	U137 T Sign, responding to rollover and mouse click
U110 P June, responding to rollover and mouse click	U124 T October, responding to rollover and mouse click	U138 I flower, haptically and aurally inaccessible
U111 B coloured, responding to rollover and mouse click	U125 Tab white, haptically and aurally inaccessible	U139 T Live, haptically and aurally inaccessible
		U140 T visitscotland.com, haptically and aurally inaccessible
		U141 T VisitOrkney, haptically and aurally inaccessible
		U142 T e.info@visitorkney.com, rollover and mouse click

AB: advertising banner; B: box; Bl: block; D: drawing; G: grid; I: icon; M: map; P: photograph; S: separator; T: text; Tab: table; MEI: menu item; SCAR: scroll arrow; SCA: scroll area; MA: menu area; SCB: scroll box; V: type of visual

B3. Homepage of the Istria region website

Table A1.3 Base units of the homepage of the Istria region website

U001 BI coloured, haptically and aurally inaccessible
U002 T Croatia, coloured, responding to mouse click
U003 I Multimedia, responding to mouse click
U004 T Multimedia, responding to mouse click
U005 I Newsletter, responding to mouse click
U006 T Newsletter, responding to mouse click
U007 I Brochures, responding to mouse click
U008 T Brochures, responding to mouse click
U009 I Contact, responding to mouse click
U010 T Contact, responding to mouse click
U011 I PR, responding to mouse click
U012 T PR, responding to mouse click
U013 I Site, responding to mouse click
U014 T Site, responding to mouse click
U015 I RSS, responding to mouse click
U016 T RSS, responding to mouse click
U017 T Hrvatski, responding to rollover and mouse click
U018 T Deutsch, responding to rollover and mouse click
U019 T Italiano, responding to rollover and mouse click
U020 I goat, haptically and aurally inaccessible
U021 T Istra, haptically and aurally inaccessible
U022 P landscape, moving, haptically and aurally inaccessible
U023 P landscape, moving, haptically and aurally inaccessible
U024 P landscape, moving, haptically and aurally inaccessible
U025 P landscape, moving, haptically and aurally inaccessible
U026 I magnifier, responding to mouse click
U027 MEI Find, responding to mouse click
U028 MA white, responding to mouse click
U029 MEI Select, responding to mouse click
U030 SCAR arrow, responding to mouse click
U031 MA white, responding to mouse click
U032 MEI Choose, responding to mouse click
U033 SCAR arrow, responding to mouse click
U034 MA white, responding to mouse click
U035 MEI Hotels, responding to mouse click
U036 SCAR arrow, responding to mouse click
U037 T Arrival, haptically and aurally inaccessible
U038 MA white, responding to mouse click
U039 MEI 29, responding to mouse click
U040 I calendar, responding to mouse click
U041 T Departure, haptically and aurally inaccessible
U042 MA white, responding to mouse click
U043 MEI 1, responding to mouse click
U044 I calendar, responding to mouse click
U045 T Persons, haptically and aurally inaccessible
U046 MA white, responding to mouse click
U047 MEI 1, responding to mouse click
U048 SCAR arrow, responding to mouse click
U049 T Rooms, haptically and aurally inaccessible
U050 MA white, responding to mouse click
U051 MEI 1, responding to mouse click
U052 SCAR arrow, responding to mouse click
U053 MA white, responding to mouse click

(continued)

Table A1.3 Continued

U054 I tick, responding to mouse click

U055 T Online, responding to mouse click

U056 S horizontal, responding to mouse click

U057 B white, responding to mouse click

U058 T Search, responding to mouse click

U059 I house, haptically and aurally inaccessible

U060 T Istra, haptically and aurally inaccessible

U061 S horizontal, haptically and aurally inaccessible

U062 T Site, haptically and aurally inaccessible

U063 B coloured, responding to type in

U064 B coloured, responding to rollover and mouse click

U065 T Search, responding to rollover and mouse click

U066 B coloured, responding to mouse click

U067 I arrow, responding to mouse click

U068 B coloured, haptically and aurally inaccessible

U069 P Experience, responding to mouse click

U070 MA coloured, responding to rollover and mouse click

U071 MEI Experience, responding to rollover and mouse click

U072 MA coloured, responding to rollover and mouse click

U073 MEI About, responding to rollover and mouse click

U074 MEI Where, responding to rollover and mouse click

U075 MEI History, responding to rollover and mouse click

U076 MEI Blue, responding to rollover and mouse click

U077 MEI Green, responding to rollover and mouse click

U078 P Where, responding to mouse click

U079 MA coloured, responding to rollover and mouse click

U080 MEI Where, responding to rollover and mouse click

U081 MA coloured, responding to rollover and mouse click

U082 MEI Regions, responding to rollover and mouse click

U083 MEI Cities, responding to rollover and mouse click

U084 P What, responding to mouse click

U085 MA coloured, responding to rollover and mouse click

U086 MEI What, responding to rollover and mouse click

U087 MA coloured, responding to rollover and mouse click

U088 MEI Coast, responding to rollover and mouse click

U089 MEI Holidays, responding to rollover and mouse click

U090 MEI Arts, responding to rollover and mouse click

U091 MEI Food, responding to rollover and mouse click

U092 MEI Natural, responding to rollover and mouse click

U093 MEI Sport, responding to rollover and mouse click

U094 MEI Children, responding to rollover and mouse click

U095 MEI Wellness, responding to rollover and mouse click

U096 MEI Conventions, responding to rollover and mouse click

U097 MEI Events, responding to rollover and mouse click

U098 P Planning, responding to mouse click

U099 MA coloured, responding to rollover and mouse click

U100 MEI Planning, responding to rollover and mouse click

U101 MA coloured, responding to rollover and mouse click

U102 MEI When, responding to rollover and mouse click

U103 MEI Accommodation, responding to rollover and mouse click

U104 MEI Travel, responding to rollover and mouse click

U105 MEI Nautics, responding to rollover and mouse click

U106 MEI Useful, responding to rollover and mouse click

U107 S horizontal, haptically and aurally inaccessible

U108 Tab coloured, haptically and aurally inaccessible

U109 B coloured, haptically and aurally inaccessible

U110 T Holiday, haptically and aurally inaccessible

U111 P New, responding to mouse click

U112 T New, responding to mouse click

U113 T In, responding to mouse click
U114 B white,
haptically and aurally inaccessible

U115 T New, responding to rollover and mouse click

U116 B coloured, responding to mouse click

U117 I arrow, responding to mouse click
U118 P diving, responding to mouse click
U119 B white, haptically and aurally inaccessible

U120 T Diving, responding to rollover and mouse click

U121 B coloured, responding to mouse click

U122 I arrow, responding to mouse click

U123 P Domus, responding to mouse click

U124 T Domus, haptically and aurally inaccessible

U125 B white, haptically and aurally inaccessible

U126 T Domus, responding to rollover and mouse click

U127 B coloured, responding to mouse click

U128 I arrow, responding to mouse click

U129 P Wellness, responding to mouse click

U130 B white, haptically and aurally inaccessible

U131 T Wellness, responding to rollover and mouse click

U132 B coloured, responding to mouse click

U133 I arrow, responding to mouse click

U134 Tab coloured, haptically and aurally inaccessible

U135 B coloured, haptically and aurally inaccessible
U136 T Links, haptically and aurally inaccessible

U137 M map, responding to mouse click

U138 T Map, responding to rollover and mouse click

U139 P Accommodation, responding to mouse click

U140 T Accommodation, responding to rollover and mouse click

U141 P Blue, responding to mouse click

U142 T Blue, responding to rollover and mouse click

U143 P Green, responding to mouse click

U144 T Green, responding to rollover and mouse click

U145 P When, responding to mouse click
U146 T When, responding

to rollover and mouse click

U147 V Convention, responding to mouse click

U148 T Convention, responding to rollover and mouse click

U149 Tab white, haptically and aurally inaccessible

U150 B coloured, haptically and aurally inaccessible

U151 T What, haptically and aurally inaccessible

U152 P Istria, responding to mouse click

U153 T Istria, responding to rollover and mouse click

(continued)

Table A1.3 Continued

U154 T If, haptically and aurally inaccessible	U172 T Honey, responding to rollover and mouse click	U190 M Croatia, responding to mouse click
U155 T More, responding to rollover and mouse click	U173 T 26, haptically and aurally inaccessible	U191 T Croatia, responding to mouse click
U156 P December, responding to rollover and mouse click	U174 T Pazin, haptically and aurally inaccessible	U192 T Istria, responding to mouse click
U157 T Forum, responding to mouse click	U175 S horizontal, haptically and aurally inaccessible	U193 M Istria, responding to mouse click
U158 T 31, responding to mouse click	U176 T Promohotel, responding to rollover and mouse click	U194 T Istria, responding to mouse click
U159 T Mor´, responding to mouse click	U177 T 24, haptically and aurally inaccessible	U195 Tab coloured, haptically and aurally inaccessible
U160 T December, responding to mouse click	U178 T Poreč, haptically and aurally inaccessible	U196 B coloured, haptically and aurally inaccessible
U161 T The, haptically and aurally inaccessible	U179 S horizontal, haptically and aurally inaccessible	U197 T Search, haptically and aurally inaccessible
U162 T More, responding to rollover and mouse click	U180 T 24, haptically and aurally inaccessible	U198 I magnifier, responding to rollover and mouse click
U163 S horizontal, haptically and aurally inaccessible	U181 T Pazin, responding to rollover and mouse click	U199 M Search, magnified, responding to mouse click
U164 T Rovinj, responding to rollover and mouse click	U182 S horizontal, haptically and aurally inaccessible	U200 M Search, Istria, responding to mouse click
U165 T 28, haptically and aurally inaccessible	U183 T View, responding to rollover and mouse click	U201 M Search, Zagreb, responding to mouse click
U166 T Rovinj, haptically and aurally inaccessible	U184 Tab coloured, haptically and aurally inaccessible	U202 D circle, responding to mouse click
U167 S horizontal, haptically and aurally inaccessible	U185 B coloured, haptically and aurally inaccessible	U203 T Zagreb, responding to mouse click
U168 T Festival, responding to rollover and mouse click	U186 T Where, haptically and aurally inaccessible	U204 M Search, Ljubljana, responding to mouse click
U169 T 06, haptically and aurally inaccessible	U187 M Europe, responding to mouse click	U205 D circle, haptically and aurally inaccessible
U170 T Rakotule, haptically and aurally inaccessible	U188 T Europe, responding to mouse click	U206 T Ljubljana, responding to mouse click
U171 S horizontal, responding to mouse click	U189 T Croatia, responding to mouse click	U207 M Search, Budapest, responding to mouse click

U208 D circle, haptically and aurally inaccessible

U209 T Budapest, responding to mouse click

U210 M Search, Istria, haptically and aurally inaccessible

U211 M Search, Umag, responding to rollover and mouse click

U212 T Umag, haptically and aurally inaccessible

U213 M Search, magnified, haptically and aurally inaccessible

U214 D spot, responding to rollover and mouse click

U215 T Savudrija, responding to mouse click

U216 D spot, responding to rollover and mouse click

U217 T Umag, responding to mouse click

U218 D spot, responding to rollover and mouse click

U219 T Novigrad, responding to mouse click

U220 D responding to rollover and mouse click

U221 T Buje, responding to mouse click

U222 D responding to rollover and mouse click

U223 T Brtonigla, responding to mouse click

U224 M Search, Poreč, haptically and aurally inaccessible

U225 T Poreč, haptically and aurally inaccessible

U226 M Search, magnified, haptically and aurally inaccessible

U227 D spot, responding to rollover and mouse click

U228 T Tar, responding to mouse click

U229 D spot, responding to rollover and mouse click

U230 T Vabriga, responding to mouse click

U231 D spot, responding to rollover and mouse click

U232 T Poreč, responding to mouse click

U233 D spot, responding to rollover and mouse click

U234 T Kaštelir Labinci, responding to mouse click

U235 M Search, Vrsar, responding to rollover and mouse click

U236 T Vrsar, haptically and aurally inaccessible

U237 M Search, magnified, haptically and aurally inaccessible

U238 D spot, responding to rollover and mouse click

U239 T Funtana, responding to mouse click

U240 D spot, responding to rollover and mouse click

U241 T Vrsar, responding to mouse click

U242 M Search, Rovinj, responding to rollover and mouse click

U243 T Search, Rovinj, haptically and aurally inaccessible

U244 M Search, magnified, haptically and aurally inaccessible

U245 D spot, responding to rollover and mouse click

U246 T Rovinj, responding to mouse click

U247 D spot, responding to rollover and mouse click

U248 T Bale, responding to mouse click

U249 D spot, responding to rollover and mouse click

U250 T Kanfanar, responding to mouse click

U251 M Search, Pula, responding to rollover and mouse click

U252 T Search, Pula, haptically and aurally inaccessible

U253 M Search, magnified, haptically and aurally inaccessible

U254 D spot, responding to rollover and mouse click

U255 T Fažana, responding to mouse click

U256 D spot, responding to rollover and mouse click

U257 T Pula, responding to mouse click

(*continued*)

Table A1.3 Continued

U258 D spot, responding to rollover and mouse click	U275 D, responding to rollover and mouse click	U292 D spot, responding to rollover and mouse click
U259 T Medulin, responding to mouse click	U276 T Rabac, responding to mouse click	U293 T Pazin, responding to mouse click
U260 D spot, responding to rollover and mouse click	U277 D, responding to rollover and mouse click	U294 D spot, responding to rollover and mouse click
U261 T Ližnjan, responding to mouse click	U278 T Kršan, responding to mouse click	U295 T Hum, responding to mouse click
U262 D spot, responding to rollover and mouse click	U279 M Search, Central, responding to rollover and mouse click	U296 D spot, responding to rollover and mouse click
U263 T Marčana, responding to mouse click	U280 T Central, responding to rollover and mouse click	U297 T Roč, responding to mouse click
U264 D spot, responding to rollover and mouse click	U281 M Search, magnified, haptically and aurally inaccessible	U298 D spot, responding to rollover and mouse click
U265 T Vodnjan, responding to mouse click	U282 D spot, responding to rollover and mouse click	U299 T Buzet, responding to mouse click
U266 D spot, responding to rollover and mouse click	U283 T Grožnjan, responding to mouse click	U300 D spot, responding to rollover and mouse click
U267 T Barbari, responding to mouse click	U284 D spot, responding to rollover and mouse click	U301 T Motovun, responding to mouse click
U268 M Search, Labin, responding to rollover and mouse click	U285 T Vižinada, responding to mouse click	U302 D spot, responding to rollover and mouse click
U269 T Search, Labin, responding to rollover and mouse click	U286 D spot, responding to rollover and mouse click	U303 T Oprtljaj, responding to mouse click
U270 M Search, magnified, haptically and aurally inaccessible	U287 T Višnjan, responding to mouse click	U304 B White, responding to rollover and mouse click
U271 D spot, responding to rollover and mouse click	U288 D spot, responding to rollover and mouse click	U305 T Show, responding to rollover and mouse click
U272 T Labin, responding to mouse click	U289 T Svetvinčenat, responding to mouse click	U306 M Search, magnified, responding to mouse click
U273 D, responding to rollover and mouse click	U290 D spot, responding to rollover and mouse click	U307 M Search, Istria, responding to mouse click
U274 T Raša, responding to mouse click	U291 T Žminj, responding to mouse click	U308 M Search, Zagreb, responding to mouse click
		U309 D circle, responding to mouse click

U310 T Zagreb, responding to mouse click
U311 M Search, Ljubljana, responding to mouse click
U312 D circle, haptically and aurally inaccessible
U313 T Ljubljana, responding to mouse click
U314 M Search, Budapest, responding to mouse click
U315 D circle, haptically and aurally inaccessible
U316 T Budapest, responding to mouse click
U317 MA White, responding to mouse click
U318 MEI Select, responding to mouse click
U319 SCAR arrow, responding to rollover and mouse click
U320 MA, white, responding to rollover and mouse click
U321 MEI Umag, responding to rollover and mouse click
U322 MEI Poreč, responding to rollover and mouse click
U323 MEI Vrsar, responding to rollover and mouse click
U324 MEI Rovinj, responding to rollover and mouse click
U325 MEI Pula, responding to rollover and mouse click
U326 MEI Labin, responding to rollover and mouse click
U327 MEI Central, responding to rollover and mouse click
U328 MA white, responding to mouse click
U329 MEI Choose, responding to mouse click
U330 SCAR arrow, responding to rollover and mouse click
U331 MA white, responding to rollover and mouse click
U332 MEI Bale, responding to rollover and mouse click
U333 MEI Barban, responding to rollover and mouse click
U334 MEI Brtonigla, responding to rollover and mouse click
U335 MEI Buje, responding to rollover and mouse click
U336 MEI Buzet, responding to rollover and mouse click
U337 MEI Fažana, responding to rollover and mouse click
U338 MEI Funtana, responding to rollover and mouse click
U339 MEI Grožnjan, responding to rollover and mouse click
U340 MEI Hum, responding to rollover and mouse click
U341 MEI Kanfanar, responding to rollover and mouse click
U342 MEI Kaštelir, responding to rollover and mouse click
U343 MEI Kršan, responding to rollover and mouse click
U344 MEI Labin, responding to rollover and mouse click
U345 MEI Labinci, responding to rollover and mouse click
U346 MEI Ližnjan, responding to rollover and mouse click
U347 MEI Marčana, responding to rollover and mouse click
U348 MEI Medulin, responding to rollover and mouse click
U349 MEI Motovun, responding to rollover and mouse click
U350 MEI Novigrad, responding to rollover and mouse click
U351 MEI Oprtalj, responding to rollover and mouse click
U352 MEI Pazin, responding to rollover and mouse click
U353 MEI Poreč, responding to rollover and mouse click
U354 MEI Pula, responding to rollover and mouse click
U355 MEI Rabac, responding to rollover and mouse click

(continued)

Table A1.3 Continued

U356 MEI Raša, responding to rollover and mouse click
U357 MEI Roč, responding to rollover and mouse click
U358 MEI Rovinj, responding to rollover and mouse click
U359 MEI Savudrija, responding to rollover and mouse click
U360 MEI Svetvinčenat, responding to rollover and mouse click
U361 MEI Tar, responding to rollover and mouse click
U362 MEI Umag, responding to rollover and mouse click
U363 MEI Vabriga, responding to rollover and mouse click
U364 MEI Višnjan, responding to rollover and mouse click
U365 MEI Vižinada, responding to rollover and mouse click
U366 MEI Vodnjan, responding to rollover and mouse click
U367 MEI Vrsar, responding to rollover and mouse click
U368 MEI Žminj, responding to rollover and mouse click
U369 B coloured, responding to mouse click
U370 T Search, responding to mouse click
U371 I arrow, responding to mouse click
U372 Tab coloured, haptically and aurally inaccessible
U373 B coloured, haptically and aurally inaccessible
U374 T Info, haptically and aurally inaccessible
U375 I telephone, haptically and aurally inaccessible
U376 T +, haptically and aurally inaccessible
U377 T Information coloured, haptically and aurally inaccessible
U378 T Fax, haptically and aurally inaccessible
U379 T plus, haptically and aurally inaccessible
U380 T E-mail, haptically and aurally inaccessible
U381 T info@istra.com, responding to mouse click
U382 S horizontal, responding to mouse click
U383 Tab coloured, haptically and aurally inaccessible
U384 B coloured, haptically and aurally inaccessible
U385 T Find, haptically and aurally inaccessible
U386 MA white, responding to mouse click
U387 MEI By, responding to mouse click
U388 SCAR arrow, responding to rollover and mouse click
U389 MA white, responding to rollover and mouse click
U390 MEI Umag, responding to rollover and mouse click
U391 MEI Poreč, responding to rollover and mouse click
U392 MEI Vrsar, responding to rollover and mouse click
U393 MEI Rovinj, responding to rollover and mouse click
U394 MEI Pula, responding to rollover and mouse click
U395 MEI Labin, responding to rollover and mouse click
U396 MEI Central, responding to rollover and mouse click
U397 MA white, responding to mouse click
U398 MEI By, responding to mouse click
U399 SCAR arrow, responding to rollover and mouse click
U400 MA white, responding to rollover and mouse click
U401 MEI Bale, responding to rollover and mouse click
U402 MEI Barban, responding to rollover and mouse click
U403 MEI Brtonigla, responding to rollover and mouse click

U404 MEI Buje, responding to rollover and mouse click

U405 MEI Buzet, responding to rollover and mouse click

U406 MEI Fažana, responding to rollover and mouse click

U407 MEI Funtana, responding to rollover and mouse click

U408 MEI Grožnjan, responding to rollover and mouse click

U409 MEI Hum, responding to rollover and mouse click

U410 MEI Kanfanar, responding to rollover and mouse click

U411 MEI Kaštelir, responding to rollover and mouse click

U412 MEI Kršan, responding to rollover and mouse click

U413 MEI Labin, responding to rollover and mouse click

U414 MEI Labinci, responding to rollover and mouse click

U415 MEI Ližnjan, responding to rollover and mouse click

U416 MEI Marčana, responding to rollover and mouse click

U417 MEI Medulin, responding to rollover and mouse click

U418 MEI Motovun, responding to rollover and mouse click

U419 MEI Novigrad, responding to rollover and mouse click

U420 MA white, responding to mouse click

U421 MEI By, responding to mouse click

U422 SCAR arrow, responding to rollover and mouse click

U423 MA white, responding to rollover and mouse click

U424 MEI Hotels, responding to rollover and mouse click

U425 MEI Family, responding to rollover and mouse click

U426 MEI Campsites, responding to rollover and mouse click

U427 MEI Private, responding to rollover and mouse click

U428 MEI Holidays, responding to rollover and mouse click

U429 Tab white, haptically and aurally inaccessible

U430 B coloured, haptically and aurally inaccessible

U431 T Weather, responding to mouse click

U432 I arrow, responding to mouse click

U433 T 28, haptically and aurally inaccessible

U434 I cloud, haptically and aurally inaccessible

U435 T 5, haptically and aurally inaccessible

U436 T 9, haptically and aurally inaccessible

U437 T 29, haptically and aurally inaccessible

U438 I cloud, haptically and aurally inaccessible

U439 T 7, haptically and aurally inaccessible

U440 T 10, haptically and aurally inaccessible

U441 T 30, haptically and aurally inaccessible

U442 I cloud, haptically and aurally inaccessible

U443 T 9, haptically and aurally inaccessible

U444 T 12, haptically and aurally inaccessible

U445 T Istria, responding to mouse click

U446 I goat, responding to mouse click

U447 T Green, responding to mouse click

U448 T About, responding to mouse click

U449 S vertical, haptically and aurally inaccessible

U450 T Contact, responding to mouse click

U451 S vertical, haptically and aurally inaccessible

U452 T Press, responding to mouse click

U453 S vertical, haptically and aurally inaccessible

U454 T Site, responding to mouse click

U455 S vertical, haptically and aurally inaccessible

U456 T Privacy, responding to mouse click

U457 S vertical, haptically and aurally inaccessible

U458 T Croatia, coloured, responding to mouse click

U459 Bl coloured, haptically and aurally inaccessible

AB: advertising banner; B: box; Bl: block; D: drawing; G: grid; I: icon; M: map; P: photograph; S: separator; T: text; Tab: table; MEI: menu item; SCAR: scroll arrow; SCA: scroll area; MA: menu area; SCB: scroll box; V: type of visual

B4. Homepage of the Perthshire region website

Table A1.4 Base units of the homepage of the Perthshire region website

U001 Bl coloured, haptically and aurally inaccessible
U002 B white, responding to mouse click
U003 T Search, responding to mouse click
U004 B coloured, responding to mouse click
U005 T Go, responding to mouse click
U006 T Perthshire, responding to mouse click
U007 T Home, responding to mouse click
U008 T Site, responding to mouse click
U009 T Contact, responding to mouse click
U010 T Links, responding to mouse click
U011 MA grey, responding to mouse click
U012 MEI Active, responding to rollover and mouse click
U013 MA purple, responding to rollover and mouse click
U014 T Introduction, responding to rollover and mouse click
U015 MA purple, responding to rollover and mouse click
U016 T Angling, responding to rollover and mouse click
U017 MA purple, responding to rollover and mouse click
U018 T Cycling, responding
o rollover and mouse click
U019 I arrow, responding to mouse click
U020 MA purple, responding to rollover and mouse click
U021 T Introduction, responding to rollover and mouse click
U022 MA purple, responding to rollover and mouse click
U023 T Road, responding to rollover and mouse click
U024 MA purple, responding to rollover and mouse click
U025 T Off, responding to rollover and mouse click
U026 MA purple, responding to rollover and mouse click
U027 T National, responding to rollover and mouse click
U028 MA purple, responding to rollover and mouse click
U029 T Cycling, responding to rollover and mouse click
U030 MA purple, responding to rollover and mouse click
U031 T ByCycle, responding to rollover and mouse click
U032 MA purple, responding to rollover and mouse click
U033 T Golf, responding to rollover and mouse click
U034 I arrow, responding to mouse click
U035 MA purple, responding
o rollover and mouse click
U036 T Introduction, responding to rollover and mouse click
U037 MA purple, responding to rollover and mouse click
U038 T Green, responding to rollover and mouse click
U039 MA purple, responding to rollover and mouse click
U040 T Highlands, responding to rollover and mouse click
U041 MA purple, responding to rollover and mouse click
U042 T Golf, responding to rollover and mouse click
U043 MA purple, responding to rollover and mouse click
U044 T Golf, responding to rollover and mouse click
U045 MA purple, responding to rollover and mouse click
U046 T Scottish, responding to rollover and mouse click
U047 MA purple, responding to rollover and mouse click
U048 T James, responding to rollover and mouse click

U049 MA purple, responding to rollover and mouse click	U065 T East, responding to rollover and mouse click	U081 MA purple, responding to rollover and mouse click
U050 T Golf, responding to rollover and mouse click	U066 MA purple, responding to rollover and mouse click	U082 T Adventure, responding to rollover and mouse click
U051 MA purple, responding to rollover and mouse click	U067 T Drovers, responding to rollover and mouse click	U083 I arrow, responding to mouse click
U052 T Walkingwild, responding to rollover and mouse click	U068 MA purple, responding to rollover and mouse click	U084 MA purple, responding to rollover and mouse click
U053 I arrow, responding to mouse click	U069 T Enchanted, responding to rollover and mouse click	U085 T Introduction, responding to rollover and mouse click
U054 MA purple, responding to rollover and mouse click	U070 MA purple, responding to rollover and mouse click	U086 MA purple, responding to rollover and mouse click
U055 T Walks, responding to rollover and mouse click	U071 T Snowsports, responding to rollover and mouse click	U087 T Water, responding to rollover and mouse click
U056 MA purple, responding to rollover and mouse click	U072 I arrow, responding to mouse click	U088 MA purple, responding to rollover and mouse click
U057 T Deer, responding to rollover and mouse click	U073 MA purple, responding to rollover and mouse click	U089 T Air, responding to rollover and mouse click
U058 MA purple, responding to rollover and mouse click	U074 T Where, responding to rollover and mouse click	U090 MA purple, responding to rollover and mouse click
U059 T The, responding to rollover and mouse click	U075 MA purple, responding to rollover and mouse click	U091 T Land, responding to rollover and mouse click
U060 MA purple, responding to rollover and mouse click	U076 T Curling, responding to rollover and mouse click	U092 MA purple, responding to rollover and mouse click
U061 T Rambles, responding to rollover and mouse click	U077 MA purple, responding to rollover and mouse click	U093 T Adventure, responding to rollover and mouse click
U062 MA purple, responding to rollover and mouse click	U078 T Other, responding to rollover and mouse click	U094 MA purple, responding to rollover and mouse click
U063 T Walkers, responding to rollover and mouse click	U079 MA purple, responding to rollover and mouse click	U095 T Adventure, responding to rollover and mouse click
U064 MA purple, responding to rollover and mouse click	U080 T Glenshee, responding to rollover and mouse click	U096 MA purple, responding to rollover and mouse click

(continued)

Table A1.4 Continued

U097 T Equestrian, responding to rollover and mouse click	U114 T VisitScotland, responding to rollover and mouse click	U132 I arrow, responding to mouse click
U098 I arrow, responding to mouse click	U115 I arrow, responding to mouse click	U133 MA green, responding to rollover and mouse click
U099 MA purple, responding to rollover and mouse click	U116 MA purple, responding to rollover and mouse click	U134 T Winter, responding to rollover and mouse click
U100 T Riding, responding to rollover and mouse click	U117 T VisitScotland, responding to rollover and mouse click	U135 MA green, responding to rollover and mouse click
U101 MA purple, responding to rollover and mouse click	U118 MA purple, responding to rollover and mouse click	U136 T Springtime, responding to rollover and mouse click
U102 T Equestrian, responding to rollover and mouse click	U119 T VisitScotland, responding to rollover and mouse click	U137 MA green, responding to rollover and mouse click
U103 MA purple, responding to rollover and mouse click	U120 MA grey, responding to mouse click	U138 T Springtime, responding to rollover and mouse click
U104 T Horse, responding to rollover and mouse click	U121 MEI Eventful, responding to rollover and mouse click	U139 MA green, responding to rollover and mouse click
U105 MA purple, responding to rollover and mouse click	U122 MA blue, responding to rollover and mouse click	U140 T Autumn, responding to rollover and mouse click
U106 T Horse, responding to rollover and mouse click	U123 T Search, responding to rollover and mouse click	U141 MA green, responding to rollover and mouse click
U107 MA purple, responding to rollover and mouse click	U124 MA blue, responding to rollover and mouse click	U142 T Explosions, responding to rollover and mouse click
U108 T Team, responding to rollover and mouse click	U125 T All, responding to rollover and mouse click	U143 MA green, responding to rollover and mouse click
U109 MA purple, responding to rollover and mouse click	U126 MA grey, responding to mouse click	U144 T Green, responding to rollover and mouse click
U110 T Relaxing, responding to rollover and mouse click	U127 MEI Green, responding to rollover and mouse click	U145 I arrow, responding to mouse click
U111 MA purple, responding to rollover and mouse click	U128 MA green, responding to rollover and mouse click	U146 MA green, responding to rollover and mouse click
U112 T Active, responding to rollover and mouse click	U129 T Introduction, responding to rollover and mouse click	U147 T Environmental, responding to rollover and mouse click
U113 MA purple, responding to rollover and mouse click	U130 MA green, responding to rollover and mouse click	U148 MA green, responding to rollover and mouse click
	U131 T The, responding to rollover and mouse click	

U149 T Gardens, responding to rollover and mouse click	U165 I arrow, responding to rollover and mouse click	U180 I arrow, responding to rollover and mouse click
U150 I arrow, responding to mouse click	U166 MA green, responding to rollover and mouse click	U181 MA green, responding to rollover and mouse click
U151 MA green, responding to rollover and mouse click	U167 T Introduction, responding to rollover and mouse click	U182 T Introduction, responding to rollover and mouse click
U152 T Introduction, responding to rollover and mouse click	U168 MA green, responding to rollover and mouse click	U183 MA green, responding to rollover and mouse click
U153 MA green, responding to rollover and mouse click	U169 T Green, responding to rollover and mouse click	U184 T Wildlife, responding to rollover and mouse click
U154 T The, responding to rollover and mouse click	U170 MA green, responding to rollover and mouse click	U185 MA green, responding to rollover and mouse click
U155 MA green, responding to rollover and mouse click	U171 T Green, responding to rollover and mouse click	U186 T Classic, responding to rollover and mouse click
U156 T Gardens, responding to rollover and mouse click	U172 MA green, responding to rollover and mouse click	U187 MA green, responding to rollover and mouse click
U157 MA green, responding to rollover and mouse click	U173 T Green, responding to rollover and mouse click	U188 T Special, responding to rollover and mouse click
U158 T More, responding to rollover and mouse click	U174 MA green, responding to rollover and mouse click	U189 MA green, responding to rollover and mouse click
U159 MA green, responding to rollover and mouse click	U175 T Greener, responding to rollover and mouse click	U190 T Wildlife, responding to rollover and mouse click
U160 T Scotland´s, responding to rollover and mouse click	U176 MA green, responding to rollover and mouse click	U191 MA green, responding to rollover and mouse click
U161 MA green, responding to rollover and mouse click	U177 T Give, responding to rollover and mouse click	U192 T Perthshire, responding to rollover and mouse click
U162 T Scottish, responding to rollover and mouse click	U178 MA green, responding to rollover and mouse click	U193 MA green, responding to rollover and mouse click
U163 MA green, responding to rollover and mouse click	U179 T Wildlife, responding to rollover and mouse click	U194 T Environmental, responding to rollover and mouse click
U164 T Green, responding to rollover and mouse click		

(continued)

Table A1.4 Continued

U195 MA grey, responding to mouse click	U211 MA grey, responding to rollover and mouse click	U227 MA orange, responding to rollover and mouse click
U196 MEI Conference, responding to rollover and mouse click	U212 MEI Things, responding to mouse click	U228 T Kinross, responding to rollover and mouse click
U197 MA red, responding to rollover and mouse click	U213 T Introduction, responding to rollover and mouse click	U229 MA orange, responding to rollover and mouse click
U198 T Conference, responding to rollover and mouse click	U214 MA orange, responding to rollover and mouse click	U230 T Perth, responding to rollover and mouse click
U199 MA red, responding to rollover and mouse click	U215 T Towns, responding to rollover and mouse click	U231 MA orange, responding to rollover and mouse click
U200 T The, responding to rollover and mouse click	U216 I arrow, responding to mouse click	U232 T Pitlochry, responding to rollover and mouse click
U201 MA red, responding to rollover and mouse click	U217 MA orange, responding to rollover and mouse click	U233 MA orange, responding to rollover and mouse click
U202 T Travel, responding to rollover and mouse click	U218 T Aberfeldy, responding to rollover and mouse click	U234 T History, responding to rollover and mouse click
U203 MA red, responding to rollover and mouse click	U219 MA orange, responding to rollover and mouse click	U235 I arrow, responding to mouse click
U204 I arrow, responding to mouse click	U220 T Auchterarder, responding to rollover and mouse click	U236 MA orange, responding to rollover and mouse click
U205 MA red, responding to rollover and mouse click	U221 MA orange, responding to rollover and mouse click	U237 T Genealogy, responding to rollover and mouse click
U206 T Travel, responding to rollover and mouse click	U222 T Blairgowrie, responding to rollover and mouse click	U238 MA orange, responding to rollover and mouse click
U207 MA red, responding to rollover and mouse click	U223 MA orange, responding to rollover and mouse click	U239 T Visitor, responding to rollover and mouse click
U208 T Perth, responding to rollover and mouse click	U224 T Crieff, responding to rollover and mouse click	U240 I arrow, responding to mouse click
U209 MA red, responding to rollover and mouse click	U225 MA orange, responding to rollover and mouse click	U241 MA orange, responding to rollover and mouse click
U210 T Links, responding to rollover and mouse click	U226 T Dunkeld, responding to rollover and mouse click	U242 T Search, responding to rollover and mouse click

U243 MA orange, responding to rollover and mouse click

U244 T Shopping, responding to rollover and mouse click

U245 MA orange, responding to rollover and mouse click

U246 T Great, responding to rollover and mouse click

U247 MA orange, responding to rollover and mouse click

U248 T Music, responding to rollover and mouse click

U249 MA orange, responding to rollover and mouse click

U250 T Perthshire´s, responding to rollover and mouse click

U251 MA orange, responding to rollover and mouse click

U252 T Romantic, responding to rollover and mouse click

U253 MA grey, responding to mouse click

U254 MEI Travel, responding to rollover and mouse click

U255 MA brown, responding to rollover and mouse click

U256 T Getting, responding to rollover and mouse click

U257 I arrow, responding to mouse click

U258 T MA brown, responding to rollover and mouse click

U259 T By, responding to rollover and mouse click

U260 MA brown, responding to rollover and mouse click

U261 T By, responding to rollover and mouse click

U262 MA brown, responding to rollover and mouse click

U263 T By, responding to rollover and mouse click

U264 MA brown, responding to rollover and mouse click

U265 T By, responding to rollover and mouse click

U266 MA brown, responding to rollover and mouse click

U267 T By, responding to rollover and mouse click

U268 MA brown, responding to rollover and mouse click

U269 T Tourist, responding to rollover and mouse click

U270 MA brown, responding to rollover and mouse click

U271 T Perthshire, responding to rollover and mouse click

U272 MA brown, responding to rollover and mouse click

U273 T Perth, responding to rollover and mouse click

U274 MA brown, responding to rollover and mouse click

U275 T Scotland, responding to rollover and mouse click

U276 MA brown, responding to rollover and mouse click

U277 T Travel, responding to rollover and mouse click

U278 MA brown, responding to rollover and mouse click

U279 T Useful, responding to rollover and mouse click

U280 MA grey, responding to mouse click

U281 MEI Accommodation, responding to rollover and mouse click

U282 MA green, responding to rollover and mouse click

U283 T Introduction, responding to rollover and mouse click

U284 MA grey, responding to mouse click

U285 MEI Media, responding to rollover and mouse click

U286 MA red, responding to rollover and mouse click

U287 T Intro, responding to rollover and mouse click

U288 MA red, responding to rollover and mouse click

U289 T Latest, responding to rollover and mouse click

(*continued*)

Table A1.4 Continued

U290 I arrow, responding to mouse click
U291 MA red, responding to rollover and mouse click
U292 T Horsecross, responding to rollover and mouse click
U293 MA red, responding to rollover and mouse click
U294 T Scone, responding to rollover and mouse click
U295 MA red, responding to rollover and mouse click
U296 T Season, responding to rollover and mouse click
U297 MA red, responding to rollover and mouse click
U298 T Perth 800, responding to rollover and mouse click
U299 MA red, responding to rollover and mouse click
U300 T First, responding to rollover and mouse click
U301 MA red, responding to rollover and mouse click
U302 T Features, responding to rollover and mouse click
U303 I arrow, responding to mouse click
U304 MA red, responding to rollover and mouse click
U305 T Perthshire, responding to rollover and mouse click
U306 MA red, responding to rollover and mouse click
U307 T Big, responding to rollover and mouse click
U308 MA red, responding to rollover and mouse click
U309 T All, responding to rollover and mouse click
U310 MA red, responding to rollover and mouse click
U311 T Angling, responding to rollover and mouse click
U312 MA red, responding to rollover and mouse click
U313 T Adventure, responding to rollover and mouse click
U314 MA red, responding to rollover and mouse click
U315 T Perth, responding to rollover and mouse click
U316 Tab coloured, haptically and aurally inaccessible
U317 B coloured, haptically and aurally inaccessible
U318 T Latest, haptically and aurally inaccessible
U319 B coloured, haptically and aurally inaccessible
U320 T Perth´s, moving, responding to mouse click
U321 T Scone, moving, responding to mouse click
U322 T Figures, moving, haptically and aurally inaccessible
U323 B white, responding to mouse click
U324 I crown, responding to mouse click
U325 T Perth, responding to mouse click
U326 T 800, responding to mouse click
U327 B coloured, responding to mouse click
U328 T 1310, responding to mouse click
U329 P landscape, haptically and aurally inaccessible
U330 D card, haptically and aurally inaccessible
U331 T Your, haptically and aurally inaccessible
U332 T [illegible], haptically and aurally inaccessible
U333 D envelope, haptically and aurally inaccessible
U334 T [illegible], haptically and aurally inaccessible
U335 I flower, haptically and aurally inaccessible
U336 T Live, haptically and aurally inaccessible
U337 T visitscotland.com, haptically and aurally inaccessible
U338 B coloured, haptically and aurally inaccessible
U339 T Home, haptically and aurally inaccessible
U340 P Active, responding to mouse click
U341 T Active, responding to mouse click

U342 T Perthshire, responding to rollover and mouse click

U343 P Eventful, responding to mouse click

U344 T Eventful, responding to mouse click

U345 T No, responding to rollover and mouse click

U346 P Green, responding to mouse click

U347 T Green, responding to mouse click

U348 T Clear, responding to rollover and mouse click

U349 V Conference, responding to mouse click

U350 T Conference, responding to mouse click

U351 T Conferences, responding to rollover and mouse click

U352 B coloured, haptically and aurally inaccessible

U353 T Welcome, haptically and aurally inaccessible

U354 I France, responding to mouse click

U355 I Germany, responding to mouse click

U356 I Netherlands, responding to mouse click

U357 P Perthshire, haptically and aurally inaccessible

U358 B coloured, haptically and aurally inaccessible

U359 T Perthshire, haptically and aurally inaccessible

U360 T bbc.co.uk, responding to mouse click

U361 S horizontal, responding to mouse click

U362 M Perthshire, haptically and aurally inaccessible

U363 B coloured, haptically and aurally inaccessible

U364 T Perthshire, responding to mouse click

U365 S horizontal, responding to mouse click

U366 T Did, haptically and aurally inaccessible

U367 T In, haptically and aurally inaccessible

U368 P visit, responding to mouse click

U369 B white, responding to mouse click

U370 T visitscotland.com, responding to mouse click

U371 B white, haptically and aurally inaccessible

U372 I Europe, haptically and aurally inaccessible

U373 I Scotland, haptically and aurally inaccessible

U374 T Europe, haptically and aurally inaccessible

U375 T Illegible, haptically and aurally inaccessible

U376 I copyright, responding to rollover and mouse click

U377 T Visit, responding to rollover and mouse click

U378 S horizontal, responding to rollover and mouse click

U379 S vertical,

haptically and aurally inaccessible

U380 T Text, responding to rollover and mouse click

U381 S horizontal, responding to rollover and mouse click

U382 S vertical, haptically and aurally inaccessible

U383 T Privacy, responding to rollover and mouse click

U384 S horizontal, responding to rollover and mouse click

U385 S vertical, haptically and aurally inaccessible

U386 T Feedback, responding to rollover and mouse click

U387 S horizontal, responding to rollover and mouse click

U388 S vertical, haptically and aurally inaccessible

U389 T Top, responding to rollover and mouse click

U390 S horizontal, responding to rollover and mouse click

U391 S vertical, haptically and aurally inaccessible

U392 T Print, responding to rollover and mouse click

U393 Bl coloured, haptically and aurally inaccessible

AB: advertising banner; B: box; Bl: block; D: drawing; G: grid; I: icon; M: map; P: photograph; S: separator; T: text; Tab: table; MEI: menu item; SCAR: scroll arrow; SCA: scroll area; MA: menu area; SCB: scroll box; V: type of visual

Bibliography

Adamzik, K. (2004) *Textlinguistik. Eine einführende Darstellung* (Tübingen: Niemeyer).

Antelmi, D., G. Held, and F. Santulli (eds) (2007) *Pragmatica della Comunicazione Turistica* (Roma: Editori Riuniti).

Austin, J. L. (1962) *How to Do Things With Words* (Cambridge, Massachusetts: Harvard University Press).

Baider, F., M. Burger, and D. Goutsos (eds) (2004) *La communication touristique. Approches discursives de l'identité et de l'altérité* (Paris: L'Harmattan).

Baldry, A. and P. J. Thibault (2006) *Multimodal Transcription and Text Analysis* (Oakville, CT: Equinox Publishing).

Bateman, J. A. (2008) *Multimodality and Genre. A Foundation for the Systematic Analysis of Multimodal Documents* (Basingstoke: Palgrave Macmillan).

Bendel, S. (2008) 'Werbestrategien hinterfragen statt reproduzieren – Plädoyer für eine kritische Wissenschaft' in G. Held and S. Bendel (eds) *Werbung grenzenlos – Multimodale Werbetexte im interkulturellen Vergleich* (Frankfurt am Main et al.: Peter Lang), 229–244.

Bendel, S. and Held, G. (2008) '"Werbung – grenzenlos" – kulturvergleichende Werbeanalysen auf dem theoretischen und methodischen Prüfstand (Einleitung)' in G. Held and S. Bendel (eds) *Werbung grenzenlos – Multimodale Werbetexte im interkulturellen Vergleich* (Frankfurt am Main et al.: Lang), 1–12.

Bernstein, B. (1972) 'Social class, language and socialization' in P. P. Giglioli (ed.) *Language and Social Context* (Harmondsworth: Penguin), 157–178.

Bernstein, B. (1975) *Class, Codes and Control: Towards a Theory of Educational Transmissions*, vol. 3 (London: Routledge and Kegan Paul).

Brinker, K. (2001) *Linguistische Textanalyse. Eine Einführung in Grundbegriffe und Methoden* (Berlin: Schmidt).

Bucher, H. J. (2010) 'Multimodalität – eine Universalie des Medienwandels: Problemstellungen und Theorien der Multimodalitätsforschung' in H. J. Bucher, T. Gloning, and K. Lehnen (eds) *Neue Medien – Neue Formate. Ausdifferenzierung und Konvergenz in der Medienkommunikation* (Frankfurt am Main, New York: Campus Verlag), 41–79.

Bucher, H. J., T. Gloning, and K. Lehnen (2010) *Neue Medien – Neue Formate. Ausdifferenzierung und Konvergenz in der Medienkommunikation* (Frankfurt am Main and New York: Campus Verlag).

Burgess, L. and J. Cooper (2000) 'Extending the Viability of MICA (Model of Internet Commerce Adoption) as a Metric for Explaining the Process of Business Adoption of Internet Commerce', *International Conference on Telecommunications and Electronic Commerce, Dallas (November).*

Burgess, L., B. Parrish, J. Cooper and C. Alcok (2009) 'A longitudinal study of the use of the web by regional tourism organisations (RTOs) in Australia', *22nd Bled eConference eEnablement: Facilitating an Open, Effective and Representative Society* (Bled, Slovenia), 14–17 June 2009, http://aisel.aisnet.org/cgi/viewcontent.cgi?article=1033&context=bled2009, date accessed 17 August 2012.

Chandler, D. (2007) *Semiotics: The Basics* (New York: Routledge).

Dann, G. (1996) *The Language of Tourism: A Sociolinguistic Perspective* (Wallingford: CAB International).

Deacon, D., M. Pickering, P. Golding, and G. Murdock (2007) *Researching Communications: A Practical Guide to Methods in Media and Cultural Analysis*, 2nd edition (London: Bloomsbury Academic).

Djonov, E. (2005) *Analysing the organisation of information in websites: From Hypermedia Design to Systemic Functional Hypermedia Discourse Analysis*, Doctoral Thesis (Australia: University of New South Wales).

Doolin, B., L. Burgess, and J. Cooper (2002) 'Evaluating the use of the Web for Tourism Marketing: A case study from New Zealand', *Tourism Management*, 23 (5), 557–561.

Dore, L. and G. I. Crouch (2003) 'Promoting destinations: An exploratory study of publicity programs used by national tourism organizations', *Journal of Vacation Marketing*, 9 (2), 137–151.

Eco, U. (1976) *A Theory of Semiotics* (Bloomington: Indiana University Press).

European Parliament (2014) Croatia joins the EU, http://europa.eu/newsroom/highlights/croatia-joins-eu/index_en.htm#, date accessed 09 March 2014.

Filipan-Zignić, B. (2007) *Analiza Jezika Reklamnih Poruka na Internetu Njemačkoga i Hrvatskoga Govornog Područja (The analysis of banner advertising on the Internet in German and Croatian)*, Doktorska Dizertacija (Doctoral Thesis) (Zagreb: Filozofski Fakultet).

Foley, A. and J. Fahy (2004) 'Incongruity between expression and experience: The role of imagery in supporting the positioning of a tourism destination brand', *Journal of Brand Management*, 11 (3).

Foucault, M. (1980) *Power/Knowledge: Selected Interviews and Other Writings, 1972–1977*, Gordon (ed.) (New York: Pantheon).

Fritz, G. (1982) *Kohärenz. Grundfragen der linguistischen Kommunikationsanalyse* (Tübingen: Narr).

Fyall, A. (2010) 'Destination Management: Challenges and Opportunities' in R. Wang and A. Pizam (eds) *Tourism Destination Management*, (CABI, forthcoming), http://rosen.hospitality.ucf.edu/faculty/raywang/documents/HFT7715/Tourism%20Future/Chapter%2023%20-%20Fyall.pdf, date accessed 17 August 2012.

Gloning, T. (1996) *Bedeutung, Gebrauch und sprachliche Handlung. Ansätze und Probleme einer handlungstheoretischen Semantik aus linguistischer Sicht* (Tübingen: Narr).

Goatly, A. (1997) *The Language of Metaphors* (London: Routledge).

Goffman, E. (1959) *The Presentation of Self in Everyday Life* (New York: Doubleday).

Gumperz, J. J. (1982) *Language and Social Identity* (Cambridge: Cambridge University Press).

Gumperz, J. J. and J. Cook-Gumperz (1982) 'Introduction: Language and the communication of social identity' in J. J. Gumperz (ed.) *Language and Social Identity* (Cambridge: Cambridge University Press), 1–21.

Hall, E. T. (1966) *The Hidden Dimension* (Garden City, New York: Doubleday).

Hallet, W. (2008a) 'Schreiben lernen mit dem Hypertext? Hypertextualität und generische Kohärenz in der Schreiberziehung', *Zeitschrift für Interkulturellen Fremdsprachenunterricht*, 13 (1), 1–10, http://zif.spz.tu-darmstadt.de/jg-13-1/beitrag/Hallet1.htm, date accessed 28 June 2012.

Hallet, W. (2008b) 'Visual culture, multimodal discourse and tasks: Die bildkulturelle Dimension des Fremdsprachenlernens' in A. Müller-Hartmann and M. Schocker-von Ditfurth (eds) (2008) *Aufgabenorientiertes Lernen und Lehren mit Medien: Ansätze, Erfahrungen, Perspektiven in der Fremdsprachendidaktik* (Frankfurt am Main: Lang), 167–183.

Hallett, W. and J. Kaplan-Weinger (2010) *Official Tourism Websites: A Discourse Analysis Perspective* (Bristol: Channel View Publications).

Halliday, M. A. K. (1978) *Language as Social Semiotic: The Social Interpretation of Language and Meaning* (London: Edwards Arnold).

Halliday, M. A. K. (1985) *An Introduction to Functional Grammar* (London: Edward Arnold).

Halliday, M. A. K. (1989) 'Part A' in M. A. K. Halliday and R. Hasan (eds) *Language, Context and Text: Aspects of Language in a Social-Semiotic Perspective* (Oxford: Oxford University Press), 1–49.

Halliday, M. A. K. and C. M. I. M Matthiessen (2004) *An Introduction to Functional Grammar*, 3rd edition (London: Arnold).

Hazeldene Guest House (2013) http://www.hazeldeneguesthouse.com/, date accessed 29 July 2013.

Held, G. (2008) 'Der Raum als Traum – intersemiotische Gestaltungsstrategien und ihre Realisierung in globalen Kampagnen der Tourismwerbung' in G. Held and S. Bendel (eds) *Werbung grenzenlos – Multimodale Werbetexte im interkulturellen Vergleich* (Frankfurt am Main et al.: Lang), 149–172.

Held, G. and S. Bendel (eds) (2008) *Werbung grenzenlos – Multimodale Werbetexte im interkulturellen Vergleich* (Frankfurt am Main et al.: Lang).

Heringer, H. J. (1974) *Praktische Semantik* (Stuttgart: Klett).

Hodge, R. and G. Kress (1993) *Language as Ideology*, 2nd edition (London: Routledge).

Holsanova, J. and A. Nord (2010) 'Multimodal design: Media structures, media principles and users' meaning-making in printed and digital media' in H. J. Bucher, T. Gloning, and K. Lehnen (eds) *Neue Medien – neue Formate. Ausdifferenzierung und Konvergenz in der Medienkommunikation* (Frankfurt/New York: Campus), 81–103.

Hommerberg, C. (2011) *Persuasiveness in the Discourse of Wine: The Rhetoric of Robert Parker*, Doctoral Thesis (Växjö: Linnaeus University Press).

Istraturist (2013) http://www.istraturist.com/en/about-umag/istria-gourmet/istrian-food, date accessed 29 July 2013.

Jack, G. and A. Phipps (2005) *Tourism and Intercultural Exchange: Why Tourism Matters* (Clevedon: Channel View Publications).

Jaworski, A. and A. Pritchard (eds) (2005) *Discourse, Communication and Tourism* (Clevedon: Channel View Publications).

Jewitt, C. (2008) 'Multimodality and literacy in school classrooms', *Review of Research in Education*, 32 (1), 241–267.

Jewitt, C. (2009a) 'An introduction: Handbook rationale, scope and structure' in C. Jewitt (ed.) *The Routledge Handbook of Multimodal Analysis* (New York: Routledge), 1–7.

Jewitt, C. (2009b) 'Different approaches to multimodality' in C. Jewitt (ed.) *The Routledge Handbook of Multimodal Analysis* (New York: Routledge), 28–39.

Jewitt, C. (2009c) *The Routledge Handbook of Multimodal Analysis* (New York: Routledge).

Just, M. A. and P. A. Carpenter (1980) 'A theory of reading: From eye fixations to comprehension', *Psychological review*, 17, 329–354.

Koffka, K. (1935) *Principles of Gestalt Psychology* (New York: Harcourt, Brace & World).

Köhler, W. (1947) *Gestalt Psychology, An Introduction To New Concepts In Modern Psychology* (New York: Liveright Pub. Corp).

Kress, G. (2009) 'What is mode?' in C. Jewitt (ed.) *The Routledge Handbook of Multimodal Analysis* (New York: Routledge), 54–67.

Kress, G. (2001) *Multimodal Discourse: The Modes and Media of Contemporary Communication* (Arnold: London).

Kress, G. (2007) *Reading Images. The Grammar of Visual Design*, 2nd edition (London and New York: Routledge).

Kress, G. and T. van Leeuwen (1996/2004) *Reading Images. The Grammar of Visual Design* (London: Routledge Falmer).

Leander, K. M. and L. Vasudevan (2009) 'Multimodality and mobile culture' in C. Jewitt (ed.) *The Routledge Handbook of Multimodal Analysis* (New York: Routledge), 127–139.

Leetaru, K. H. (2012) *Data Mining Methods for the Content Analyst. An Introduction to the Computational Analysis of Content* (New York and London: Routledge).

Lüger, H. H. and H. E. H. Lenk (2008) 'Kontrastive Medienlinguistik. Ansätze, Ziele, Analysen' in H. H. Lüger and H. E. H. Lenk (eds) (2008) *Kontrastive Medienlinguistik* (Landau: Verlag Empirische Pädagogik), 11–28.

Martin, J. R. (1992) *English Text: System and Structure* (Amsterdam/Philadelphia: John Benjamins Publishing Company).

Martin, J. R., C. Matthiessen, and C. Painter (1997) *Working with Functional Grammar* (London: Edward Arnold).

Martin, J. R. and D. Rose (2003) *Working with Discourse: Meaning beyond the clause*, 2nd edition (London; New York: Continuum).

Martinec, R. and A. Salway (2005) 'A system for image-text relations in new (and old) media', *Visual Communication*, 4 (3), 337–371.

Matthiessen, C. M. I. M. (2009) 'Ideas & new directions' in M. A. K Halliday and J. J. Webster (eds) (2009) *Continuum Companion to Systemic Functional Linguistics* (London and New York: Continuum), 12–58.

Matthiessen, C. M. I. M., K. Teruya and M. Lam (2010) *Key Terms in Systemic Functional Linguistic* (London and New York: Continuum).

Ministry of Foreign Affairs and European Integration of the Republic of Croatia (2006) 'Economy', http://www.mvpei.hr/MVP.asp?pcpid=972, date accessed 09 April 2008.

Ministry of the Sea, Transport and Infrastructure, Ministry of Tourism (2008), 'Nautical Tourism Development Strategy of the Republic of Croatia (2009–2019)', 1–48, http://hidra.srce.hr/arhiva/995/55957/www.mmpi.hr/UserDocsImages/Strategija%20razvoja%20nautickog%20turizma%20ENGL%201.pdf, date accessed 28 June 2012.

Ministry of Tourism of the Republic of Croatia (2010) 'Croatian tourism to be advertised on BBC, CNN, Euronews, Eurosport this spring', http://www.mint.hr/default.aspx?id=4942, date accessed 28 June 2012.

Muckenhaupt, M. (1986) *Text und Bild. Grundfragen der Beschreibung von Text- Bild-Kommunikationen aus sprachwissenschaftlicher Sicht* (Tübingen: Narr).

National Development Agency, Managing Authority for International Co-operation Programmes (2011), 'Handbook to Tourism Projects in the Hungary-Croatia IPA Cross-border Cooperation Programme 2007–2013', 1–126, http://www.nfu.hu/download/36118/Tourism%20Handbook%20DRAFT.pdf, date accessed 28 June 2012.

Nekić, M. (2009), review, 'Tourist Language Learning: A Way of Grasping Human Interaction', KULT Online 19 (ed.), on Phipps, A. (2007) *Learning the Arts of Linguistic Survival. Languaging, Tourism, Life* (Clevedon: Channel View Publications), http://cultdoc.uni-giessen.de/wps/pgn/kd/det/KULT_online/1/1889/, date accessed 17 August 2012.

Neumann, S. (2003) 'Exploitation of an SFL-annotated multilingual register corpus' in A. Abeillé, S. Hansen-Schirra, and H. Uszkoreit (eds), *Proceedings of the 4th International Workshop on Linguistically Interpreted Corpora (LINC-03)* (Budapest: ACL).

Nilsson, T. (2000) 'Noun phrases in British travel texts' in C. Mair and M. Hundt (eds) *Corpus Linguistics and Linguistic Theory: Papers from the twentieth International Conference on English Language Research on Computerized Corpora (ICAME 20)* (Amsterdam: Editions Rodopi B.V), 267–272.

Norris, S. (2004) *Analyzing Multimodal Interaction: A Methodological Framework* (London: Routledge).

Norris, S. (2009) 'Tempo, **Auftakt**, levels of actions, and practice: Rhythm in ordinary interactions', **Journal of Applied Linguistics**, 6 (3), 333–355.

Norris, S. (ed.) (2011) **Multimodality in Practice: Investigating Theory-in-Practice-through-Methodology** (London: Routledge).

Norris, S. and R. H. Jones (eds) (2005) *Discourse in Action: Introducing Mediated Discourse Analysis* (London: Routledge).

O'Neill, F., S. Barnard, and D. Lee (2004) 'Best Practice and Interpretation in Tourist/Wildlife Encounters: A Wild Dolphin Swim Tour Example', *Wildlife Tourism Research Report Series*, No. 25, (Gold Coast, Australia: CRC Sustainable Tourism), http://www.innz.net.nz/Interp101/Ecotourism%20and%20interpretation/InterpWildlifeEncounters.pdf, date accessed 17 August 2012.

O'Neill, S. (ed.) (2008) *Interactive Media: The Semiotics of Embodied Interaction* (London: Springer).

Page, S. and J. Connell (2006) *Tourism: A Modern Synthesis* (London: Thomson).

Phipps, A. (2007) *Learning the Arts of Linguistic Survival. Languaging, Tourism, Life* (Clevedon: Channel View Publications).

Pritchard, A. and Jaworski, A. (2005) 'Introduction: Discourse communication and tourism dialogues' in A. Jaworski and A. Pritchard (eds) *Discourse, Communication and Tourism* (Clevedon: Channel View Publications), 1–16.

Royce, T. D. (2007) 'Intersemiotic complementarity: A framework for multimodal discourse analysis' in T. D. Royce and W. D. Bowcher (eds) *New Directions in the Analysis of Multimodal Discourse* (Mahwah and New Jersey: Lawrence Erlbaum Associates), 63–109.

Salazar, N. B. (2012) 'Community-based cultural tourism: issues, threats and opportunities', *Journal of Sustainable Tourism*, 20 (1), 9–22.

Schmidt, S. J. (2004) '"Vorwort"' in B. Cha and S. J. Schmidt (eds) *Interkulturalität: Theorie und Praxis. Deutschland und Korea* (Münster: Lit-Verlag), VII–VIII.

Scholz, O. R. (2004) *Bild, Darstellung, Zeichen. Philosophische Theorien bildhafter Darstellung*, 2nd edition (Frankfurt/M: Klosermann).

Scotland map (2014) Scotland Map and Area Guide http://www.scotland.com/maps/, date accessed 8 January 2014.

Scotland's national tourism organization (2011) Surprise Yourself http://www.visitscotland.org/what_we_do/marketing/uk_and_ireland_campaigns/surprise_yourself_2011.aspx, date accessed 26 June 2011.

Screenshot of the homepage of the Zadar region website http://www.zadar.hr/English/Default.aspx, date accessed 10 September 2009.

Screenshot of the homepage of the Orkney region website http://www.visitorkney.com/index.html, date accessed 10 December 2009.

Screenshot of the homepage of the Istria region website http://www.istra.hr/en, date accessed 26 December 2009.

Screenshot of the homepage of the Perthshire region website http://www.perthshire.co.uk, date accessed 26 December 2009.

Searle, J. R. (1969) *Speech Acts. An Essay in the Philosophy of Language* (Cambridge: Cambridge University Press).

Sharpley, R. (2011) *The Study of Tourism: Past Trends and Future Directions* (Abingdon: Routledge).

Simon-Vandenbergen, A. M. (2003) 'Lexical metaphor and interpersonal meaning' in A. M. Simon-Vandenbergen, M. Taverniers, and L. Ravelli (eds) *Grammatical Metaphor: Views from Systemic Functional Linguistics* (Amsterdam: John Benjamins), 223–256.

Snow, P. (2004) 'Tourism and small-language persistence in a Panamanian Creole village', *International Journal of the Sociology of Language*, 166, 113–129.

Spitzmüller, J. and I. Warnke (2011) 'Discourse as a "linguistic object": methodical and methodological delimitations', *Critical Discourse Studies*, 8 (2), 75–94.

Stöckl, H. (2004) *Die Sprache im Bild – Das Bild in der Sprache. Zur Verknüpfung von Sprache und Bild im massenmedialen Text. Konzept – Theorien – Analysemethoden* (Berlin [de Gruyter]).

Storrer, A. (2008) 'Hypertextlinguistik' in N. Janich (ed.) (2008) *Textlinguistik. 15 Einführungen* (Tübingen: Narr Francke Attempto Verlag), 211–227, http://www.hytex.tu-dortmund.de/pdf/Storrer_2008_Hypertextlinguistik.pdf, date accessed 17 August 2012.

The Scottish Government (2011) 'Tourism', http://www.scotland.gov.uk/Topics/Business-Industry/Tourism, date accessed 28 June 2012.

Thibault, P. J. (1987) 'An interview with Michael Halliday' in R. Steele and T. Threadgold (eds) *Language Topics: Essays in Honour of Honour of Michael Halliday* (Amerstam/Philadelphia: John Benjamins), 2, 601–627.

Thibault, P. J. (2001): 'Multimodality and the school science textbook' in C. T. Torsello, G. Brunetti, and N. Penello (eds) *Corpora Testuali per Ricerca, Traduzione e Apprendimento Linguistico* (Padova: Unipress), 293–335.

Trim, J. (2002) 'Multilingualism and the interpretation of languages in contact' in A. Tosi *Crossing Barriers and Bridging Cultures: The Challenges of Multilingual Translation for the European Union* (Clevedon: Multilingual Matters), 8–21.

Verheugen, G. (2005) 'A Renewed EU Tourism Policy: Towards a Stronger Partnership for European Tourism', 4th **European Tourism** Forum: Malta, 20 October 2005, 1–6, http://www.aer.eu/fileadmin/user_upload/MainIssues/Tourism/2005/SPEECH-05-626_EN.pdf, date accessed 17 August 2012.

Webopedia: Online Computer Dictionary for Computer and Internet Terminology (2012), www.webopedia.com, date accessed 28 June 2012.

Whittaker, R., M. O'Donnell, and A. McCabe (2007) 'Introduction: Responses to the changing face of education' in A. McCabe, M. O'Donnell, and R. Whittaker (eds) *Advances In Language And Education* (London: Continuum), 1–12.

Index

CPSIA information can be obtained at www.ICGtesting.com
Printed in the USA
LVOW05*0849221214

419926LV00005B/18/P

9 781137 397904